HISTORY OF LAKE CHAMPLAIN

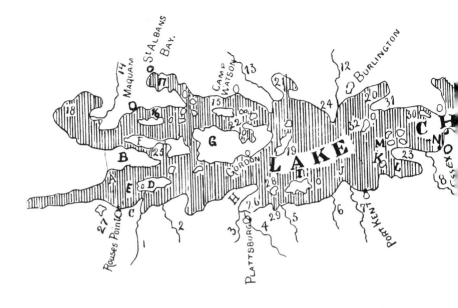

A. Windmill Point.
B. Alburgh Tongue.—*Pointe Algonquin.*
C. Point au Fer.—*Pointe au Feu.*
D. Isle la Motte.—*Isle la Mothe.*
E. Site of old French Fort St. Anne.
F. North Hero.—*Isle Longue.*
G. Grand Island.—*La Grand Isle.*
H. Cumberland Head.—*Cap Scononton.*
I. Valcour Island.—*Valeur.*
J. Sand Point.—*Pointe au Sable.*
K. Schuyler's Island.—*Isle aux Chapons.*
L. Willsborough Bay.—*Perue Bay.*
M. Four Brothers.—*Isle de Quatre Vents.*
N. Split Rock.—*Rocher Fendre.*
O. Thompson's Point.—*Pointe Regiochene.*
P. Crown Point.—*Pointe de la Couronne.*
   Site of old Fort Frederic.
Q. Chimney Point.—*Pointe a la Chevelure.*
R. Probable locality of Champlain's battle with the Iroq
S. Fort Ticonderoga and old Fort Carillon.
T. Mount Independence.
U. Mount Defiance.
V. South Bay.—*Grande Baie.*
W. Skenesborough.—*Kal-cho-quah-na.*
X. Fort Anne on Wood Creek.—*Fort la Raine.*
Y. Bulwagga Bay.
Z. Fort William Henry and Fort George.

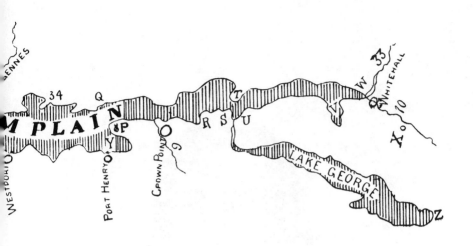

1. Great Chazy River } *Chassy.*
2. Little Chazy River
3. Dead Creek.—*Scononton.*
4. Saranac. —*Salasanac and St. Amant.*
5. Salmon River.—*Riviere au Canot.*
6. Little Ausable.
7. Great Ausable.—*Riviere au Sable.*
8. Bouquet River.
9. Put's Creek.—*Riviere a la Barbue.*
10. Wood Creek.—*Riviere du Chicot.*
11. Otter Creek.—*Riviere aux Loutre.*
12. Winooski, or Onion River.—
    Riviere Ouinousque.
13. Lamoille River.—*Riviere a la Mouille.*
14. Missisco River.—*Michiscouy.*
15. Savage Island.—*Isle a la Couverte.*
16. Butler's Island.
17. St. Albans Bay.
18. Missisco Bay.—*Michiscouy.*
19. Providence Island.
20. Shelburne Bay.

21. Mallet's Bay.
22. Keeler's Bay.
23. Willsborough **Point.**
24. Colchester Point.
25. Pelot's Point.
26. Cumberland Bay.
27. Fort Montgomery.
28. Crab or Hospital Island.—*St. Michel.*
29. Bluff Point, near which the
    French vessels were sunk
    on retreat to Canada.
30. Sloop Island.
31. Pottier's Point.—*Erkly's Point.*
32. Juniper Island.
33. Poultney River and East Bay,
    where the hulks of
    American and British vessels
    were laid up in 1814.
34 Adams' Bay, where Arnold burned
    several of his vessels
    of the battle of Valcour.

SAMUEL DE CHAMPLAIN

HISTORY

OF

LAKE CHAMPLAIN

FROM ITS FIRST EXPLORATION BY THE FRENCH

IN

1609

TO THE CLOSE OF THE YEAR

1814

BY

PETER S. PALMER

FOURTH EDITION
Illustrated

PURPLE MOUNTAIN PRESS
Fleischmanns, New York

The text of this edition has been reproduced from
the third (undated) edition published in New York by
Frank F. Lovell & Company between 1886 and 1889.
Nearly all illustrations and maps are new to this
fourth edition which was originally published by
Harbor Hill Books in 1983.

First paperback edition published by
PURPLE MOUNTAIN PRESS, LTD.
Main Street, PO Box E3
Fleischmanns, New York 12430-0378

1992

Library of Congress Cataloging-in-Publication Data

Palmer, Peter Sailly, 1814-1890.
  History of Lake Champlain from its first exploration by the French
in 1609 to the close of the year 1814 / by Peter S. Palmer. -- 4th
ed.
      p.   cm.
  Originally published: 3rd ed. New York : F. Lovell, 1886? With new
illus.
  Includes index.
  ISBN 0-935796-31-2 (pb : acid-free)
  1. Champlain, Lake, Region--History. 2. Champlain, Lake--History,
I. Title.
F127.C6P2   1992
974.7'54--dc20   92-15003
                                                            CIP

Manufactured in the United States of America

Printed on acid-free paper

TABLE OF CONTENTS

CHAPTER I.   16

Progress of discoveries by the French in Canada—Character of the Indian tribes—Champlain's visit to Lake Champlain in 1609—Battle between the Canada Indians and the Iroquois—Fort erected on Isle La Motte—De Courcelle's Expedition to the Mohawk River.

CHAPTER II.   30

M. De Tracy collects a large army at Isle La Motte—He marches against and destroys the Mohawk villages—Condition of Canada—De Callieres' project for the invasion of New York—Burning of Schenectady—Captain John Schuyler's attack upon Fort Laprairie —Major Philip Schuyler's expedition to Canada—De Frontenac marches against the Mohawks.

CHAPTER III.   44

Indian Depredations on the Frontier—Forts built by the New York Colonists on Wood Creek—Two Expeditions organized against Canada—Condition of the Country about Lake Champlain—The French build a Fort at Crown Point—French Grants on the Lake —Troubles among the New York Colonists—Attempt to settle the Lands lying between the Hudson River and Lake Champlain.

CHAPTER IV.   56

Sir William Johnson's Expedition against Crown Point—Battle of Lake George—The French fortify Ticonderoga—Montcalm attacks the English at Lake George—Massacre at Fort William Henry— Defeat of Abercrombie at Ticonderoga—English Scouting Parties— Putnam in trouble.

CHAPTER V.   72

General Amherst marches against Ticonderoga and Crown Point— Retreat of the French to Canada—Naval operations on Lake Champlain—Progress of the settlement of the country bordering on Lake Champlain, prior to the revolution—New Hampshire Grants— Dispute with tenants of Colonel Reed—A new Province projected by Colonel Skene and others.

CHAPTER VI.   85

War of the Revolution—Surprise of Ticonderoga—Arnold at St. Johns—Sentiments of the Canadians—Invasion of Canada—Seige of St. Johns—Death of General Montgomery at Quebec—Retreat of the " Army of Canada."

CHAPTER VII. 102

1776—The Americans and British Build Armed Vessels on Lake Champlain—Arnold's Cruise on the Lake—Battle of Valcour Island—Defeat of the American Fleet near Split Rock—The British occupy Crown Point—Condition of the American Army at Ticonderoga.

CHAPTER VIII. 116

1777—1783.—Burgoyne invades the United States— Evacuation of Ticonderoga by General St. Clair—Battle of Hubbardton—Surprise and Indignation of the People—Vindication of St. Clair and Schuyler—Lincoln's Expedition against Ticonderoga—Surrender of Burgoyne—Retreat to Canada—Operations on Lake Champlain from 1778 to 1783.

CHAPTER IX. 137

From 1783 to 1800—Progress and extent of Settlements on the borders of Lake Champlain—Personal Sketches—Trade and Commerce of the Country—Population, etc., etc.

CHAPTER X. 156

Difficulties between Great Britain and the United States—Henry's Mission to New England—President Madison's Message to Congress—Report of Committee on Foreign Affairs—Declaration of War in June, 1812—Troops ordered to the Champlain Frontier—General Dearborn's " Morning Visit " in Canada—His Army go into Winter Quarters—Affairs at St. Regis—Operations on the Ontario Frontier during the Summer of 1813—British and American Naval force on Lake Champlain—Loss of the Growler and Eagle—Colonel Murray burns the Barracks and Public Buildings at Plattsburgh.

CHAPTER XI. 171

Plan of the Campaign of 1813—Hampton at Lacolle and Chateaugay—Colonel Clark at Missisquoi Bay—Skirmishes—Operations on the Lake—Dispute between the Vermont volunteers and Governor Chittenden—Failure of the Campaign of 1813—Battle of Lacolle Mill—British attack the works near Otter Creek—Operations during the summer—Death of Colonel Forsyth—Izard ordered to the West—Condition of Affairs after his departure.

CHAPTER XII. 189

Sir George Provost invades the United States—Preparations at Plattsburgh to resist his advance—Description of the American Forts, etc. The British encamp at Chazy—Battle of Beekmantown—Provost's position on the north banks of the Saranac—Captain McGlassin attacks a British battery—American and British force on the lake—Naval engagement off Plattsburgh—Battle of Plattsburgh—Provost retreats to Canada—The Peace.

APPENDIX 211

INDEX 245

HISTORY OF LAKE CHAMPLAIN.

INTRODUCTORY.

General description of the Lake and of the most important points along its borders—Ancient and Modern names of places—Distances —Old Forts—Scenery—Original Indian name.

LAKE CHAMPLAIN extends from the 43°30″ to the 45° north latitude, and lies between Vermont and New York—the boundary line of those States running through its centre. The lake is about ninety miles in length, in a right line from North to South, with a length of coast, on each side, of about one hundred and twenty-five miles : its southern extremity, or head, being at Whitehall, and its northern near the boundary line between the United States and Canada. The lake varies in width from one-fourth of a mile to thirteen miles, and its waters cover an area of about five hundred square miles. It receives the waters of Lake George, at Ticonderoga, and discharges itself into the St. Lawrence, through the river Richelieu. There is no perceivable current in the body of the lake, and, its waters, at ordinary stages, pass into the Richelieu with a velocity of only one-third of a mile per hour.

The Lake has two arms ; one on the west side, near its southern extremity, called South Bay, the other, on the east side, near its northern extremity, called Missisco Bay. This last mentioned bay stretches into Canada and covers about thirty-five square miles. The area of country, drained into the lake, is variously estimated from seven thousand to nine thousand square miles. It probably approaches nearest to the larger estimate. Numerous rivers and creeks discharge themselves into the lake, among the principal of which are, on the New York side, Wood Creek, the outlet of Lake George, the Bouquet, Great and Little Ausable, the Salmon, the Saranac, and the Big and Little Chazy rivers. On the Vermont side are the Poultney river, Otter Creek, and the Winooski, Lamoille and Missisco rivers. The lake is subject to a rise and fall of from four to six feet during the year; the waters attaining their greatest height about the twentieth of May, after which they fall, gradually, until about the twentieth of September, when they usually reach the lower level of the remainder of the season. In 1869 the water reached a point nine feet nine inches above ordinary low-water mark, while in 1880 it fell to a point nine inches below low-water mark. The average between the highest and lowest water for thirteen years from 1875 to 1887— was five feet two inches.

Lake Champlain commences at the junction of Wood Creek with East Bay, in the town of Whitehall. The Indian name of this place was kah-cho-quah-na, " *the place where dip fish.*" Philip K. Skeene, an English Major under half pay, located here in 1763, and established a settlement at the mouth of Wood Creek, which was called Skeenesborough. This, for many years, was the most important settlement upon Lake Champlain. In 1773 it numbered seventy-three families, all of whom, with but two exceptions, were Skeene's tenants. The name of the town was changed to Whitehall in 1788.

About two miles north of the village of Whitehall is South Bay, an arm of the lake seven miles long and one mile wide extending to the south-west and separating the town of Whitehall from the town of Dresden. It was on the shores of this bay that the Baron de Dieskau landed, in 1755, with an army of fifteen hundred French and Indians, when marching against the English encampment at the head of Lake George.

Twenty-four miles below Whitehall is old fort Ticonderoga on the west, and Mount Independence on the east side of the lake. The waters of Lake George here discharge themselves into Lake Champlain through an outlet called, by the Indians, Cheonderoga; a word signifying "noisy," and which was applied in allusion to the falls on the outlet near its mouth. The French erected a fortress here in 1756, which they called Fort Carillon, and which was a place of great strength. Mount Defiance lies on the south side of the mouth of the outlet of Lake George, opposite Ticonderoga. The summit of this mountain is seven hundred and fifty feet above the lake, and within cannon shot of the old fortress.

Twelve miles north of Ticonderoga is Crown Point, called by the French *Pointe à la Chevelure*. Here the French built a fort in 1731, which they called Fort St. Frederic. This fort was destroyed by them on their retreat to Canada in 1759, and the same year General Amherst commenced a much larger work, the ruins of which are still to be seen.

Opposite Crown Point is a landing called Chimney Point, which was settled by the French, about the time they commenced building Fort St. Frederic, and was destroyed by them in 1759. So complete was the destruction of the settlement that when the English arrived, a few days after the retreat of the French, they saw nothing but the blackened chimneys of the consumed houses, standing as grim sentinels amid the surrounding ruin. These chimneys were permitted to stand for years, and gave the name of Chimney Point to that locality; a name it yet retains.

At the present day Lake Champlain is regarded as extending as far up as Whitehall, but among the early writers its head was knocked about in a manner most perplexing to modern readers. Kalm, who visited the lake in 1749, fixes upon Crown Point as the head, and speaks of that portion south of Crown Point, as "the river which comes out of the lake St. Sacrement to Lake Champlain." Doctor Thatcher, who was with St. Clair's army in 1777, considers the lake to reach no further south than Ticonderoga, and refers to South Bay as extending from that place to Skeenesborough "a distance of about thirty miles." By several the passage between Ticonderoga and Skeenesborough was called South River. Some writers have run the head of the lake as far up as the falls of Wood Creek, in the present village of Whitehall, while others describe Wood Creek as running as far north as the outlet of Lake George. I refer, at this time, to this difference of opinion among the early writers to guard the reader against the confusion which it has frequently produced and to explain an occasional discrepancy, apparently, between this work and the narratives of the events here collected.

Two miles north of Crown Point, and on the same side of the lake is Port Henry, and about eleven miles farther north is North-west Bay, called Bay *du Rochers Fendus*, in Sauthier's map of 1779. The village of Westport stands at the foot of this bay. On the opposite side of the lake, about ten miles north of Crown Point, is a small bay in which Arnold grounded and burned his galley and five gondolas after the engagement with the English, of the 13th October, 1776. Otter Creek, called by the French *la rivière aux Loutres* empties into the lake about seven miles north of this spot. The creek is navigable for lake vessels as far up as the falls of Vergennes, a distance of eight miles. In this creek Macdonough fitted out the fleet with which he gained the victory of the 11th of September, 1814. During the last war a small breast-work was thrown up on the north side of the creek at its mouth, where Lieutenant Cassin of the Navy, and Captain Thornton of the Artillery, with two hundred men, repulsed a large British force, sent out from Canada to destroy the American fleet fitting out at Vergennes. A few miles north, and on the opposite side of the lake, is Split Rock, called by the French *rocher fendu*. This rock has always been considered a great natural curiosity. It projects one hundred and fifty feet into the lake, and is elevated about thirty feet above the level of the water. The part detached contains half an acre, and is separated from the main rock by a channel about fifteen feet wide. The popular opinion is, that this rock was separated from the main land by an earthquake, *but Professor Emmons, who examined it particularly, supposes the separation to have been occasioned by the wearing away or decomposition of a mass of rock containing a large amount of pyritous iron.

The lake between Split Rock and Thompson's Point, formerly called Point *Regiochne*, is not quite one mile wide. A light-house has been erected by the general government, upon the main land, a few rods south of the rock. From this point the lake increases in width as it extends towards the north. Between Essex and Charlotte, four miles north, it is three miles wide. Opposite Burlington it is nine and three-quarters miles, and from shore to shore, opposite Plattsburgh, about thirteen miles wide.

Between Essex and Charlotte is Sloop Island, so called because an English vessel of war, during the revolution, fired upon it, mistaking, in the fog, the stump of a pine tree standing near its centre for the mast of a sloop. A short distance below Essex, on the New York side, is the mouth of Bouquet river. At the falls, two miles up this river, Burgoyne encamped and gave a war feast to a party of about four hundred Indians, previous to his attack on Ticonderoga in 1777. Fourteen miles north-east from Essex and on the opposite side of the lake, is the city of Burlington. About midway between these two places are four small islands called the Four Brothers. They are called *Isle de quatre vents* on Charlevoix's map of 1744 and the Four Winds Islands on Sauthier's map. Two and one-half miles south of Burlington is Pottier's Point, called *Erkly's* by Sauthier. It forms the west side of the mouth of Shelburne bay. Three miles south-west of Burlington is Juniper Island, on which stands a light-house erected in 1826.

North-west from Juniper Island and near the west

* In the winter of 1663 there was a severe earthquake in Canada. "Lakes appeared where none ever existed before; mountains were overthrown; rivers sought other beds or totally disappeared. The earth and the mountains entirely split and rent in innumerable places, creating chasms and precipices, whose depths have never been ascertained."—*Jesuit's Journal, Quebec*, 1663.

shore of the lake is Schuyler's Island, called by the
French, *Isle Au Chapon.* Under this island Arnold
collected his fleet on the morning of the 12th of October after his retreat from Valcour Island.   A little to
the south of this island is Douglass' Bay, called *Corlear*
by the French and Indians.   It is supposed by some
that the humane and noble Corlear was drowned in this
bay in 1667.

A mile to the north of Schuyler's Island is a bold
promontory called Point Trembleau.   At the foot of a
small bay, formed by this point, stands the village of
Port Kent, and about two miles to the north are the
mouths of the Great and Little Ausable rivers, which
empty into the lake near a sandy point, called point
Au Sable.   Six miles farther north and half a mile
from the main shore lies the island of Valcour, or Valeur, as it is sometimes called.   This island is celebrated on account of a severe naval engagement fought
near it between the Americans and English on the 11th
day of October, 1776.*   One mile north of Valcour is
St. Michel's, or Crab Island, and about three miles farther north is the mouth of the Saranac river, called
Salasanac on Sauthier's map.   The village of Plattsburgh lies on both sides of this river at its mouth.
Three miles east from Plattsburgh is Cumberland
Head, on which a light-house has been erected.   Cumberland Head was called by the French Cape *Scoumon-
ton* or *Scononton.*   It extends about three miles into
the lake in a southerly direction, and forms Cumberland Bay.   This bay was the scene of Macdonough's
naval victory of the 11th of September, 1814.   To the
east of Cumberland Head is a large island called Grand
Isle.   The Lamoille river empties into the lake on the
Vermont side near the south end of this island.   Eight
miles south of the Lamoille is the mouth of the Winooski.   North of Grand Isle, and separated from it

---

*A light-house has been erected upon the western side of the
island, and nearly opposite is a bold promontory called Bluff Point,
upon which a spacious hotel is being erected (1888-9) for a summer
resort.

by a narrow channel, is another large island called North Hero. This is the *Isle Longue* of the French.

Twelve miles north of Cumberland Head, and lying between North Hero and the western side of the lake is Isle La Motte. This island was named after Sieur la Mothe, a French officer who built a fort on the north end of the island in 1665, called Fort St. Anne. It was afterwards called Fort la Mothe. Kalm says this was a wooden fort or redoubt, standing on the west side of the island near the water's edge. It had disappeared when he passed through the lake in 1749, but he was shown the spot where it stood, which he describes as then "quite overgrown with trees." Opposite the north end of this island, and on the New York side, is the mouth of the Little Chazy river, and a short distance further north is the mouth of the Big Chazy. These rivers are called *Chasy* on a map of the survey of the lake made in 1732, and were originally named from Lieut. de Chasy, a French officer of distinction who, in 1665, was killed by a party of Mokawk Indians, while hunting in that vicinity. King's Bay lies north of the mouth of the Big Chazy. The north side of this bay is formed by Point Au Fer, which separates it from Rouse's Point Bay.

Point Au Fer was formerly separated from the main shore by a channel or deep morass connecting Rouse's Point Bay with King's Bay. Kalm says that the first houses he saw, after leaving Fort St. Frederic, were on the western side of the lake about ten French miles above St. Johns, in which the French had lived before the last war, but which were then (1749) abandoned. These houses probably stood either on Point Au Fer or near the mouth of the Big Chazy river. Prior to the revolution a brick house was built on this point, which was known as the " *White House.*" It was fortified with an entrenchment and cannon by General Sullivan, at the time of the invasion of Canada in 1775, and was then considered as a very advantageous position to command the navigation of the north end of the lake. Burgoyne, when he entered the United States, threw a body of troops into this place and it was retained by the British as a military post until after the Peace.

Opposite the northern part of Isle La Motte, on the Vermont side of the lake, is Alburgh Tongue, called by the French, *Pointe Algonquin.* The entrance to Missisco Bay is on the east side of this point. About eight miles north of Isle La Motte, also on the Vermont side, is Windmill Point. The French built a windmill here about the time of the erection of Fort St. Frederic at Crown Point, and had collected a small settlement near the mill; but the English having burnt the houses several times during their incursions into Canada, the settlement was at length abandoned. In 1749 nothing but the mill, which was built of stone, remained.

Opposite Windmill Point is the village of Rouse's Point. This is the terminus of the Ogdensburg (Northern) Railroad. It is also the terminus of the New York & Canada Railway of the Delaware & Hudson Canal Company's system of Railroads. The Canada Atlantic also has a station here. A connection is here formed between the Ogdensburg and the Vermont & Canada Railroads by a bridge and floating draw. The boundary line between the United States and Canada, as fixed by the Ashburton Treaty of 1842, is about one mile below this bridge. This line is located 4,200 feet north of the true parallel of the 45° of latitude, and was so established in order to secure to the United States the site of an old fort commenced by that government soon after the close of the war of 1812.

The parallel of 45° was originally correctly located by the French, but, in 1766, Governor Moore and Brigadier General Carleton visited Lake Champlain and fixed the boundary between Canada and the Province of New York about two and a half miles below Windmill Point, which Governor Moore says was further to the northward than they expected to find it from the observations said to have been made by the French some years before. Moore's line was recognized as the true one until about the year 1818, when, on taking new observations, it was found to be too far to the north. As soon as the error was discovered the United States suspended work on the fort, and the unfinished walls were long known as "Fort Blunder." Since the treaty of 1842 a new and larger fort has been built on the site of the old one, called Fort Montgomery.

Fort Montgomery stands at the foot of the lake. Here the river Richelieu commences and conveys the waters of the lake to the St. Lawrence. This river, for several years after the first settlement of Canada, was called the river of the Iroquois. Charlevoix says it was afterwards called the Richelieu on account of a fort of that name which had been built at its mouth, in 1641. This outlet of Lake Champlain is also called the Sorel or Chambly River.

Three and a half miles below the boundary line is Bloody Island, said to be so called on account of the murder of two lumbermen who were killed there by a party of soldiers sent out from Montreal to protect them from the Indians, on their return to the lake after having sold a raft of timber. Three-fourths of a mile below Ash Island or *Isle aux Tetes.* One mile below Ash Island is Hospital Island and six miles lower down the river is Isle Aux-Noix, where the French established a military post on their retreat from Crown Point in 1759. Thirteen miles below Isle Aux-Noix is the village of St. Johns. This place was selected for a military post by Montcalm in 1758. It was occupied by the French prior to 1749.

About thirteen miles below St. Johns is the village and fort of Chambly. A fort was built here by the French in 1664, which was called Fort St. Louis. It was at first built of wood, but had prior to 1721 been replaced by a strong work of stone, flanked with four bastions, and capable of containing a large garrison. Fort Richelieu, which we have already stated to have stood at the mouth of the river, was afterwards demolished and a new fort built there by Mons. de Sorel, to which his name was given.

Lake Champlain is situate on the western side of a valley lying between the Adirondacks of New York and the Green Mountains of Vermont. This valley is from one to thirty miles in width and about one hundred and eighty miles in length, north and south. Its greatest depression has been found to be between Westport, Burlington and Port Kent. A survey of the lake was made in the years 1870–5, when it was found that the depression commenced at Crown Point and extended as far north as Isle La Motte. The main channel, opposite Port Henry, has a depth of 40 feet; opposite Barber's Point, of 133 feet; opposite Westport, of 220 feet; opposite Split Rock, 392 feet; between Essex and McNiels Ferry, 399 feet; opposite Juniper Island, 338 feet; opposite Colchester light-house, 291 feet; opposite Valcour Island, 205 feet; opposite the point of Cumberland Head, 191 feet; opposite Pointe Au Roche light-house, 140 feet, and at the south end of Isle La Motte, 86 feet. South of Crown Point the depth varies from 15 to 30 feet, and north of Isle La Motte from 17 to 27 feet, The broad lake generally freezes over in January or February and remains closed until the month of March or April. In the years 1837, 1872, 1875 and 1884 it was closed by ice from 101 to 103 days. It was closed 7 days only in 1834, and was not frozen over during the years 1828, 1842 and 1850. The average duration of ice in the broad lake for 69 years, was 68 1-2 days. As soon as the broad lake closes between Port Kent and Burlington the channel opens at Rouse's Point.

Mr. Colvin states the mean level of the lake for eleven years—1871 to 1881—to have been 96,-561-1000 feet above tide. It is the popular opinion that the waters of the lake are gradually subsiding, but I judge this to be a mistake for the reason that the soundings made one hundred years ago do not differ materially from those of the present day. The water in the bays and along the shores is not as deep as it was formerly, from the washing of the banks and the deposit of earth, saw-dust and rubbish brought down by the creeks and rivers, but the surface is probably as high above tide as it was when the lake was first visited by Champlain in 1609. It is evident, however, from an examination of the adjacent shores and rocks, that the lake at one time filled a much larger portion of the valley than it does at present. Geologists suppose this entire valley to have been twice occupied by the ocean—but these speculations are of but little interest to the general reader, who, usually, is satisfied to take things as they have existed for the last five thousand years.

This lake has ever been celebrated for the beauty of its scenery and the bold and imposing configuration of the surrounding country. Upon the eastern side, the valley is wide and fertile, until we pass Mount Independence, going south, when the hills approach the lake, and, in some places, rise abrupt from its shores. On the New York side, the mountains in many places extend to the water's edge, as in the case of the Black Mountains south of Ticonderoga; the Kayadarosseras range which terminates with Bulwagga Mountain near Crown Point; the northern end of the West Moriah range at Split Rock, and of the Adirondack Mountains at Trembleau Point, near Port Kent. These several ranges run from the lake in a south-westerly direction, increasing in altitude as they recede, and presenting a scene at once bold and beautiful; hill after hill rising gradually above each other, until the highest peaks attain an elevation of five thousand feet. From the west the snow-crowned rocks of Mount Marcy, old White Face, and half a dozen other giants among the hills, look down in solemn grandeur on the lake; while, on the east, the eye passes over green fields to trace along the horizon the clear blue outline of Jay's Peak, Old Mansfield's "Chin" and "Nose," and Camel's Hump, the poetic *Lion Couchant* of the French.*

* The following are the elevations, above tide, of some of the peaks seen from Lake Champlain.

On the New York side, Mt. Marcy 5,344 feet. Dix's Peak, 4,916; Nipple Top, 4,604; Whiteface, 4,871; Raven Hill, 1,902; Bald Peak, 2,120; Lyon Mountain, 3,809 (Colvin).

On the Vermont side, The Chin, 4,348; The Nose, 4,044; Camel's Hump, 4,083; Jay's Peak, 4,018; Killington Peak. 3,924.

The original Indian name of Lake Champlain has been a subject of much speculation and research. By some it is supposed to have been called Peta-wa-bouque, meaning *alternate land and water*, in allusion to its numerous islands and projecting points of land. Among the other names ascribed to the lake are Caniaderi— Garunte, *the door or mouth of the country*; Petow-pargow, the *great water*, and Ska-ne-togh-ro-wah-na, *the largest lake.* These names, however, seem to have been selected more from the peculiar aptness of their meaning than from any known application to the lake itself. The early French writers do not refer to its Indian name, but speak of the lake as the passage that leads to the country of the Iroquois. Among the papers published in O'Callaghan's Documentary History of New York in relation to the old French Grants on Lake Champlain, is a letter from Governor Tryon to Lord Dartmouth, in which he states that this lake is called on Blain & Ogelby's and other ancient maps the " mer des Iroquois," the Richelieu river " riviere des Iroquois," and the tract on the east side of the lake " Iroscosia." From this it has been conjectured that the lake was called *Yroquois* by the Indians. But this is explained by Charlevoix, who says that the name was given to the river and lake by the French because the Mohawk Iroquois were in the habit of passing through their waters in their incursions into the French plantations on the St. Lawrence. Champlain affixed his own name to the lake during his exploration of its shores in July, 1609. It was, at a later day, sometimes called " Lake Corlear," in honor of a Dutchman who, in 1766, saved a party of French and Canada Indians from being destroyed by a war party of the Mohawks, and who, the year after was accidentally drowned there while on his way to Canada.

———

In the following chapters I propose to collect many facts connected with the history of Lake Champlain. No part of the United States is more interesting from its historic incidents. Every bay and island of the lake and nearly every foot of its shore has been the scene of some warlike movement—the midnight foray of the predatory savage, the bloody scout of frontier settlers, the rendezvous of armed bands or the conflict of contending armies. These stirring incidents extend in tradition far beyond the first discovery of the lake, and are brought down, by scattered and unconnected history, in an almost uninterrupted series of strifes and contentions, to the close of the war of 1812.

The first 150 years of French dominion over the Champlain Valley are described in great detail by Guy Omeron Coolidge in his The French Occupation of the Champlain Valley from 1609 to 1759 published in 1938 and reprinted by Harbor Hill Books.

CHAPTER I.

Progress of discoveries by the French in Canada—Character of the Indian tribes—Champlain's visit to Lake Champlain in 1609—Battle between the Canada Indians and the Iroquois—Fort erected on Isle La Motte—De Courcelle's Expedition to the Mohawk River.

BUT little progress was made by the French in their American discoveries until the spring of 1534, when Jacques Cartier sailed from France with two small vessels and, in the month of May, reached Bonavista in Newfoundland. Cartier coasted around the north shore of the island and along the gulf of St. Lawrence and, in September, returned to France. The following year he left France with three ships and, entering the mouth of the St. Lawrence, ascended that river as far as the St. Croix (St. Charles) near the Indian village Stadacona (Quebec), where he passed the winter. While his party were preparing their winter quarters, Cartier, with thirty-five armed men, proceeded up the river as far as Hochelaga (Montreal), where he arrived on the second day of October.

" Hochelaga," says Warburton,* " stood in the midst of great fields of Indian corn ; it was of a circular form, containing about fifty large huts, each fifty paces long and from fourteen to fifteen wide, all built in the shape of tunnels, formed of wood, and covered with birch bark ; the dwellings were divided into several rooms, surrounding an open court in the centre, where the fires burned. Three rows of palisades encircled the town, with only one entrance ; above the gate, and over the whole length of the outer ring of defence, there was a gallery, approached by flights of steps, and plentifully provided with stones and other missiles to resist attack. This

* Conquest of Canada, Volume 1.

was a place of considerable importance, even in those
remote days, as the capital of a great extent of country,
and as having eight or ten villages subject to its sway.
The inhabitants spoke the language of the Great Huron nation and were more advanced in civilization than
any of their neighbors ; unlike other tribes, they cultivated the ground and remained stationary." This was
Hochelaga in 1534. Seventy years later it had sunk
into a decayed and unimportant place.

On the 11th of October Cartier rejoined his party at
St. Croix, and, the following spring, returned to France.
Early in the spring of 1541 he again sailed for America
and, entering the St. Lawrence, passed up that stream
as high as the rapids of Lachine. The next spring he
returned to Europe and soon afterwards died. No effort
was made by the French to colonize Canada, after the
return of Cartier and his associates, until the year 1603,
when an armament was fitted out, under the command
of Pontgrave, to make further dicoveries in the St.
Lawrence. Among the officers who accompanied this
expedition was SAMUEL DE CHAMPLAIN, a captain in
the French navy and a native of Saintonge. Pontgrave
and Champlain explored the St. Lawrence as far as the
Lachine Rapids, which was the highest point reached by
Cartier sixty-eight years before. In 1604 Champlain
accompanied De Monts to Canada and again returned
to France in the fall of that year.

In 1608, De Monts, who was at the head of a trading
company, equipped two ships at Honfleur, and sent
them out under the command of Champlain and Pontgrave, for the purpose of establishing the fur trade at
Tadousac. Champlain reached Tadoussac on the 3d
day of June, and, after a brief stay there, ascended the
St. Lawrence, and on the 3d day of July arrived at the
ancient village Stadacona, which he selected as the site
of the future capital of Canada.

When the French first visited Canada the Indians
residing north of the river St. Lawrence were engaged
in war with the Five Nations of Indians who occupied
the territory south of the St. Lawrence. The Five Na-

tions were a powerful confederacy, consisting of the Mohawks, the Oneidas, the Cayugas, the Onondagas and the Senecas. They called themselves the Aganuschioni, or United People.* The French called them the Iroquois; the Dutch the Maquas. By the Delawares they were called Mingoes. Lafitau gives them the name of the Agonnonsionni, as does Charlevoix, who says, " Leur nom propre est Agonnonsionni, qui veut dire, Fraiseurs de Cabannes; parcequ'ils les batissent beaucoup plus solides, que la plupart des autres sauvages."† In 1712 the Tuscaroras, who had been driven from the south by the English, were admitted into the confederacy, which was afterwards known as the " Six Nations."

Prior to the settlement of Canada by the French the Iroquois occupied all the country south of the river St. Lawrence and resided in numbers around Montreal and in the valley of Lake Champlain, but they had been driven off towards Lake Ontario by the Adirondacks, who lived near the Three Rivers. The success of the Adirondacks was of short duration, for soon afterwards they, in their turn, were driven from their ancient seats to a safer position below Quebec.‡ In 1608 the Iroquois resided upon the banks of the Mohawk and in several villages to the west of that river. They claimed the whole country lying on both sides of Lake Champlain, as far north as the St. Lawrence. The northern bank of the St. Lawrence was held by the Algonquins, the ancient and inveterate enemies of the Iroquois. The Hurons, a numerous nation residing west of Lake Ontario, were in alliance with the Algonquins and joined them in their wars against the Iroquois.

The Iroquois were powerful, politic, warlike and courageous. They have been termed among Europeans the Romans of the West.§ Charlevoix says the name

* Governor Clinton's discourse before the N. Y. Historical Society.
† Charlevoix, Tom 1.
‡ Gordon.
§ Warburton, Vol. 1.

of Iroquois was formed from the Indian *Hiro*, which means *I have said*, with which these Indians always finished their speeches, and *de koue*, a word often used by them and which, when pronounced with a drawl was a cry of grief, and, when spoken short and quick, one of exultation.* They lived in villages, around which they had extensive cultivated fields. These villages were enclosed with strong quadruple palisades of large timber, about thirty feet high, interlocked with each other, with an interval of not more than half a foot between them. On the inner side of the palisades were galleries in the form of parapets defended with double pieces of timber.† The Algonquins were a warlike nation and the most polished of the northern tribes. They were a migratory people, disdaining the cultivation of the soil and depending altogether on the produce of the chase. The Hurons had some slight knowledge of husbandry, but were more effeminate and luxurious than the other tribes, and inferior in savage virtue and independence.‡ They lived in villages, of which the nation possessed twenty, but which were inferior in construction and strength to those of the Iroquois.

When Champlain landed at Quebec he found the Algonquins and Hurons engaged in active war with the Mohawks, one of the oldest and most powerful branches of the Five Nations. Learning from some Indians who visited his encampment in the winter, that they intended an inroad into the country of their enemy in the course of the approaching summer, he determined to accompany them, and, by that means, not only explore a river and large lake through which the war party would pass, but by his powerful assistance strengthen the friendship which then existed between the French and the neighboring Indians. For this purpose, on the 18th of April, 1609, he left Quebec on board a pinnace accompanied by a small party of followers, and ascending the St. Lawrence as far as the mouth of the Riche-

* Charlevoix, Tome 1.
† Champlain's Voyage de la Nouv: France.
‡ Warburton, Vol. 1.

lieu, passed up that stream to the foot of the rapids near Chambly. Here a war party of sixty Algonquins and Hurons joined him, and commenced preparations for the incursion.

It would seem that it was Champlain's intention to take his whole party with him, but the men, intimidated by the small number of the Indians or from some other cause, refused to proceed any further, and, after the strongest appeals on the part of Champlain, but two would accompany him. With these alone he determined to join the Indians on their long and perilous expedition. All their arrangements being completed, Champlain and his two companions, on the 2d of July, embarked with the Indians in twenty-four canoes and that day proceeded up the river to a point about nine miles above the island of St. Theresa, where they encamped for the night. The next day they continued on as far as the lake, which they entered on the following morning, and coasted along its west shore until they came within two or three days' journey of the place where they expected to meet the enemy. After this they travelled only by night, each morning retiring into a barricaded camp to pass the day. The party advanced with the utmost caution, keeping their canoes close together, and making no noise which might be heard by the enemy should they happen to be near. During the whole journey they used no fire but lived upon dried Indian meal soaked in water.

Champlain, in his account of this expedition, particularly refers to the superstition of the Indians and the importance they attach to dreams.* Whenever he awoke they would eagerly inquire whether he had dreamed of or seen their enemies. One day, while the party lay concealed near Crown Point, Champlain fell

---

* The Indian trusts to his dreams and invariably holds them sacred. Before he engages in any important undertaking, particularly in war, diplomacy, or the chase, the dreams of the principal chiefs are carefully watched and examined; by their interpretation his conduct is guided. In this manner the fate of a whole nation has often been decided by the chance vision of a single man.—*Conquest of Canada, Volume* I, *page* 192.

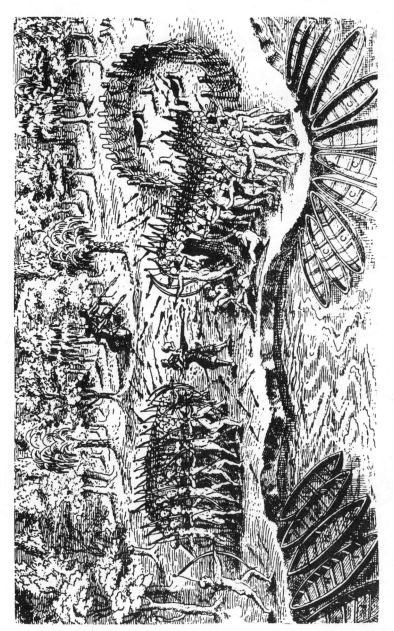

Champlain's Battle with Iroquois. A drawing by Champlain.

Auguste Rodin's bust "La France" placed on the Champlain
Memorial Lighthouse at Crown Point on May 3rd, 1912.

asleep and thought he saw the Iroquois drowning in the lake within sight of the encampment. On awaking he related the dream to the Indians, which, he says, gained such credit among them that they no longer doubted but they should meet with success." That same night about ten o'clock, while proceeding cautiously along, they met a war party of the Iroquois, who were passing down the lake in canoes.

As soon as the two parties discovered each other the Iroquois hastened to the shore and, having first secured their canoes, began to cut down trees and form a barricade. The others pushed out towards the centre of the lake and proceeded to fasten their canoes together, and then secured them, with poles, in a position within arrow-shot of the barricade. Two canoes were then sent towards the shore to inquire whether the Iroquois wished to fight, who answered they did, but proposed, as it was then dark, that the battle be deferred until morning. To this the Algonquins and Hurons agreed and both parties passed the night in singing and taunting their rivals with cowardice and imbecility. Champlain and his two companions were equipped in light armor, and each carried an arquebus. They were placed in different canoes and kept themselves concealed from sight, lest the Iroquois might be alarmed at their appearance and decline the combat.

On the following morning an engagement took place which is thus recorded by Champlain.* " The moment we landed they (the Algonquins and Hurons) began to run about two hundred paces toward their enemies who stood firm, and had not yet perceived my companions, who went into the bush with some savages. Our Indians commenced calling me in a loud voice, and, opening their ranks, placed me at their head, about twenty paces in advance, in which order we marched until I was within thirty paces of the enemy. The moment they saw me they halted, gazing at me and I at them. When I saw them preparing to shoot at us, I raised my arquebus, and, aiming directly at one of

* Voyages de la Nouv: France.

the three chiefs, two of them fell to the ground by this
shot, and one of their companions received a wound of
which he died afterwards. I had put four balls in my
arquebus. Our party on witnessing a shot so favorable
for them, set up such tremendous shouts that thunder
could not have been heard; and yet, there was no lack
of arrows on one side and the other. The Iroquois
were greatly astonished at seeing two men killed so
instantaneously, notwithstanding they were provided
with arrow-proof armor woven of cotton thread and
wood ; this frightened them very much. Whilst I was
re-loading, one of my companions in the bush fired a
shot, which so astonished them anew, seeing their
chiefs slain, that they lost courage, took to flight and
abandoned the field and their fort, hiding themselves
in the depth of the forests, whither pursuing them I
killed some others. Our savages also killed several of
them and took ten or twelve prisoners. The rest
carried off the wounded. Fifteen or sixteen of our
party were wounded by arrows ; they were promptly
cured."

This battle was fought on the 30th of July, near
what Champlain describes as "the point of a Cape
which juts into the lake on the west side." Some writers have located the battle-ground on Lake George.
Doctor Fitch* thinks it took place upon one of the
points of land in the town of Dresden or Putnam, south
of Ticonderoga ; but, from an examination of Champlain's map of New France,† it is evident that the engagement took place somewhere between Crown Point
and Lake George, probably in the town of Ticonderoga.

As soon as the victorious party had gathered the
weapons and other spoils left behind by the Iroquois,
they embarked on their return for Canada. After proceeding about eight leagues down the lake they landed,
after night fall, when the Indians put one of their pris-

* Historical Survey of Washington County.
† A copy of this map will be found in Vol. 3 of O'Callaghan's Documentary History of New York.

oners to death with the most horrible and protracted tortures. The rest of their prisoners were taken to Canada. At the rapids of the Richelieu the party separated and the Indians returned to their homes, well satisfied, says Champlain, with the result of the expedition and uttering strong professions of gratitude and friendship for the French.*

The above is, in substance, Champlain's narrative of the first visit of civilized man within the limits of the state of New York. Two months later Henry Hudson entered New York Bay and ascended the North River as far as the present village of Waterford.† Thus were the northern and southern sections of the state almost simultaneously explored by the European. How unlike was the subsequent fate of these bold explorers. Hudson returned to Europe in the autumn of the same year, and, in April, 1810, again sailed in search of unknown lands. It was his last voyage. Steering westward from Greenland he discovered and passed through the straits now known by his name, and entered Hudson Bay. He decided to winter upon the border of this bay, but the sailors mutinied, and placing him and a few others, who remained faithful, in an open boat, and abandoned them to the mercy of the waves. No trace of the brave captain, or his companions, was ever discovered.

After the departure of the Indians Champlain returned to Quebec. He continued Governor of Canada until 1629, when he surrendered the government to the English and returned home. In 1632 Canada was restored to France, and, the next year, Champlain was

---

* Charlevoix and most English writers say that Champlain, on this expedition, ascended a rapid and passed into another lake afterwards called Lake St. Sacrament. Champlain, in his account, says the Indians told him of a waterfall and of a lake beyond, *three or four leagues long*, and adds that he saw the waterfall, but says nothing of the lake. Had he explored the lake he would not have represented it as only three or four leagues long.

† Hudson first entered New York Bay in September 1609. He sailed up the river as far as Albany and embarking in small boats continued on to Waterford, where he arrived on the 22d of that month.

re-appoined Governor of the colony; which situation he continued to hold until his death, at Quebec, in 1635.

Champlain was brave, high-minded, active and generous, and eminent for his Christian zeal and purity. "The salvation of one soul," he often said, "is of more value than the founding of a new empire." During his life he fostered Christianity and civilization and succeeded in planting them among the snows of Canada. The only great mistake of his administration was an injudicious interference in the quarrels between the Indians. By this means he directed the hostility of the warlike Mohawks against the French, and created an implacable hatred on the part of that powerful nation, which time could not heal, nor the blood of a thousand victims soften. The Mohawks never forgot that fatal 30th of July, 1609. The names of the three chiefs who then fell at the fire of the Frenchman's arquebus were not appeased until rivers of blood had flowed beneath the tomahawk of the avenger. For every feather in the waving plumes of those chieftains a bloody scalp was counted — for every triumphant shout of the victorious Hurons and Algonquins, in after years, an answering shout was returned.

Mons. de Montmagny succeeded Champlain as Governor of New France. In 1641 he erected a fort at the mouth of the Richelieu, as a protection against the repeated inroads of the Indians by the way of Lake Champlain. M. de Montmagny was succeeded by M. D' Ailleboust, in the course of whose administration, of three years,* the Iroquois made several inroads into the territory of the Hurons and drove them from the fertile banks of the Ottawa. These victories of the Iroquois rendered them more audacious than ever. Breaking a solemn treaty of peace made with M. de Montmagny several years before, they again appeared among the French settlements, despising forts and

* The Governors of New France held office for three years only; in consequence of a decree that no one man should hold the government of a colony for more than that length of time.—Warburton.

impunity. In their attacks no force was too strong for them to overcome; no hiding place too secret for them to discover. So great, at length, became the audacity of these savages that they suddenly fell upon a body of Algonquins, under the very guns of the fortress of Quebec, and massacred them without mercy.

A dark and unpropitious gloom hung over the affairs of the colony until the arrival of the Marquis de Tracy, as viceroy, in 1664. M. de Tracy brought with him the Carignan-Salieres, a veteran regiment which had greatly distinguished itself in the wars against the Turks.* Immediately on the arrival of these troops they were sent, accompanied by the allied Indians, against the Iroquois and soon cleared the country of those troublesome enemies. Having established peace throughout the colony, M. de Tracy prepared to adopt measures to make that security permanent. The hostile Indians had been accustomed to approach the French settlements by the way of Lake Champlain and the Richelieu River, and to effectually block up this avenue three Captains of the Carignan regiment, MM. de Sorel, de Chambly and de Salieres, were ordered to erect forts on that river.

M. de Sorel built a fort at the mouth of the river, on the site of old fort Richelieu erected by de Montmagny in 1641. M. de Chambly built a fort at the foot of the rapids, in the present village of Chambly, which he called fort St. Louis, and M. de Salieres built one nine miles above, which he named St. Theresa, because it was finished on that Saint's day. The next year M. de La Mothe, another Captain in the Carignan regiment, was sent to Lake Champlain to construct a fort on an island near the lower end of the lake, which was intended to serve as a place of rendezvous, "from which continual attacks could be made on the enemy."† This fort was called St. Anne.

---

* This regiment was raised in Savoy by the Prince of Carignan in 1644, and was subsequently incorporated in the French army. When ordered to America it was placed under the command of Col. de Salieres—hence its double name, Carignan-Salieres.

† Relations, etc., de la Nouv: France.

As soon as tidings of the erection of these forts reached the Iroquois, three of those tribes sent deputies to Quebec with proposals of peace. M. de Tracy gave them a friendly audience and sent them back with valuable presents.

About the same time he determined to invade the country of the Mohawks, who with the Oneidas, remained stubborn and inflexible, and inflict summary punishment upon them for their former insolence and treachery. With this view M. de Courcelles was ordered to fit out a military expedition with the utmost dispatch. On the 9th of Jan., 1666, he started with three hundred men of the regiment of Carignan-Salieres, and two hundred volunteers, *habitans*, for Fort St. Theresa, which had been designated as the place of rendezvous. The weather was so severe that before they had advanced three days' journey many of the men would have perished, had they not been carried along by their companions. On the 24th Sieurs de la Fouille, Maximin and Lobiac, Captains of the Carignan regiment, joined the army with sixty men and some *habitans*, but before they reached St. Theresa so many men had become disabled that it was necessary to withdraw four companies from the forts on the Richelieu to supply the vacancies in the ranks.

On the 30th of January De Courcelles marched out of Fort St. Theresa at the head of five hundred men, and passing the lake on the ice, crossed the country towards the Mohawk villages. The snow was nearly four feet deep, and the men were obliged to use snow-shoes to pass over it. As horses could make no progress through the deep snow, a large number of slight sledges were prepared which were loaded with provisions and dragged along by the men, or by large dogs brought on for that purpose. Each man, including all the officers, carried upon his back from twenty-five to thirty pounds of biscuit or other supplies.* The intention of the French had

* Relations de ce qui s'est passes en la Nouv. France en annees 1665—6.

been to march direct against the Mohawk villages, but
having lost their way, through the ignorance of their
guides, they turned too far to the south, and on the 9th
of February arrived within two miles of Schenectady,
where they encamped. Here they were met by a small
party of Mohawks, who, pretending to retreat, were
carelessly pursued by sixty of the French Fusileers,
who were thus drawn into an ambuscade of about two
hundred Indian warriors securely posted behind the trees
of the forest. At the first volley of the Indians eleven
of the French, including a Lieutenant, were killed and
several wounded. The fusileers discharged their pieces
and immediately fell back upon the main body of the
army, while the Indians retired with a loss of three
killed and six wounded, taking with them the scalps of
four Frenchmen, which they exhibited in the streets of
Schenectady. It is said the whole company of fusileers
would have been massacred, but for the intercession of
Corlear, a Dutchman greatly beloved by the Mohawks,
who humanely interceded in their behalf.*

Information of the approach of the French having
been sent to Fort Albany by the authorities of Schenectady, three of the principal citizens were sent to M. de
Courcelles to inquire what were his intentions in invading the country belonging to the English. De Courcelles replied that he had no desire to molest the English in their possessions, but came solely to seek out and
punish the Mohawks, who were the unrelenting enemies of the French. He also represented to them the
state of his army, worn out with fatigue and hunger,
and requested that they would sell him provisions and
consent that be might send his wounded to Albany.
The English readily assented to do as he desired, and
the next day seven wounded Frenchmen were sent to
Albany. The inhabitants also carried large quantities
of beans, bread and other provisions to the French camp,
for which they were liberally paid.

De Courcelles, having rested his men until the 12th

---

* Gordon says the whole of De Courcelles' party would have been
destroyed but for intercession of Corlear.

suddenly broke up his camp and hastily retraced his steps to Lake Champlain and from thence to Canada. The Mohawks, who were at their first village, learning the retreat of the French, immediately started in pursuit and followed them as far as the lake, where they took three prisoners and found the bodies of five men who had perished of cold and hunger.*

The expedition of M. de Courcelles, although it had failed to reach the Mohawk villages, through the mistake of the guides, caused much anxiety to the Indians, nor were their fears diminished by the information communicated by the prisoners that M. de Tracy intended to send a much larger force into their country the next summer. To avert the threatening storm, they determined to make immediate overtures of peace. Accordingly, in June, 1666, ten ambassadors from the Mohawks, accompanied by a delegation of Oneidas, repaired to Quebec asking protection for their people and a renewal of the old treaties of peace. M. de Tracy at first refused to receive their wampum belts, but perceiving that this caused them great anxiety, he finally accepted their proposals. But while the negotiations were in progress at Quebec, and just as the French viceroy began to congratulate himself upon the future security of his colony, a tragedy took place on Lake Champlain, which for the time defeated his plans and destroyed all his confidence in the professions of the Indian deputies.

Fort St. Anne was at this time garrisoned by several companies of the Carignan regiment, one of which was commanded by Sieur de Chasy, a nephew of the viceroy. Apprised of the friendly professions of the Mohawks and their desire for peace, the ambassadors of that nation having passed the fort on their way to Quebec, the officers relaxed their usual vigilance and amused themselves by fishing and hunting in the neighborhood. While a small party of French officers and soldiers were thus engaged, they were suddenly

* London Document II. In 1st Volume Documentary History of New York.

attacked by a band of Mohawk Indians, who killed two
Carignan captains de Travesy and de Chasy, and took
several volunteers prisoners. Information of this treach-
erous act was immediately sent to Quebec, and one of
the Indian deputies had the vain audacity to boast, at
M. de Tracy's table, that he had slain the officers with
his own hand. The Indian was seized and strangled
on the spot ; and M. de Tracy, breaking off all negotiations, sent M. de Sorel, at the head of three hundred
men, against the Mohawk villages with orders to over-
run the whole country and to put every inhabitant to
the sword. M. de Sorel had by forced marches crossed
Lake Champlain, and was pushing rapidly towards the
Indian villages,when he was met by a new deputation
from the Mohawks, bringing back the Frenchmen taken
prisoners near Fort St. Anne and offering every satis-
faction for the murders committed there.

Still desirous to secure peace, and in the belief that
the demonstration already made had over-awed the Indian, M. de Sorel retraced his steps to Quebec, where
negotiations were again resumed with such success that,
on the 12th of July, a treaty was signed by which the
Indians agreed to restore the Canadian, Algonquin and
Huron prisoners in their hands, and to become the fast
friends and allies of the French. On the other part, the
viceroy promised to extend his protection over their
nation, " to send some black-gowns (Jesuit missionaries)
among them " and " to open a trade and commerce by
the lake du Saint Sacrement." *

* Relations, en années, 1665—6.

CHAPTER II.

M. De Tracy collects a large army at Isle La Motte—He marches against and destroys the Mohawk villages—Condition of Canada—De Callieres' project for the invasion of New York—Burning of Schenectady—Captain John Schuyler's attack upon Fort Laprairie —Major Philip Schuyler's expedition to Canada—De Frontenac marches against the Mohawks.

WAR is the delight of the savage. It furnishes an excitement necessary to his happiness. Without it he pines and wastes in insufferable quiet; a restless, miserable. being. To gratify his passion for war he does not hesitate to violate the most sacred treaties or break the ties of long continued friendship, " We must either," says Sir William Johnson,* " permit these people to cut each other's throats, or risk their discharging their fury on our traders and defenceless frontiers."

M. de Tracy soon found that he could only secure permanent peace and quiet to the colony, by an expedition into the Mohawk country, of such force as to make that implacable nation feel the destructive power of the French Arms. With such an army he now prepared to march against the Indian villages on the Mohawk River. Never had Fort St. Anne presented so lively a scene as was beheld there in September, 1666. Within the fort and close under its defences were collected six hundred veterans of the Carignan-Salieres, while on the main shore opposite lay encamped an equal number of volunteers, *habitans* of the colony. One hundred Huron and Algonquin warriors, bedaubed with paint and bedecked with feathers, stalked majestically among the crowd, and rendered the night boisterous with their war songs and dances. The labor of preparing this expedition, the largest which had yet been collected on Lake Champlain, was confided to M. Talon, Intendant of New France.

* Letter to Earl of Hillsborough.

On the 1st of October, M. de Courcelles started from the fort at the head of four hundred men. On the 3d the main body of the army moved off under the immediate command of M. de Tracy, who despite his advanced years, was determined to lead the expedition in person. Four days afterwards Sieurs de Chambly and Berthier followed with the rear guard. The progress of the army, after it reached the upper end of the lake, was slow and laborious, as the men dragged with them two small pieces of cannon and three hundred bateau or bark canoes, which had been provided for crossing the lakes and rivers on the route. It was De Tracy's intention to surprise the Indians before they should learn of his advance; but, notwithstanding the great caution of the troops, the Mohawks received timely information of their approach, and, abandoning the villages, secreted themselves in the surrounding forests, or ascended the mountains, and from a distance fired random shots at the soldiers. The French found the cabins of this nation larger and better built than any they had seen elsewhere. The villages were surrounded by a triple palisade twenty feet in height, newly repaired and strengthened and flanked by four bastions. Large quantities of Indian corn, beans and other provisions were stored away in magazines sunk in the ground, and numerous bark tanks filled with water stood about the enclosure to supply the inhabitants with water, and to extinguish fires when necessary. Everything indicated that the Indians intended to make a strong defence, had they not been intimidated by the strength and numbers of the invaders. But as it was, not a warrior or able-bodied man was to be seen; they had fled, leaving behind only the women and a few old and decrepit men, too feeble to escape. These M. de Tracy retained as prisoners. In this manner he passed through the whole country until he reached the most remote Mohawk village, which he burned. After celebrating Mass and returning thanks to God for the success of the enterprise, the French retraced their steps towards Canada, on their way burning the other villages and detroying all the provisions they could not carry off.*

While the army was passing near Schenectady on its return, M. de Courcelles called upon Corlear, who it will be remembered had rendered the French such signal service the preceding winter, and invited him to visit Canada. On Lake Champlain the fleet of boats encountered a heavy storm, which capsized two canoes with eight persons on board, all of whom were unfortunately drowned. Among the persons thus lost were Corlear and Lieut. Sieur de Luges, an officer of great merit and distinction.†

The expedition of M. de Tracy effectually subdued the Mohawks, and, for the next twenty years, secured the settlements on the St. Lawrence from the inroads of that nation. But Canada was not destined long to enjoy the blessings of profound peace. Ten years had scarcely elapsed before she found herself again engaged in a destructive war with the Western Iroquois, which continued, with short intervals of truce and with varied success, until the treaty of Utrecht in 1713. For several years after the commencement of this war the English colonists were on friendly terms with those of Canada, and repeatedly refused to aid the Western Iroquois in their controversy with the French. They were equally careful to do nothing to prevent it. "The Five Nations are a bulwark between us and the French," said Governor Dongan.‡ That bulwark was strongest in war. In times of peace it might crumble into atoms.

The accession of William and Mary to the throne of England, in 1689, was followed by a war between the English and French, which continued until the peace

* Relation, etc., en la Nouv. France, en années 1665—6.

† The accounts of these expeditions through Lake Champlain do not clearly indicate the route followed by the French, but it was probably along the western border of the lake as far south as the outlet of Lake George, then up the outlet and through that lake to its head, from whence it crossed the country to the waters of the Hudson River. In the treaty between the French and Iroquois, referred to at the close of the preceeding chapter, it was expressly provided that trade and commerce be opened to the Iroquois, with New France, "by the lake du saint Sacrement."

‡ Dongan's Report to the Committee of Trade, 1687.

of Ryswick in 1697. The news of the quarrel between the mother countries soon reached America, and found the colonists of both nations, not only willing, but anxious to participate in the struggle. The Chevalier de Callieres, who was Governor of Montreal and Commander-in-chief of the troops and militia in Canada, visited France in the year 1689, and submitted to the King a project for the reduction of the Province of New York, the re-establishment of French ascendency over the Five Nations, and the consequent control of the lucrative fur trade of America.

De Callieres' plan was to lead an army of two thousand men up the Richelieu River and Lake Champlain as far as the carrying place between Wood Creek and the Hudson River, where he would build a small log fort, and garrison it with two hundred men to guard the bateau during his absence. With the rest of his army he would march direct against Fort Orange (Albany) which he would seize, and then, embarking in the boats and canoes found there, would push on for New York. This town he represented as containing two hundred houses, protected by a small fort which could offer but a slight resistance to his attack. To prevent succor reaching the town from Boston or England, he required that two ships of war should be sent to cruise in the mouth of the river until his arrival. De Callieres predicted the highest benefits to France from the success of his project. " It will," he declared, " firmly establish the Christian religion as well among the Iroquois as among the other savages to whom we shall be able to speak as masters, when they are encircled on the side of Canada as well as of New York. It will secure and facilitate the cod-fishery, which is carried on along our coasts of Lacadie and on the Great Bank. It will give His Majesty one of the finest harbors in America which can be entered during almost all seasons of the year, in less than one month of very easy navigation." Accept the favorable opportunity which presents itself of becoming masters of New York, adds de Callieres in conclusion, and the trade of our

Colony will flourish; reject it and English intrigues with the Iroquois and other savages will destroy Canada in a little while.*

The French King received de Callieres with favor and in June of the same year sent instructions to Count de Frontenac, then viceroy of Canada, to organize an expedition to carry out the proposed plan, and directed that De Callieres should be appointed Governor of the conquered Province.—The King also ordered Sieur Begon to send out two ships of war under command of Sieur de la Caffiniere, who was instructed to place himself under the direction of de Frontenac. Should the proposed expedition fail, de Caffiniere was ordered " to make war against the English, and to range along the coasts of New England and New York, to capture as many prizes as possible, and to remain there until he have no more provisions than are necessary for his return to France."†

While the French were engaged in prosecuting the war with the Indians at the west they seem to have been regardless of the exposed state of the frontier towards Lake Champlain. The old forts of St. Anne and St. Theresa, which had proved so great a protection twenty years before, were suffered to decay. Montreal was not fortified ; a triple palisade, in poor repair, being its main defence. Indeed the only work in that quarter of any strength was the fort at Chambly, which had been rebuilt of stone and was surrounded by a small but flourishing settlement. On the 12th of November, 1687, a formidable party of the Iroquois suddenly attacked this fort. The garrison made a successful resistance, but the settlement around was ravaged and several of the inhabitants taken prisoners. A few days later the whole country between the St. Lawrence and the Richelieu swarmed with a savage host, who demanded immediate audience with the Governor, M. de Denonville, and haughtily dictated peace to the weak and terrified inhabitants. " Look," cried the proud

---

* De Callieres to the Marquis of Seignelay.　January, 1689.
† Instructions to Count de Frontenac, June 7th, 1689.

Chief, pointing towards a band of twelve hundred warriors at his back, " we are like the leaves of the forest in number and stronger than the mighty oak. Your people are few and weak. We have no occasion to lift our whole hand, for our little finger is sufficient to destroy you." Denonville bowed before a storm he could not resist, and concluded a treaty of peace upon the terms proposed by the savages.

Of short duration was this boon of peace to the French, the acceptance of which alike proclaimed their own humiliation and the power *of their savage foe. On the 26th of July, 1688, twelve hundred Indian warriors landed on the island of Montreal, and having overpowered a force of one hundred and fifty Canadians and fifty Indians imprudently sent against them, devastated the whole settlement, killing nearly a thousand of the inhabitants and carrying two hundred of them into captivity.* The St. Lawrence frontier was now at the mercy of the fierce and relentless Iroquois. The power of the French was paralyzed; trade languished, agriculture was interrupted and the very existence of the colony threatened.

Such was the gloomy condition of affairs when the instructions of the King, for an invasion of New York, reached the Count de Frontenac. The troops in Canada consisted of thirty-five companies of regulars, each of which, when full, numbered fifty men. But at least four hundred and fifty were required to fill the ranks, so that the actual number did not exceed thirteen hundred.† Of the *habitans*, about three thousand were able to bear arms.‡ Although de Frontenac could not send out an expedition of the magnitude and strength proposed in his instructions, he nevertheless determined to organize three small detachments to march against the English. One was to rendezvous at Montreal and was to proceed against Albany, another was to assemble

* Gordon—Warburton, Vol. 1.
† De Callieres to the Marquis of Seignelay.
‡ This was the estimated number in 1687. It had probably decreased during two succeeding years--See Gov. Dongan's Report to Board of Trade.

at Three Rivers, from whence a descent was to be made
upon the settlements near the Connecticut, and the third
was to start from Quebec to attack the settlements, on
the seaboard, east of Boston.

The party which left Three Rivers surprised and
destroyed the English settlement of Salmon Falls and
on their retreat, falling in with M. de Mamerval, who
had marched from Quebec, joined him in an attack on
the fortified village of Kaskebe upon the sea coast,
which they captured after a severe struggle.*

The third and most important detachment numbered
two hundred and ten men, including ninety-six Huron
and Algonquin Indians. This detachment was placed
under the command of two Canadian officers, Sieur la
Moyne de St. Helene and Lieutenant Daillebout de
Mantet, having under them D'Iberville and De Mon-
tesson. Attached to the expedition as volunteers were
Sieurs de Bonrepos and de la Brosse, two Calvinist officers, and Sieurs de Blainville and de Montigny. The
party left Montreal about the middle of the month of
January 1690, crossing to the Richelieu and ascending
that river and Lake Champlain on the ice. At the
close of the sixth day's march a consultation was held to
determine the route to be taken and to regulate the
plan of attack. The Indians asked where the officers
proposed to lead them. To this De St. Helene replied
that he had received no orders to march against any
particular place, but generally to act as he should think
best, and that he wished to attack and surprise Fort
Orange, which he represented as the capital of New
York and a place of considerable importance. The
Indians, remembering the defeats of the French during
the preceding year, and holding their prowess in slight
esteem, opposed this plan as rash and impracticable.
"Attack an armed fort indeed," cried a swarthy warrior sarcastically, "Since when have the French become so desperate!" "We wish to regain our honor,
"replied de Mantet, "or perish in so glorious an enterprise." The Indians, however, remained unconvinced

* Warburton, Vol. 1.

and the party moved on without coming to a decision.

Eight days after this the party reached the point where the two routes to Albany and Schenectady diverged. The Indians took the road leading towards Schenectady, and the French followed without objection. Nine days afterwards they arrived, about four in the evening, within two miles of that place. Here the savages were addressed by one of their Chiefs, who urged them to lose all recollection of their fatigue and to prepare to take ample revenge for the injuries they had received from the Iroquois at the instigation of the English. Having remained here to refresh themselves and prepare their arms, the party moved on, and about 11 o'clock came within sight of the village. The night was intensely cold and the citizens had retired early to bed—even those who usually guarded the gates of the palisade had withdrawn, leaving those avenues open and undefended. In profound silence the Canadian officers marched into the village and distributed their forces among the scattered houses. As soon as each man was properly posted, the savages raised the war cry and the whole force rushed upon the unconscious inhabitants. De Mantet, at the head of one party, assulted a small fort which he captured and burned; putting to death all who defended it. De St. Helene rushed against the barricaded doors of the private houses, beating them down with muskets and slaughtering every one who opposed his progress. In the confusion, M. de Montigny was wounded by the thrust of a spear. The massacre lasted for two hours, and during that time sixty of the inhabitants, including women and children, were butchered in cold blood. Having pillaged and burned every house in the village but two, the French and Indians, early the next morning, started on their return to Canada taking with them twenty-seven prisoners and carrying off fifty horses, besides a quantity of other property.*

* M. de Monseignat's account. In this account it is stated that "some twenty Mohawks were spared, in order to show them that it was the English and not they against whom the grudge was entertained.

The news of this murderous assault reached Albany about five o'clock the next morning, and created the greatest consternation among its inhabitants. Alarm guns were fired from the fort, messages were sent to Esopus for assistance, and Laurence, a Mohawk chief then in Albany, hurried to the Mohawk castles to bring down the warriors of that nation. In three days a party of fifty young men from Albany and one hundred and fifty Indians were collected at Schenectady, and started in pursuit of the retreating marauders. At Crown Point the young men gave out, but Laurence and his Indians continued on as far as Canada and succeeded in overtaking a party of Canadians, who had dropped to the rear of the main body, of whom they killed six and took twelve prisoners.

The accounts given by these prisoners were of the most startling nature. Count de Frontenac, they said, was busily engaged preparing for an invasion of New York. He had already built one hundred and twenty bateaux and one hundred birch canoes, and intended, in the spring, to pass up Lake Champlain at the head of fifteen hundred regular troops and one thousand allied Indians. Letters were now addressed, by Lieutenant-Governor Liesler, to the Governors of the different Provinces, calling earnestly for aid to protect the exposed frontier beyond Albany. The Five Nations were also assembled in council and agreed to furnish eighteen hundred warriors to fight the French.

Nor were the authorities of Albany idle. On the 26th of March they ordered Captain Jacob d' Warm to proceed to Crown Point with seventeen English and twenty Indians, and there watch the movements of the enemy. Four days later Captain Abram Schuyler was sent, with nine men and a party of Mohawks under Laurence, to take post at Otter Creek, for a similar purpose. Captain Schuyler, while posted at Otter Creek, led a scout of eight Indians as far as Chambly, where he encountered a small party of the French, of whom he killed two and took one prisoner.*

* Documentary History of New York.

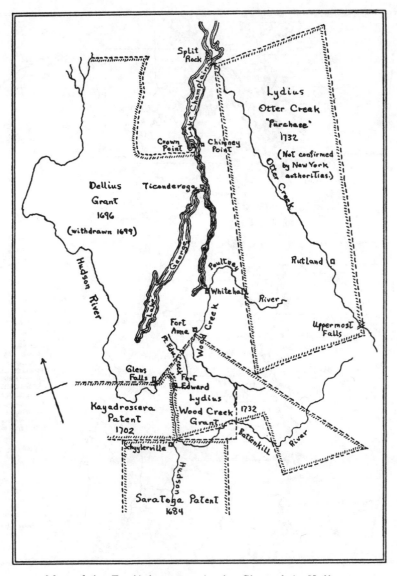

Map of the English grants in the Champlain Valley

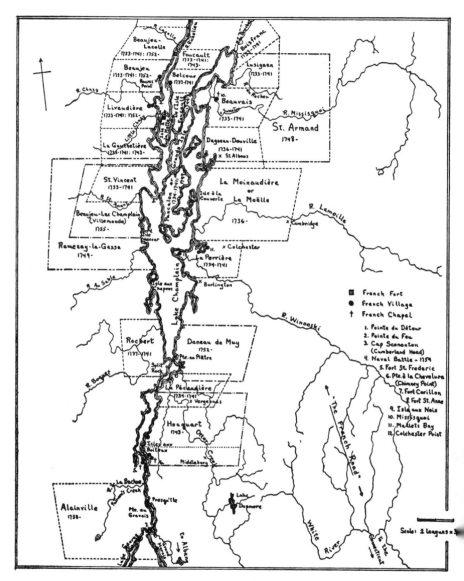

Map of the French grants in the Champlain Valley

About the 10th of April, one of the parties on Lake Champlain sent in word that they had discovered the track of twelve French and Indians, proceeding in the direction of Albany. Warning of danger was immediately sent throughout the country and the inhabitants were advised to retreat into the neighboring towns for safety. Two families, residing near Schenectady, neglected the advice and were attacked during the night and eleven of their number killed or captured.*

The fear that this success might excite the French to further outrage hastened the preparations of the New York Colonists for the invasion of Canada. On the 1st of May an agreement was concluded between the provinces of Massachusetts, Connecticut and New York by which each was to furnish its quota of troops for the expedition.† At the urgent request of New England the command of the expedition was conferred upon John Winthrop.

A naval expedition was also fitted out by the Colonists and sent against Quebec, under command of Sir William Phipps.

The army under Major-General Winthrop, numbering eight hundred men, left Albany about the 1st of August and proceeded on its march as far as Wood Creek. There Winthrop waited a few days for the promised reinforcements of Indians, but these not arriving, nor furnishing a supply of canoes to cross the lake, as they had promised to do, he called a council of war, who decided it inexpedient to proceed further. The expedition was therefore abandoned and the troops returned to Albany, where they were disbanded.

Attached to Winthrop's army was Captain John Schuyler of Albany, a man of great bravery and energy of character and of considerable experience in border warfare. Schuyler was dissatisfied with the decision of the council of war, which he considered weak and cow-

* Documentary History of New York.
† New York was to furnish four hundred men; Massachusetts, one hundred and sixty; Connecticut, one hundred and thirty-five, and Plymouth, sixty. Maryland promised one hundred men.

ardly, and declared the campaign should not be abandoned so easily. Beating up for volunteers he soon
gathered around him a little band of twenty-nine followers, each as bold and daring as himself. To these
he added one hundred and twenty Indians who had arrived at the camp under command of Juriaen, called the
ferocious, and having loaded a number of canoes with
provisions, proceeded, on the 13th of August, as far as
Canaghsionie (probably Whitehall) where he encamped
for the night. The next day he again embarked with
his party and on the 21st of the month reached a point
"one mile below the sand bank of Chambly."* In the
course of the journey one of the Indians died. "He
died of sickness," adds the brave Captain, evidently
surprised that so quiet a death should be reserved for
a Mohawk.

On the 22d the little party, having first secreted
their canoes and provisions, started by land for Laprairie, which lay on the south shore of the St. Lawrence
River about fifteen miles distant. While Schuyler was
slowly approaching Laprairie, the inhabitants of that
place were having a gala day in honor of their Governor, the brave old Frontenac, who having learned
from his scouts that Winthrop's army had retired, was
marching with eight hundred men to Quebec, to repel
the threatened attack of Sir William Phipps in that
quarter. Little did the quiet husbandmen imagine, as
they sat near their doors at evening, chatting over the
stirring incidents of the day, repeating to listening ears
the wonders each had seen, and, perhaps, rejoicing at a
security which the departure of the troops seemed to
confirm, that a band of fierce and determined warriors
lay secreted under the trees which bordered the little
settlement, ready with the morrow's sun to bring destruction and death about those rude but happy homes.

* Schuyler in his journal of this expedition gives the Indian names
of several localities on Lake Champlain. On the 16th the party, he
tells us, reached *Kanondoro*, and, traveling all night, arrived the next
morning at *Oghraro*. The next night they travelled as far as *Ogha-
ronde*, where "they determined by the majorities, to fall upon Fort
Laprairie."

Early on the morning of the 23d Schuyler sent forward his spies, who soon returned with the information that the inhabitants were leaving the fort to go into the fields to cut corn. It was Schuyler's intention to wait quietly until they reached the fields and then place his party between them and the fort, so as to intercept their retreat, but, through the eagerness of some young savages, the war cry was prematurely raised and both the English and Indians rushed to the attack without waiting for orders. The French, taking alarm, hastily retired to the fort, but not until six of their number were killed and nineteen taken prisoners. As soon as the prisoners were secured the assailants fell upon the cattle feeding around the fort and killed one hundred and fifty head of oxen and cows. They also set fire to all the houses and barns outside the fort, which were speedily consumed. The English wished to attack the fort itself, but did not do so, as the Indians refused to aid them. The forts at Montreal and Chambly now answering the alarm guns fired at Laprairie, Schuyler hastened his departure, lest his retreat might be cut off; but, before leaving, his Indians burned the body of one of their number, who had been killed during the affray.

The party retreated about seven miles, when they halted for dinner. The same evening they reached the river and embarked in their canoes. The next day they went as far as the ruins of old Fort St. Anne and, on the 15th, stopped on the long sand point near Port Kent, where they killed two elk. The next day's journey took them to a place which Schuyler calls " The Little Stone Fort,"* from which a canoe was sent forward with the news. On the 27th the party reached the mouth of Wood Creek, and on the 31st arrived with their prisoners at Albany.†

During the winter of 1690-91 the New York Colonists

* This was probably a slight work thrown up by Capt. de Warm at Crown Point the March previous, or one erected at Ticonderoga by Capt. Sanders Glen while he was waiting there for the advance of Winthrop's army.

† Journal of Capt. John Schuyler.

were too much occupied with their internal disputes to give much attention to military affairs. In the spring however their difficulties ceased, and active measures were at once adopted to carry on the war with Canada. The frontier posts of Albany, Schenectady and Half-Moon were repaired, the Militia reorganized and a conference held with the Five Nations, with whom the French emissaries had begun to tamper. The Indians not only promised to abandon all negotiations with the French, but pledged themselves to make war upon that people so long as they should live. An expedition was now planned against Canada ; the English Colonists wisely concluding that the only way to secure the co-operation of the savages was to give them active employment.

On the 22d day of June, 1691, Major Philip Schuyler left Albany at the .head of one hundred and fifty English and three hundred Indians, and crossing Lake Champlain by the route taken by his brother Capt. John Schuyler, appeared, unexpectedly, before Fort Laprairie, which he carried by surprise, killing several of its defenders. De Callieres, then Governor of Montreal, hastily collected eight hundred troops and crossed the river, when the English retreated to the woods, where they met and destroyed a small detachment sent forward to cut off their retreat. A short time afterwards, M. de Valrenes coming up with a large force, a severe and desperate battle was fought between the two parties. Schuyler posted his men behind trees, and, for an hour and a half, withstood the fire and repelled the charges of the Canadian troops. In this engagement the loss of the English was trifling, while not less than two hundred of the French were killed or wounded. Schuyler, fearing to be overpowered by superior numbers, now hastily withdrew and returned to Albany.

The favorable result of this expedition gave a new impetus to the warlike temper of the Iroquois and, strengthened their friendship for the English. These Indians, for the next two years, so harassed the French that De Frontenac determined again to invade their territory. For this purpose he collected a force of six or seven hundred French and Indians and, about the middle of January, 1693, set out from Montreal, for the Mohawk valley. The march, upon the frozen surface of the lake and through the deep snows of the forest, was attended with great hardships, yet such was the energy of the invaders that early in February they passed Schenectady unobserved, and falling suddenly upon the first Mohawk village, killed many of the inhabitants and took more than three hundred prisoners. As soon as the intelligence of this incursion reached Albany, Major Schuyler collected a party of about three hundred men, principally Indians, and started in pursuit of the assailants, who, according to their custom, had retreated immediately after the attack. Schuyler continued the pursuit as far as the Hudson, and would have overtaken the enemy had not a severe storm of snow and wind prevented his crossing the river. As it was he succeeded in recapturing about fifty of the prisoners, with whom he returned to Albany. The sufferings of those engaged in this expedition were so great that the Indians fed upon the dead bodies of the enemy, and the French were compelled to eat their own shoes.*

Although the contest between the French and English continued several years longer, this was the last expedition of any importance which entered the valley of Lake Champlain during this war. The peace of Ryswick, in 1697, was soon followed by a formal treaty between the French and the Five Nations.

* Gordon.

CHAPTER III.

Indian Depredations on the Frontier—Forts built by the New York
Colonists on Wood Creek—Two Expeditions organized against
Canada—Condition of the Country about Lake Champlain—The
French build a Fort at Crown Point—French Grants on the Lake
—Troubles among the New York Colonists—Attempt to settle the
Lands lying between the Hudson River and Lake Champlain.

THE history of events connected with Lake Champlain
brings us down to the year 1709. During "Queen
Anne's War," which commenced in 1702, the frontier
towns of New England were severely scourged by ma-
rauding parties from Canada. Deerfield was destroyed
in 1704 by a party of three hundred French and Indians under command of the inhuman De Rouville.*
In 1708, a party of four hundred men, including savages,
crossed the almost impracticable mountains of Vermont and New Hampshire, and attacked the little fort,
and village of Haverhill which, after a sharp defence,
they carried and reduced to ashes.

These and other repeated and unprovoked aggressions at length aroused the British Ministry who, in
1709, at the earnest solicitation of the colonists, adopted a plan for the conquest of the French possessions in
America. This plan contemplated an attack by water
upon Quebec, whilst fifteen hundred men, from New
York and the New England Provinces, were to attempt
Montreal by the way of Lake Champlain. The inhabitants of New York entered cordially into the scheme.
They not only furnished their quota of troops, but several volunteer companies were organized to join the

* This expedition followed the route up Lake Champlain to the
Winooski and then ascended that river and crossed the mountains to
the Connecticut. On their return they secreted the "bell of St.
Regis" in the sands of Burlington, where it remained until the following spring, when it was taken to Canada.

expedition. The Five Nations, through the exertions of Col. Peter Schuyler, were induced to take up the hatchet and to send five hundred warriors into the field. New York, also, at her own expense, opened a road from Albany to Lake Champlain, which greatly facilitated the movements of the troops and the transportation of supplies.

This road commenced near the present village of Schuylerville and ran up the east side of the river to Fort Edward, and thence by the way of Wood Creek to the head of Lake Champlain. It ran the whole way through a dense forest. Along the route three forts were erected; one on Wood Creek near the present village of Fort Ann ; another at the commencement of the carrying place between the Hudson River and the head of Wood Creek, which was at first called Fort Nicholson ; and a third on the summit of one of the hills opposite Schuylerville. These forts were built of timber and were surrounded by palisades so constructed as to protect the garrisons from the fire of musketry. One hundred bateaux and a large number of canoes were built at the mouth of Wood Creek for the transportation of the troops across Lake Champlain. All the arrangements for the campaign being complete, the army left Albany under the command of Col. Nicholson and encamped at Fort Ann, where they awaited intelligence of the arrival of the expedition destined for the attack of Quebec.

These demonstrations on the part of the English Colonists created great alarm among the inhabitants of Canada, who were but ill prepared to resist the large force which threatened both extremes of the Colony. A council of war was called by M. de Vaudreuil, under whose advice a force of fifteen hundred men was sent to Lake Champlain to oppose the advance of Nicholson's army ; but a misunderstanding between the Governor General and some of his principal officers embarrassed the enterprise and ultimately caused the army to return.

The two expeditions against Canada proved equally

abortive. The fleet destined for the attack of Quebec
was sent to Lisbon instead, to support the Portuguese
against the power of Castile, while Nicholson's army,
discouraged by delays and almost decimated by a malignant and fatal malady which broke out in the camp,*
returned to Albany, where they were soon afterwards
disbanded.

In 1711 preparations were again made by the Colonists for the invasion of Canada. Colonel Nicholson,
under whom served Colonels Schuyler, Whitney and
Ingoldsby, mustered at Albany a strong force comprising two thousand English, one thousand Germans and
one thousand Indians, who, on the 28th of August,
commenced their march towards Lake Champlain,
taking the Lake George route, instead of the unhealthy
one by the way of Wood Creek, which had proved so
fatal to the troops on the former expedition. At the
same time an army of six thousand four hundred men,
under Brigadier General Hill, sailed from Boston on
board of sixty-eight transports, under convoy of Sir
Hovedon Walker, for a simultaneous attack on Quebec.†

As soon as M. de Vaudreuil received intelligence of
these movements he hastened to Quebec, and, having
strengthened its defences, confided to M. de Bou-
court the responsible duty of resisting the debarka-
tion of the English troops, and then returned to the
rescue of Montreal. But the plans of the invading
army were destined to be again defeated. The British
Admiral had neglected the warnings of an experienced
French navigator, named Paradis, who accompanied
him, and approached too near a small island in the
narrow and dangerous channel of the Traverse. While
embarrassed amid its rocks, a sudden squall scattered
the fleet, driving eight of the vessels on the shore,

---

* This sickness is said to have been caused by the Indians who
poisoned the waters of the Creek. But Doctor Fitch in his "Survey
of Washington County" questions the truth of this accusation, and
presumes the malady to have been a malignant dysentery, brought on
by the troops drinking the stagnant water which flowed into the
creek from the surrounding marshes.
† Gordon.

where they were wrecked.* Charlevoix says nearly three thousand men were drowned, whose bodies were afterwards found scattered along the banks of the river. After this severe disaster the Admiral bore away for Cape Breton, and the expedition was abandoned. The advance corps of Nicholson's army had scarcely reached the head of Lake George, when intelligence arrived of the failure of the northern expedition. Orders were at once given for their return to Albany.

These two abortive attempts upon Canada cost the Province of New York, alone, over thirty thousand pounds sterling. Their failure disheartened the Colonists and chilled for a time the affections of the Five Nations, who began to look upon the English as a weak and cowardly people. The situation of the New York Colonists was now most critical. Clouds of adversity lowered darkly over the Province. The river Indians became restless and evinced a strong and growing disposition to break their allegiance; the Five Nations listened favorably to the renewed propositions of peace from the French, who threatened an invasion of the Province by sea and land. Happily these impending evils were averted by the treaty of Utrecht, which was concluded in the spring of 1713. By this treaty the French King released his nominal sovereignty over the Iroquois and recognized their country as subject to the dominion of Great Britain.

As yet no settlements had been permanently established in the valley of Lake Champlain. Fort St. Anne, built in 1665, had been occupied for a few years and then abandoned. The "little Stone Fort" mentioned by Schuyler in 1690, was a structure of no importance except as it served for the immediate protection of those by whom it was erected. Fort Ann, erected by Colonel Nicholson on Wood Creek in 1709, was burned by him on the return of his army to Albany in 1711. Kalm saw the remains of the burnt palisades, when he passed there thirty-eight years afterwards. In 1713 Fort Saratoga was the nearest post to the lake on the south, and Forts Laprairie and Chambly on the north.

* Warburton, Vol. 1.

No settlements were commenced within the present limits of Vermont until after the erection of Fort Dummer, on the Connecticut river, in 1724.

We have already seen that, from the first settlement of the country, Lake Champlain had been used as a thoroughfare through which predatory excursions were directed against both the French and English frontiers. Its control was therefore a matter of great importance. No movements was however made to obtain the command of this important avenue until the year 1731, when the Marquis de Beauharnois, then Governor General of Canada, erected a fort at Crown Point, which he called St. Frederic, in honor of Frederic Maurepas the, then, French Secretary of State. The English claimed the title to the territory on both sides of the lake, by virtue of their treaties with the Five Nations, and strongly remonstrated against, but took no steps to prevent its unauthorized occupation by the French. The first work erected by the French was a small stockade which could accommodate a garrison of 30 men only. This was replaced in 1734 by a "redoubt à machi coulis," sufficient for a garrison of 120 men. It was subsequently enlarged, and in 1742 was, with the exception of Quebec, the strongest work held by the French in Canada.*

"Fort St. Frederic," says Kalm, "is built on a rock consisting of black lime slates,† and is nearly quadrangular, has high and thick walls, made of the same limestone, of which there is a quarry about half a mile from the fort. On the eastern part of the fort is a high tower, which is proof against bomb shells, provided with very thick and substantial walls, and well stored with cannon from the bottom almost to the very top, and the Governor lives in the tower. In the terre plaine of the fort is a well built little church and houses of stone for the officers and soldiers. There are sharp rocks on all sides towards the land beyond cannon shot from the fort, but among them are some

* Paris document in Colonial History.
† Chazy Limestone—Emmons.

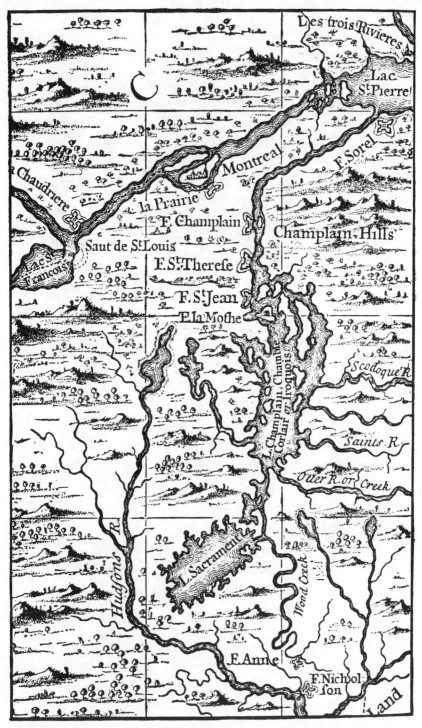

The Champlain Valley. From: A Map of the British Empire
in America, by Henry Popple. 1733.

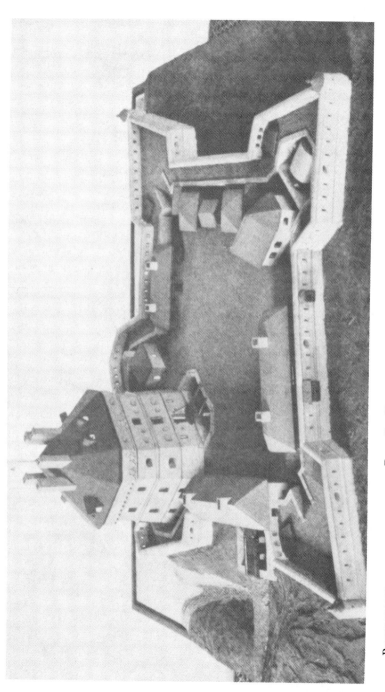

Photograph of a scale-model of Fort St. Frederic, made from the original plans by Mr. A. S. Hopkins, State Conservation Department, Albany, N. Y.

which are as high as the walls of the fort and very near them. Within one or two musket shots to the east of the fort is a windmill, built of stone, with very thick walls, and most of the flour, which is wanted to supply the fort, is ground here. This windmill is so constructed as to serve the purpose of a redoubt and at the top of it are five or six small pieces of cannon."* Subsequently a trench or wide ditch was dug around the fort, on the land side, enclosing the hill referred to by Kalm. This trench commenced at the water's edge about two rods north and terminated about fifteen rods south of the fort. Its greatest distance from the fort, in the rear, was thirty rods. An enclosure was also erected about twenty-five rods north-west of the fort which reached the water's edge and surrounded several buildings used for soldier's quarters.†

Soon after the erection of the fort a settlement of considerable size was formed about it, on both sides of the lake, composed, principally, of the families of old soldiers who had been paid off and discharged from service The houses of some of the settlers were convenient and comfortable, but the majority lived in mere cabins built of boards. To each soldier in service was allotted a small piece of ground near the walls of the fort, which was cultivated as a garden, and occasionally occupied as a summer residence.*

A small village stood about half a mile southwest of the fort, and one-half mile further south was a hamlet, containing four houses, surrounded by wheat fields.†

The boats used by the inhabitants were of three kinds; bark canoes, dugouts or canoes made of a log of wood hollowed out, and bateaux. The last mentioned were constructed with flat bottoms of oak and sides of pine, and were used for the transportation of troops or supplies upon the lake. When Kalm visited the fort, in 1749, a yacht or large sail vessel made regular trips between that place and St. Johns in Canada.‡

---

* Kalm's Travels in 1749.
† Journal of the New Hampshire Scout.
‡ Kalm says this was the first sail vessel built on the lake.

Until 1759 St. Frederic was the seat of French power
on the lake. Here was a rallying point for the fierce
Abenaquis from the St. Francis, the Arundacks of the
fertile Ottawa, and the warlike Wyandots of the west
—drawn together by a common love of revenge or the
hope of plunder. Here the ferocious Outagamis, the
restless Algonquin and the vindictive Huron met to
recount their deeds of horrid barbarity. It was a
strange and varied scene often presented at this
frontier post. At one moment would be heard the
vesper bell of the little chapel calling the rude but
virtuous husbandman, the scarred veteran of France
and the voluble Canadian to their evening prayers, while
at the next, the rocky shore would echo to the loud
whoop of the merciless savage, returning from some
successful attack upon the neighboring settlements.
Long had the English Colonists cause to regret the
want of vigilance and forecast on the part of their
rulers, which permitted the French to seize and retain
this controlling position on the lake.

We have no data by which to ascertain the exact population of the French settlements around St. Frederic;
but it probably at no time exceeded six or eight hundred, exclusive of the garrison at the fort. The period of
the existence of these settlements was confined to the
twenty-eight years of French ascendency on the lake.
Prior to 1731, the borders of the lake, in every direction, were wild and uncultivated; no building stood
upon its shores, not an acre of its majestic forest had
been cleared, nor had its fertile soil been touched by
the hand of the husbandman.

The Governor of Canada did not confine the encroachments on Lake Champlain to the vicinity of Crown
Point, for, soon after the erection of Fort St. Frederic,
he issued grants, for large tracts of land lying on both

In September, 1736, M. de Beauharnois asked permission of the
King to construct a sloop on the lake if it should be ascertained to
be navigable for sloops. The King authorized the building of sloops,
but added "before hazarding their construction it will be well to
cause the lake to be surveyed. with a view to become acquainted
with the rocks to be met there.'

sides of the lake, to several persons holding office under the French King. The first of these grants was made to Sieur Pean, Major of the town and castle of Quebec, on the 10th day of April, 1733, and embraced a tract " two leagues or two and a half in front, by three in depth along the river Chambly and Lake Champlain, together with the river Chazy included therein and Isle a la Motte."* Two days afterwards another grant was issued to Sieur St. Vincent, ensign of Foot, for " two leagues in front by three leagues in depth on lake Champlain,†" and another, on the 20th of the same month, to Sieur la Gauchetiere, Captain of Marines, of " two leagues front by three leagues deep on said lake." ‡

On the 7th of July, 1734, a grant was issued to Sieur Contrecour Jr., ensign of Infantry, for a tract of land which was described as "beginning at the mouth of the *Riviere Aux Loutres* (Otter Creek, Vt.) one league and a half above and one league and a half below, making two leagues in front by three in depth, together with so much of said river as is found included therein with three islets which are in front of said concession and depend thereon." On the 20th of the same month, another grant was made to Sieur de Beauvis of lands " two leagues in front and three in depth on Lake Champlain together with the peninsula which is found to be in front of said land."§ In the same month another was issued to Sieur de la Periere, " beginning at the mouth of the river Ouynouski (Winooski) one league above and one below, making two leagues front by three in depth, with the extent of said river which will be found comprehended therein, together with the islands and *battures* adjacent." Also one to Sieur Douville, on the 8th of October, 1736 for lands on the east side of the lake, " two leagues front by three leagues deep; "‖ and another on the 13th of June,

* Now, northern part of the town of Champlain, N. Y.
† Remainder of Champlain.
‡ In town of Chazy, N.Y.
§ Now parts of Swanton and Highgate, Vt.
‖ In town of Georgia, Vt.

1737, to Sieur Robart, King's Store-keeper at Montreal, "three leagues front by two leagues in depth on the west side of Lake Champlain, taking in going down one league below the river Boquet and in going up two and a half above .said river." The island of North Hero or *Isle Longue* was granted to Contrecour, Captain of Infantry, and M. Raimbault received a large concession north and adjoining the lands granted to M. de la Periere.

These grants were issued subject to forfeiture in case the lands were not settled and improved within a certain time. This condition not having been fulfilled, all but the two last mentioned were re-united to the King's domains by an ordinance of the Governor and Intendant of Canada of the 10th of May, 1741. The grantees gave various reasons why their lands had not been settled within the prescribed time. Pean could find no farmers to place upon his seigniory, St. Vincent had been absent on the King's service, and Contrecour had offered very advantageous inducements to settlers, including a bonus of three hundred livres, but without success. La Fontaine promised to go on to his grant immediately with three men, to build there, and was willing to furnish grain and money to any who should commence a settlement. Sieur Robart had surveyed his lands and had neglected no inducements for young men to settle upon them. These excuses were not satisfactory to the Government Officers. They however, declared that patents would be re-issued to any who should place settlers on the land within one year from that time. This was not done; but soon after settlements were formed near the mouth of the Big Chazy river and at Windmill Point,* which were occupied for a short time and then abandoned.

---

* The first houses I saw after leaving Fort St. Frederic were some on the western side of the lake, about ten French miles from St. Johns, in which the French lived before the last war and which they then abandoned. * * * A Windmill, built of stone, stands on the east side of the lake, on a projecting piece of ground. Some Frenchmen lived near to it. From this mill to Fort St. Johns they reckon eight French miles. The English, with their Indians, have

The lands originally granted to Pean were, in 1752, conceded to Sieur Bedon, Councillor in the Superior Council of Quebec, and by him afterwards transferred to M. de Beaujeu, who owned a seigniory adjoining on the north. In April, 1743 and 1745, two patents of concession were issued to Sieur Hocquart, Councillor of State and Intendant of the naval forces at Brest, for a large tract embraced in the present towns of Panton, Addison and Bridport, Vt., which Hocquart conveyed to Michael Chartier de Lotbiniere in 1764, and in November 1758, the Marquis de Vaudreuil, Governor General of Canada, granted to the same De Lotbiniere the seigniory of Alainville embracing over four leagues front by five leagues depth and lying partly on Lake George and partly on Lake Champlain.

The aggregate of these concessions embraced more than eight hundred square miles of territory. No permanent settlements were however made under any of the grants, except on parts of the seigniories of Hocquart and Alainville, in the immediate vicinity of Crown Point and Ticonderoga. After the conquest of Canada the grantees petitioned for a confirmation of their titles, but this the British Government refused, at the same time, however, declaring that the claimants should be entitled to so much of the concessions as should be proportionate to the improvements made on them, at the rate of fifty acres for every three acres improved, provided they took out new grants for the same under the seal of the Province of New York, subject to the usual quit-rents. No new grant to one person was to exceed twenty thousand acres, nor did this privilege extend to the grants of La Gauchetiere and others annulled by the ordinance of the 10th of May, 1741.

The claimants refused the smaller grants from the Province of New York, and declined to pay the required quit-rents. They fell back upon the original title of the French King who, they contended, first discovered the country and had held undisturbed posses-

burned the houses here several times, but the mill remained unhurt.
—*Kalm in* 1749.

sion of it to the year 1758. To this the authorities of
New York replied, that the country south of the St.
Lawrence River belonged originally to the Five Nations, from whom it passed to the English by virtue of
a treaty made as early as 1683. That the treaty of
Utrecht recognized the sovereignty of Great Britain
over these nations, and that the possession of the
French at Crown Point was an encroachment on British
soil, which could confer no title to the French King.
They also referred to an ancient grant (1696) to God-
frey Dellius of a large tract along the head of the lake,
extending upwards of twenty miles to the north of
Crown Point, as proof that the English had claimed
the lake to be within their jurisdiction. But the
strongest position taken against these claims and which,
considering the weakness of the French title, induced
the British Government to disaffirm them, was the
fact that a large portion of the lands covered by the
French grants were then held by old officers and soldiers of the provincial army, under patents issued
under the seal of the Province of New York.*

New York was the central point of English influence
in America. It held the keys of Canada and of the
great western lakes. Within its limits burned the
Council Fire of the Six Nations,† the most powerful
confederacy ever formed among the Indians ; whose
sway extended west to the Mississippi, and beyond the
Ohio on the south. But though strong in position,
New York was weak in power. Its history, from the
death of Governor Montgomery in 1731, to the close
of Mr. Clinton's administration in 1753, is one of
almost continued distrust and contention between the
Executive and the Assembly. In this war of party the
public business of the Province was neglected and the
security of the inhabitants disregarded. Occasionally,
however, the Government would awake from its
lethargy and, for a moment, return to the performance

---

* For interesting documents relating to the French Grants on Lake
Champlain see Documentary History of New York, Vol. 1.
† The Tuscaroras joined the Confederacy in 1712.

of its legitimate duties. During one of these periods of quiet, a plan was projected for the settlement of the wilderness between Lake Champlain and the Hudson River, to serve as a check upon the French positions on Lake Champlain. The Governor issued a proclamation, describing in glowing language, the beauty and fertility of the country, and offering the most liberal terms to those who might settle there.

Seduced by this proclamation, Captain Laughlin Campbell came from Scotland, in 1737, to examine the land, and was so well satisfied with its appearance that he returned to Isla, sold his estate and brought over, at his own expense, eighty-three Protestant families, comprising four hundred and twenty-three adults and many children. The Governor of New York had promised Campbell a grant of 30,000 acres, free of all charge, except those of survey and the usual quit-rents. But, on his arrival, the mercenary officers of Government refused to fulfill this engagement, unless they were allowed a share in the grant. This Campbell refused to give them. A dispute arising between him and the Government on this account, in which the Assembly joined with the emigrants, the negotiations were broken off. The emigrants were saved from starvation by enlisting in an expedition to Carthagena, while Campbell, broken down in spirits and fortune, sought a home elsewhere.

The Colonists long had cause to regret the folly of the Government in not securing, at this time, the settlement of their northern frontier. The Protestant Highlanders, brought over by Campbell, were a race of hardy and industrious people, indued by nature and habit with great power of indurance. They would have formed a bulwark against the French, who, for twenty years afterwards, retained absolute control of the lake and sent out, from their stronghold at Crown Point, bands of marauders to plunder and devastate the frontier settlements.*

* The fort was erected by the French at Crown Point, as much for offensive operations as for defence. " When," writes M. de Beauhar-

CHAPTER IV.

Sir William Johnson's Expedition against Crown Point—Battle of Lake George—The French fortify Ticonderoga—Montcalm attacks the English at Lake George—Massacre at Fort William Henry—Defeat of Abercrombie at Ticonderoga—English Scouting Parties—Putnam in trouble.

NOTWITHSTANDING the repeated depredations of the French upon the northern and western frontier, no attempt was made to weaken their power until 1755. On the 14th of April of that year, the Governors of the several Provinces met in conference in Virginia, and determined upon the plan of a campaign, by which to repel the encroachments of the French upon the northern frontier. This campaign contemplated three separate expeditions; one under Sir William Johnson against Crown Point,* another under Governor Shirley, of Massachusetts, against Niagara, while Major General Braddock, the Commander-in-Chief, with a third, was to move upon the French Fort on the Ohio.

The expedition against Crown Point was to be composed of provincial troops and Indians. But the six Nations did not enter into the scheme with their usual spirit and alacrity. They were dissatisfied at the long continued inaction of the English, which contrasted

nois to Louis XV., " When in possession of Crown Point the road will be blocked on the English should they wish to pass over our territory, and we will be in a position to fall on them when they least expect it. Should they on the contrary anticipate us in this establishment we could never show ourselves on Lake Champlain except with open force, nor make war against them except with a large army; whilst, seizing on this fort we could harass them by small parties, as we have done from 1689 to 1699 when we were at war with the Iroquois."

* Sir William Johnson's Commission bears date the 16th of April, 1755, and recites that the troops are placed under his command " to be employed in an attempt to erect a strong Fortress upon an eminence near the French Fort at Crown Point, and for removing the encroachments of the French on His Majesty's land there."

unfavorably with the activity and vigilance of the French. Nor had the Indians been backward to express their disapprobation. "You are desirous that we should open our minds and our hearts to you," said the celebrated Mohawk Sachem Hendrick, at one of their Councils. "Look at the French: they are men, they are fortifying everywhere; but we are ashamed to say it, you are like women, bare and open without fortifications."* This difference in the condition of the two countries was the natural result of the characteristics and genius of their inhabitants. The English colonists were bold, intelligent and self-dependent. They understood and cherished the principles of self government. Jealous of their rulers they kept a constant watch upon their conduct, refused to vote supplies unless they knew the money would be appropriated for the public good, and opposed the erection of forts on the frontier, lest their guns might be used to overawe the people. On the other hand, France kept her colonies in a state of dependence upon the Mother Country. The Canadians were allowed neither freedom of thought nor action. By this means the latter became, as subjects, more faithful but less independent than their neighbors.† France directed forts to be built in the wilderness, and her orders were obeyed. England also required forts, but, instead of building them, the colonists questioned their necessity, objected to the expense and neglected to provide means for their erection.

The words of the Mohawk sachem were true. When the Governors met at Alexandria, England had no works of defence upon her frontier, while the French were fortified at Du quesne, Niagara, Crown Point and Beau-Sejour. But notwithstanding their avowed re-

---

*Documentary History of New York, Vol. 2.
† "Let us beware how we allow the establishment of manufactures in Canada ; she would become proud and mutinous like the English. So long as France is a nursery to Canada, let not the Canadians be allowed to trade, but kept to their wandering laborious life with the savages, and to their military services. They will be less wealthy, but more brave and more faithful to us."—*Montcalm to M. de Berryer : 1757.*

luctance, the Six Nations at length renewed their cov-
enant of friendship, and promised to support the Colonies in the approaching struggle.

Considerable land carriage had to be encountered in
passing from the Hudson River to Lake Champlain.
The portage commenced at the Hudson, near the present
village of Fort Edward, from whence two routes diverged; one leading by the way of Fort Ann to the
mouth of Wood Creek, a distance of twenty-four miles;
the other passing by the way of Glen's Falls to the
head of Lake George, a distance of fourteen miles.
From the first route a third diverged near Fort Ann,
which led to the waters of Lake Champlain at the head
of South Bay. By the aid of boats on Wood Creek
the portage on the first route was usually reduced to
from six to ten miles. This portage was called " The
great carrying place," and was selected as the point
of rendezvous for General Johnson's Army, from
whence it was to move to Lake Champlain.

Early in July Major-General Phinehas Lyman arrived
at the portage with about six hundred New England
troops and commenced the erection of a fort, which was
afterwards called Fort Edward, in honor of Edward,
Duke of York, the grandson of the English sovereign.
Johnson reached the camp on the 14th day of August,
and found the army increased to two thousand eight
hundred and fifty men, fit for duty. New recruits continued to arrive so that the General found himself, by
the end of August, at the head of thirty-one hundred
Provincials and two hundred and fifty Indians,* By
the 3rd of September the main army had reached the
head of Lake George, while a great number of teamsters
were engaged in dragging six hundred boats over the
portage, to be used for the transportation of troops
across that lake. Here Johnson halted for the boats to
come up, and to announce the plan of his future operations. " I propose," said he, " to go down this lake
with a part of the army, and take post at the end of it,
at a pass called Tionderogue, there wait the coming up

*Johnson to Lt.-Gov. De Lancey.

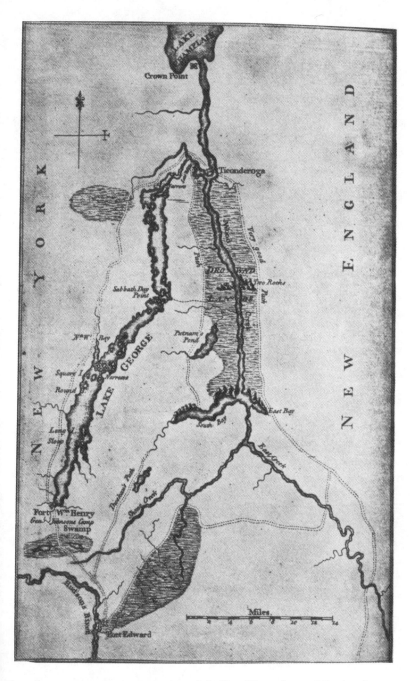

Map drawn during the French and Indian War shows Dieskau's route

GRENADIER, 42ⁿᵈ REGᵗ 1751.
(From a painting at Windsor Castle.)

42ND HIGHLANDERS, THE BLACK WATCH 1751

of the rest of the army and then attack Crown Point." *
While the English Commander was thus planning his
advance upon Fort St. Frederic, the French General had
left that post and was hastening towards South Bay.

When General Lyman stopped on the banks of the
Hudson to await the arrival of the main army, the
whole available French force on Lake Champlain, did
not exceed eight hundred men, exclusive of Indians.
Early in the summer, however, the Baron Dieskau, a
brave old officer, who had distinguished himself under
the celebrated Marshal Saxe, arrived at Quebec, accompanied by several veteran regiments from France.
These troops were immediately ordered to Lake Ontario,
but Dieskau, hearing that the English were in motion
towards Lake George, changed his route and passed
rapidly forward towards Crown Point, where he arrived
about the 1st of August. For the defence of this fortress seven hundred regulars, sixteen hundred Canadians
and seven hundred savages were now assembled.†

Dieskau left a strong garrison at Fort St. Frederic,
encamped a portion of his army at Ticonderoga, and
with six hundred savages, as many Canadians and two
hundred regular troops, ascended the lake to the head
of South Bay, and after four days' march, arrived
within four miles of Fort Edward, on the Lake George
road. The Indians now refused to proceed further in
the direction of the fort, but were willing to go against
the open camp of the English at Lake George. The
head of the column was therefore turned towards the
lake.

As soon as the English Commander learned that the
French had left South Bay, he determined, with the
advice of a council of war, to send a strong party to
reinforce Fort Edward, then guarded by two hundred
and fifty New Hampshire troops and five companies of
the New York regiment.‡ This reinforcement consisted

* Johnson to the Board of Trade.
† Bancroft's History of U. S. Vol. 4. Baron de Dieskau to Count
d'Argents, Sept. 14, 1855.
‡ Johnson to the Governors of the several colonies.

of one thousand Provincial troops, under command of Colonel Ephraim Williams of Massachusetts,* and two hundred Indian warriors led by Hendrick, the Mohawk sachem. They started from the camp about nine o'clock on the morning of the 8th of September, expecting to find the French at or near Fort Edward. When Dieskau learned, from his scouts, the approach of Williams' party, he extended his line on both sides of the road in the form of a half moon, and in this order continued slowly and cautiously to advance. Colonel Williams, in the meantime, pushed forward with rash confidence, and had proceeded about four miles from the lake, when he suddenly found himself in the very centre of the half circle. At that moment the French opened a fire of musketry in front and on both flanks. Thus attacked on all sides by an unseen enemy the Provincials offered but a slight resistance. For a short time the slaughter of the English was dreadful. Williams fell dead at the head of his regiment, and the brave and faithful Hendrick was mortally wounded; but the troops were withdrawn with great skill and coolness by Lieutenant Col. Whitney, who succeeded to the command on the death of Williams.

Johnson lay at Lake George without entrenchment or defence of any kind. Aroused by the noise of the firing, he sent Lieutenant-colonel Cole with a reinforcement of two hundred men to the aid of Williams, and hastened to form a sort of breastwork with fallen trees, drawing up a few pieces of cannon which had been left five hundred yards distant from the front.† At ten o'clock the defeated troops began to arrive at the camp in large bodies, and, at half-past eleven, the French appeared in sight, marching in regular order against the centre of the breastwork.

It had been Dieskau's purpose to rush forward and

---

* Before joining Johnson, Colonel Williams made a will by which he bequeathed his property to the town of Williamstown, Massachusetts, on condition that the money should be used for the establishment and maintenance of a free school. The school was incorporated as a College, in 1773, by the name of Williams College.

† Review of Military operations in North America.

to enter the camp with the fugitives; but the Iroquois (Caughnawagas) took possession of a rising ground and stood inactive. At this the Abenakis halted also; and the Canadians became intimidated.* A few shots from the artillery drove them all to the shelter of the neighboring swamps, and left the French commander and his handful of veteran troops unsupported. As the regulars advanced against the centre they suddenly halted for several minutes about one hundred and fifty yards from the breastwork, and then again advanced, firing by platoons. Finding it impossible to break the centre, Dieskau moved to the right and attacked Williams, Ruggles and Titcomb's regiments, where a warm fire was kept up for nearly an hour.

About four o'clock in the afternoon the English suddenly leaped over the slight breastwork and charged upon the assailants, who precipitately retreated, leaving almost all the regular troops dead on the field. The Canadians and Indians retired in small parties, to the scene of Williams' defeat in the morning, where they were surprised and defeated by a party of one hundred and twenty New Hampshire and ninety New York troops, who, under command of Captain McGinnes, had been sent from Fort Edward to reinforce the army at Lake George. The loss of the English this day was about two hundred and sixteen killed and ninety-six wounded; of the French the loss was much greater.* Dieskau was found, after the retreat, leaning against the stump of a tree, thrice wounded and helpless. Early in the action General Johnson received a painful wound in the thigh and retired to his tent; the command then devolved on General Lyman. Johnson, by this victory, became a Baronet, and re-

---

* Bancroft's History of the U, S., Vol. 4. Baron Dieskau had no confidence in the Iroquois. After his defeat he writes M. de Vaudreuil, " I prophesied to you, sir, that the Iroquois would play some scurvy trick. It is unfortunate for me that I am such a good prophet."—*Paris Doc*.

† Johnson in his official report of this battle estimates the loss of the French at from five to six hundred. Warburton states it as a "little short of eight hundred."

ceived a gratuity of five thousand pounds, while Lyman is not mentioned in the official bulletin.

A rapid movement upon Crown Point would have forced the French to evacuate that post; but Johnson instead of following up his victory by a quick and well directed blow, wasted the rest of the season in building Fort William Henry; a pile of wooden barracks, surrounded by an embankment and ditch, which stood on an elevated spot about three hundred yards from the temporary breastwork attacked by Dieskau.

While the army remained at the head of Lake George, in inaction, Captain Robert Rodgers and Captain Israel Putnam, two daring and active officers belonging to the New England troops, made repeated demonstrations against the French, cut off many of their working parties and obtained correct information of all their proceedings. Upon one of these occasions Rodgers and his men spent the night in the trench under Fort St. Frederic, and at another time, surprised a Frenchman within gun-shot of its walls.*

The season of 1756 passed without any military movement of importance being made, by either party in the vicinity of Lake Champlain. The English completed the defences of Fort William Henry, and, at one time, contemplated building a fort at the head of South Bay; but this last work was at first delayed and ultimately abandoned. On the other hand the French were busily engaged in fortifying the peninsula of Ticonderoga. After the defeat of Dieskau the remnant of his army sought shelter there, where they established a camp and commenced building a fort, afterwards called Fort Carillon. During the season of 1756 upwards of two thousand French were constantly engaged upon the work. The lake now presented a most lively appearance. Canoes, bateaux, and schooners were constantly passing and repassing between Canada, Crown Point and Ticonderoga, transporting troops from point to point, or loaded with supplies and ammunition.

* Journal of the New Hampshire Scouts.

Small scouting parties would occasionally leave Fort William Henry and penetrate as far as the French works, to gather information and beat up the outposts of the enemy. Upon one occasion Capt. Robert Rogers was sent on a scout with a party of fifty men and five whale boats. Rogers drew his boats over the mountain into Lake Champlain and, passing Ticonderoga in the night, on the morning of the 7th of July, secreted his party on the east side of the lake, about twenty-five miles north of Crown Point. While lying here, Rodgers counted thirty boats passing towards Canada, and, about three o'clock in the morning, discovered a schooner of thirty-five or forty tons at anchor a short distance below. As he was preparing to attack this vessel, two lighters with twelve men on board approached the shore, into which his party fired, killing three of the Frenchmen and wounding two others. The lighters were taken and found loaded with wheat, flour, rice, brandy and wine. Destroying all but the two last, Rodgers hastened back, his men rowing none the less stoutly, when the prisoners informed them that a party of five hundred men were only two leagues below, on their way to Crown Point.*

Major Rodgers was not always successful. In January, 1757, with about eighty rangers he intercepted a party transporting supplies from Crown Point to Ticonderoga and captured seven men, three loaded sleds and six horses. On his return to Lake George he was met by a party of French and Indians sent against him from Ticonderoga. A desperate and bloody action ensued in which the rangers were defeated with a loss of fourteen killed, six wounded and six taken prisoners. Major Rodgers was twice wounded, and Captain Spikeman, Lieutenant Kennedy and Ensign Page of the Rangers killed. The survivors were rescued, through the bravery and firmness of Lieutenant Stark, who conducted the retreat to Lake George. Two hundred and fifty French and Indians were in the action, of whom, ac-

* Rodgers' Journal.

cording to Rodgers' estimate, one-third were killed or wounded.

The campaign of 1757 opened early and briskly on the northern frontier. While the strong ice yet covered the surface of the lake and the snow lay in heavy drifts along its shores, eleven hundred French and four hundred Canada Indians, under Vaudreuil and the Chevalier Longueuil, marched from Ticonderoga to surprise the garrison of Fort William Henry. During the night of the 16th of March the party lay upon the snow behind Long Point, and, early the next morning, appeared suddenly before the fort, expecting to carry it by surprise; but Stark—the same who, twenty years later, was ready to make his Molly a widow for the cause of liberty—was there with his rangers, and the assailants were forced back, not however until they had burned several sloops, a large number of bateaux, and some store houses which stood beyond reach of the guns of the fort.

Soon after the return of the French, Colonel Parker was sent from Fort William Henry, with a command of four hundred men, to attempt the works at Ticonderoga. The detachment crossed the lake in whaleboats and bateaux, but before reaching Ticonderoga, were decoyed in an ambuscade, and the whole party, with the exception of two officers and seventy men, either killed or taken prisoners.

The French still urged forward the defenses of Fort Carillon. Montcalm, brave, sagacious and active, was at Montreal preparing to carry out his favorite project of reducing Fort William Henry. Everything favored the enterprise. The Indians, including many stern warriors of the Six Nations, gathered around the little fort of St. Johns on the Richelieu, and there danced their war dances beneath the white banner of France.

Six days afterwards they landed, from two hundred canoes, upon the rock-bound shores of Ticonderoga, where they were met by Marin, returning from a foray near Fort Edward; his canoes decorated with the bleeding scalps of forty-two Englishmen. Six thousand

French and Canadians, and seventeen hundred Indians were now collected at Ticonderoga, armed to the teeth, and anxious to be led against the enemy. On the last day of July M. de Levy was sent forward by land, under guidance of the Indians, with twenty-five hundred men, and Montcalm followed the next day, with the main body of the army, in two hundred and fifty boats.

General Webb, a man of weak, irresolute and timid character, was in command of the Provincial troops, and had five thousand men with him at Fort Edward, while a body of one thousand men garrisoned Fort William Henry. It so happened that Webb started for Lake George, with an escort of two hundred men, under command of Major Putnam, at the very time Montcalm was embarking his army at the lower end of the lake. On his arrival at the fort, Putnam was sent to reconnoitre as far as Ticonderoga, and had proceeded part of the way, when he discovered the boats of the French moving slowly up the lake. Returning to the fort, Putnam informed Webb of the approach and strength of the enemy, and urged that the whole army should be brought forward immediately to repel their attack ; but to this Webb would not consent. Enjoining secrecy upon Putnam he returned, with dastard haste, to Fort Edward, from whence he sent Colonel Monro, with one thousand men, to reinforce and take command of the garrison at the lake.

Montcalm landed about the time of Colonel Monro's arrival, and immediately laid seige to the fort, at the same time sending proposals for its surrender. " I will defend my trust to the last," was the spirited reply of the brave Monro. The seige lasted six days, in the course of which the French General pushed his advances within musket shot of the fort, while a body of over five thousand regulars, Canadians and Indians, under De Levy and De la Corne held the road leading to Fort Edward in rear of the English works. Then it was that Monro, finding his provisions and ammunition nearly exhausted, and having received a letter from his

pusillanimous chief declining to send him further assistance, consented to surrender. By the terms of capitulation the English were to march out with their arms
and baggage, and were to be escorted by a detachment
of French troops as far as Fort Edward ; the sick and
wounded remaining under Montcalm's protection until
their recovery, when they were to be allowed to return
to their homes.

At the time of the capitulation four hundred and fifty-
nine English occupied the fort, while seventeen hundred
and fifty were posted in a fortified camp standing on
an eminence to the east, now marked by the ruins of
Fort George.   The troops marched out of the works on
the morning of the 10th of August, and had scarcely
passed the gates, when they were attacked by a large
party of Indians attached to the French army.*   These
savages rushed on with the fury of demons.   Men,
women and children were murdered in cold blood, and
in the most barbarous manner.   The massacre continued until the English had proceeded half way to Fort
Edward, when the scattered and terrified troops were
met by an escort of five hundred men, sent out for
their protection.   The French officers endeavored in
vain to arrest the terrible onslaught.   " Kill me,"
cried Montcalm, baring his breast, "but spare the
English who are under my protection."   The appeal
was in vain.   The vindictive savages had tasted blood
and neither prayers, nor menaces nor promises availed
while a victim was to be found.†

Immediately after the victory the fort was levelled to
the ground ; the cannon and stores were removed to
Ticonderoga and the boats and vessels taken to the
lower end of the lake.   Thus closed the military operations of the year.   The French returned to resume their
labor upon the walls of Carillon, Webb shrunk back to

---

* Montcalm, in a letter to Lord Loudon, of 14 Aug., 1757, says he
had " three thousand Indians of thirty-three different nations" in
his army on Lake George.

† Bancroft's History of U. S., Vol. 4; Conquest of Canada, Vol.
2 ; Williams' Vermont, Vol. 2.

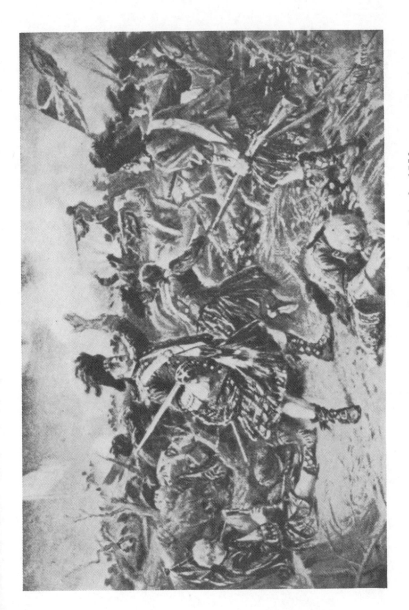

Scottish Highlanders at Ticonderoga July 8, 1758

THE MARQUIS DE MONTCALM

Albany and the timid deer again drank, undisturbed, of the cool waters of the silver Horicon.

The British Government decided to press the campaign of the succeeding year (1758) with uncommon vigor. Twelve thousand troops were to attempt the reduction of Louisburg on the island of Cape Breton, sixteen thousand were to march against Ticonderoga and Crown Point, and eight thousand were to attack Fort Duquesne. The command of the troops destined for Lake Champlain was entrusted to Major-general Abercrombie, who had succeeded the imbecile Loudon to the chief command in America.

On the first of July, six thousand three hundred and sixty-seven Regulars and nine thousand and twenty-four Provincials were collected around the decaying ruins of Fort William Henry. Four days later the whole armament struck their tents, and in nine hundred bateaux and one hundred and thirty-five whale-boats embarked on the waters of Lake George ; a large number of rafts, armed with artillery and loaded with provisions, accompanied the expedition. That night, the proud host rested for five hours on Sabbath-day Point, and, early on the morning of the 6th, reached the landing at the lower end of the lake.

Fort Carillon, against which the English were now advancing, stood near the point of the peninsula formed by the junction of the outlet of Lake George with Lake Champlain. This peninsula contains about five hundred acres, and is surrounded on three sides by water. One half of the western or land sides was then covered by a swamp. The fort was nearly one hundred feet above the water, and stood on the south side of the peninsula adjoining the outlet, which here expands into a bay of some size. On the extreme easternmost point of the peninsula, at a short distance from the main work, was a strong redoubt of earth and stones, which commanded the narrow part of the lake. A battery also stood on the bank of the bay, a short distance west of the fort, while the low land to the north was covered by two batteries, standing behind its walls. The road from

Lake George to Ticonderoga crossed the river or outlet,
twice, by bridges.　Near the lower bridge, and less than
two miles from the fort, the French had built saw-mills,
which were defended by a slight military work.　They
had also built a log camp near the landing at the foot
of Lake George.

To oppose the powerful army now advancing against
them, the French had only twenty-eight hundred
Regulars and four hundred and fifty Canadians.　The
apparent hopelessness of resistance excited Montcalm
to action.　With consummate judgment he marked out
his lines, half a mile west of the fort, and pushed the
work with such ardor that, in ten hours, a wall as many
feet high had been thrown up across the high ground
which lay between the swamp and the bank of the outlet.　On the 1st of July three regiments, under M. de
Bourlemaque, occupied the log camp at the foot of the
lake, while the battalion of La Barre was posted near
the mills.　When the English first appeared in sight,
Bourlemaque fell back upon the mills, leaving Captain
de Trepeze, with three hundred men, to watch the approaching column.

Immediately on landing, Abercrombie, leaving his
baggage, provisions and artillery in the boats, formed
his men into three columns and advanced towards Ticonderoga.　The route lay through a thick and tangled
wood which prevented any regular progress, and the
troops, misled by the bewildered guides, were soon
thrown into confusion.　While thus pressing forward
in disorder, the head of the advance column under
Lord Howe, fell in with a party of the French troops,
who had lost their way likewise, and a warm skirmish
ensued.　At the first fire the gallant Howe fell and instantly expired.　He was the idol of the army and had
endeared himself to the men by his affability and virtues.
Infuriated by the loss of their beloved leader, his men
rushed forward and swept the French from the field.
Abercrombie's bugles now sounded the retreat, and
the fatigued soldiers returned to the landing-place,
where they encamped for the night.

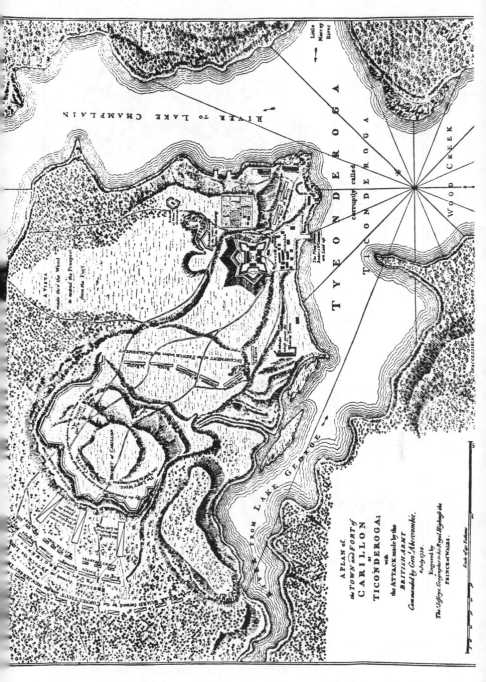

Thomas Jefferys' map of Abercrombie's attack on Fort Carillon
on July 8th, 1758

EXPLANATION.

A. Cheonderoga.
B. Intrenchment & front of the Attack in 1758.
C. Lake Champlain.
D. Wood Creek.
E. A Mountain over looking the Fort.
F. Our Rafts with 3 Cannon & 1 Howhits.
G. Where the Army lay the 7th.
H. Saw Mill & Fall. } The carrying Place is from
I. Ovens.   } H to I.X is about 2 Miles.
K. Where the Army lay the 6th.
L. Where the Army fell in with 450 of the Enemy, and Lord Howe was Kill'd
M. The Army marching in four Columns.
N. Landing Place.
O. Mutton Island.
P. Bare Mountain. Entrance of the Narrows.
Q. Saw Mill Creek.

LAKE GEORGE

Jn° Lodge Sculp

Another map of Abercrombie's attack, engraved by Jn. Lodge.

Early on the morning of the 7th, Lieutenant-colonel Bradstreet moved forward with a strong party and took possession of the saw-mills, while Abercrombie again formed his men in order of battle, and prepared to advance against the French works. But the attack was not made until the morning of the 8th, when the whole army was brought up, except a small detachment left to guard the boats, and a Provincial regiment stationed at the saw-mills. Montcalm had that morning received a reinforcement of four hundred men, under M. de Levy, which increased his force to about thirty-six hundred. Behind the newly erected lines, which were now strengthened by a wide and difficult abattis, he posted the tried battalions of La Reine, La Sarre, Bearn, Guiene, Berry, Languedoc and Roussillon, and calmly awaited the onset.

As the English approached, the rangers, light infantry, bateau men and Ruggles', Doley's, Partridge's. Williams' and Baglay's regiments of Provincials, with a battalion of the New York regiment, took post in front, out of cannon-shot of the French works, Next came the regulars destined for the attack, while the Connecticut and New Jersey troops were drawn up in the rear. At one o'clock the English bugles sounded to attack, when the regular battalions moved forward with quick and steady step—the veteran fifty-fifth leading, closely followed by the gallant Colonel Graham, at the head of Murray's Highlanders. As the columns approached, and when the ranks became entangled among the logs and fallen trees which protected the breastwork, Montcalm opened a galling fire of artillery and musketry, which mowed down the brave officers and men by hundreds. For four hours the English vainly strove to cut their way through the impenetrable abattis, until Abercrombie, despairing of success, and having already lost nineteen hundred and forty-four men in killed and wounded, ordered a retreat. Montcalm did not pursue, for the English still outnumbered him fourfold. Having refreshed his exhausted soldiers, he employed the night in strengthening his lines—a useless labor, for the frightened Abercrombie did not stop until he reached the head of Lake George and, even then, he sent his artillery and ammunition to Albany for safety.*

Soon after the retreat of the English, Majors Putnam and Rogers were sent, with their rangers, towards the head of Lake Champlain, to watch the movements of a party of five hundred Canadians and Indians, who, it was understood, intended to pass up the lake from Ticonderoga, under command of the famous Marin. Rodgers, with the main body, took a position near Wood Creek, about twelve miles from its mouth, while Putnam, with thirty-five men, took post on the bold rocky shore of the lake about half a mile north of the Creek. Near the edge of these rocks he constructed a wall of stones, and placed young trees before it in such a manner as completely to hide the defense from the water below. Learning four days afterwards, that the enemy were approaching, under cover of the night, Putnam called in his sentinels and stationed his men where their fire would prove most effective ; ordering them to remain perfectly quiet until they received his orders. The canoes advanced in solemn silence, and had passed the wall of stone, when they became alarmed by a slight noise, caused by one of Putnam's men carelessly striking his gun against a stone. Crowding together beneath the rocks, a brief consultation was held by the party, when the canoes were turned back towards Ticonderoga. As they turned, Putnam gave the order to fire. This fire was returned from the lake, and for a short time the contest was warmly kept up on both sides. Great was the carnage among the canoes, which lay exposed upon the smooth surface of the water. Ma-

*Abercrombie's Dispatch—Conquest of Canada.   Bancroft's History of the United States. Williams, Vermont, etc.

The loss of the English on that day was 551 killed, 1356 wounded and 37 missing. Montcalm reported his loss at 110 killed and 248 wounded.

In the centre of the French lines a lofty cross was erected, in celebration of the victory, on which was affixed a plate of brass with this inscription:

'Pone principes, eorum sicut Oreb, et Zebec et Zalmanna'— Warburton, Vol. II.

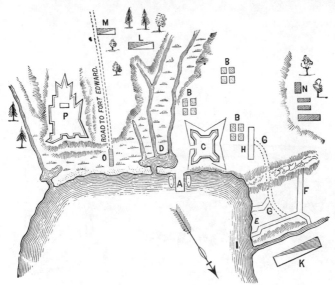

A.—Dock.	K.—Montcalm's Camp.
B.—Garrison Gardens.	L —M. DeLevy's Camp.
C.—Fort William Henry.	M.—M. De La Corne with Canadians and Indians.
D.—Morass.	
E.—Montcalm's 1st Battery.	N.—English Encampment before the retrenchments was made.
F.—Montcalm's 2d Battery.	
G.—Montcalm's Approaches.	O.—Bridge over the Morass.
H.—Two Intended Batteries.	P.—English retrenchment.
I.—Place where Montcalm landed his Artillery.	

A plan of Fort William Henry 1757, and the English camp and retrenchments, with the French camps and the attack thereupon

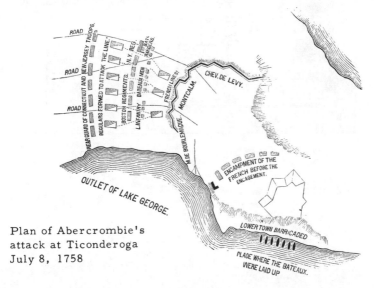

Plan of Abercrombie's
attack at Ticonderoga
July 8, 1758

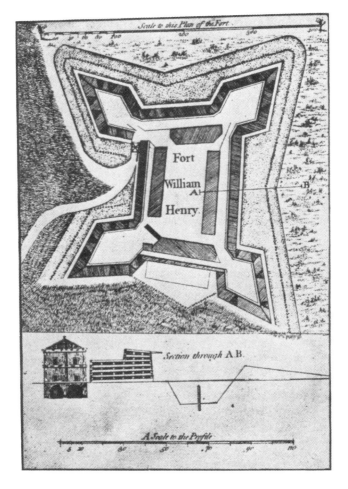

Scale to this Plan of the Fort.

Fort
William
Henry.

Section through A.B.

A Scale to the Profile

FORT WILLIAM HENRY

rin at length withdrew and landed his men a short distance below, intending to surround the rangers; but Putnam was upon the alert and immediately withdrew towards Fort Edward. While retreating through the thick forest an unexpected enemy fired upon the party, and wounded one man. Putnam instantly ordered his men to charge, when his voice was recognized by the leader of the other party, who cried out, "Hold, we are friends." "Friends or foes," answered Putnam, "you deserve to perish for doing so little execution with so fair a shot." The party proved to be a detachment sent to cover his retreat.

A few days afterwards, Putnam was taken prisoner by some of the Indians attached to Marin's command. The Indians bound Putnam to a tree. A young savage then amused himself by seeing how near he could throw a tomahawk to his prisoner's head, without touching it —the weapon struck in the tree a number of times, at a hair's breadth from the mark. When the Indian had finished this novel, but, to one of the parties, not very agreeable sport, a Canadian came up, snapped his fusee at Putnam's breast, then violently and repeatedly pushed the muzzle against his ribs, and finally gave him a severe blow on the jaw with the butt-end of the gun. Putnam was then stripped of his clothes and taken to the place selected for their night encampment, where the Indians determined to roast him alive. For this purpose they bound him to a tree, piled dried bushes in a circle around him, and then set fire to the pile. At the moment when Putnam began to feel the scorching heat, and had resigned himself to the keen agonies of certain death, Marin rushed through the crowd, opened a way, by scattering the burning brands, and unbound the victim.*

This humane officer, having reprimanded the savages in severe terms, took Putnam under his own protection and delivered him to Montcalm, by whom he was sent to Montreal.—Thus, through hardships, privations and blood, were the sturdy Provincials schooled for the great and heroic deeds of the American Revolution.

* Thacher's Military Journal.

CHAPTER V.

General Amherst marches against Ticonderoga and Crown Point—
Retreat of the French to Canada—Naval operations on Lake Cham-
plain—Progress of the settlement of the country bordering on Lake
Champlain, prior to the revolution—New Hampshire Grants—
Dispute with tenants of Colonel Reed—A new Province projected
by Colonel Skene and others.

NOTWITHSTANDING the great importance attached
by the Provincial and Home Governments to the control of Lake Champlain—the key of Canada—three
campaigns, under three different Generals, had been
undertaken without any progress towards the attain-
ment of that object. Johnson was inefficient, Webb
pusillanimous, and Abercrombie wanting in military
skill and firmness. The first halted his army to build
a fort when he should have captured one ; the second,
with four thousand men under his immediate command,
abandoned the brave Monro to the tomahawk of the
merciless savage; while Abercrombie, though far superior to both, by a false move and " the extremest fright
and consternation," allowed less than four thousand
men to repel the advance of fifteen thousand troops,
truly said to have been " the largest and best appor-
tioned army in America." Success, however, had attended the British arms in other quarters. Louisburg
capitulated to General Amherst in July, and in November General Forbes was in possession of Fort Duquesne.

Pitt, the then English Secretary of State, had long
desired the conquest of Canada, and was determined to
leave no efforts untried to accomplish that object.
Fully appreciating the skill, bravery and activity of
Amherst, he appointed him to the chief command in
America. Amherst entered upon his work with zeal.
Wolfe was placed in command of one expedition des-

tined to the attack of Quebec; Prideaux was sent with another against Niagara, while the Commander-in-Chief led a third in person, against the French posts on Lake Champlain.

Montcalm was indefatigable in his preparations for the approaching struggle. Three armed vessels were built to command the navigation of Lake Champlain, and the strong walls of Carillon again echoed with the noise of workmen. Still the French General, sorely pressed on every side, feared for the safety of that post. He could spare but few troops for its defence, and besides he well knew that its batteries were commanded by the controlling summit of Mount Defiance. "Had I to besiege Fort Carillon," said he the year before, while wondering at the retreat of Abercrombie, "I would ask but six mortars and two pieces of artillery."* Bourlemaque was sent forward to protect the fort with three batalions of Regulars and a body of Canadians and Indians, but he received instructions, at the same time, if necessary, to blow up the works on the approach of the English, to retire to Isle Aux Noix and there make a strong resistance.

On the 21st of June, Amherst reached the head of Lake George with an army of six thousand men, where he remained for a month, waiting for the remainder of the troops to come up. On the 21st he embarked with fifty-seven hundred and forty-three Regulars and five thousand two hundred and seventy-nine Provincials, and crossing the lake in four columns landed, the next day, near the spot where Abercrombie had disembarked the year before. That night his army lay under arms at the saw-mills, while the French held their old lines in force. On the night of the 23d, De Bourlemaque withdrew his men and leaving a party of four hundred in Fort Carillon, to mask his retreat, embarked with the

* Bancroft's History of U. S. See, however, Paris Doc. in Vol. X Col. His. of N. Y. Where M. de Pont le Roy, chief engineer under Montcalm, closes his memoir with these words. "From this description it will be seen how little susceptible of defence is this fort. * * Were I intrusted with the seige I should require only six mortars, and two cannon."

main body for Crown Point. The English Grenadiers immediately occupied the deserted intrenchments.

During the 24th and 25th, the French kept up a continuous fire upon the English camp, which was warmly returned. In the meantime, Amherst advanced his approaches within six hundred yards of the fort, and was prepared to assault the works, but the French, having now held their opponents at bay long enough to secure the retreat of De Bourlemaque, prepared to blow up and abandon them. Several mines were constructed under the walls and a fuse connected with the powder magazine. At ten o'clock, on the night of the 26th, they sprung the mine and hastily retreated to their boats.* The explosion scattered the flames in every direction — breastworks, barracks and storehouses were consumed, while the report of the bursting guns, following each other in quick succession, announced to the retreating French the progress of the work of destruction.

Amherst immediately commenced repairing the fort, the stone work of which remained mostly uninjured. He also sent forward Major Rodgers, with two hundred rangers, to examine the position of the French at Crown Point, and to seize, and, at all hazards, hold some strong post near the fort. But this haste was useless, for before the Rangers could reach their post, the French had destroyed the fort, burned the surrounding settlements and retreated to Isle Aux Noix. The glory of St. Frederic was gone.

On the 4th of August, Amherst reached Crown Point with the main army and immediately traced out the lines of a new fort, about two hundred yards west of the old French works. This fort, although never completed, is said to have cost the English Government over two millions of pounds sterling. The ramparts were about twenty-five feet thick and nearly the same in height and were built of solid masonry. The curtains varied in length from fifty-two to one hundred yards, and the whole circuit, measuring around the

* Conquest of Canada, Vol. II.

CROWN POINT, 1851.

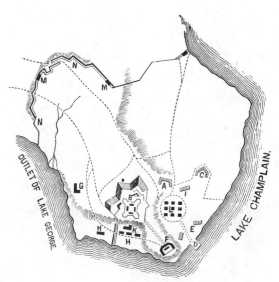

A.—Stone Battery.
B.—The Fort.
C.—Earth Battery.
D.—Wharf.
E —Stone Houses for Naval
      Stores.
F.—Redoubt.

G.—Battery.
H.—Stone Houses for Prisoners.
I. —Lime Kilns.
K.—Nine Ovens.
L.—Gardens.
M.—Batteries in the Lines.
N.—French Lines.

Plan of Fort Carillon, 1759

Lord Jeffery Amherst

ramparts and including the bastions, was eight hundred and fifty-three yards. A broad ditch surrounded the work. On the north was a gate, and from the north-east bastion a covered way leading to the water.

While engaged upon this work, Amherst directed Captain Loring, who superintended the naval operations on the lake, to build with the greatest dispatch, a sloop of sixteen guns, a radeau or raft eighty-four feet long, capable of carrying six large cannon, and a brigantine. These were completed by the 11th of October, when the English commander embarked his whole army in bateaux and started for Canada. Towards the evening of the next day the wind commenced blowing a gale, and the general was obliged to anchor his bateaux under the west shore of the lake. Captain Loring, however, kept at sea with his armed vessels, and at daylight in the morning, discovered the French about forty-five miles down the lake. He immediately gave chase and drove a schooner and three sloops under shelter of Valcour Island. The sloops were sunk, and the schooner run aground. The crew escaped into the woods.*

Amherst, after remaining wind-bound for several days, again started for Canada, but he had scarcely reached Valcour Island, when the autumn winds threatened to swamp his vessels. Satisfied that he could accomplish nothing at that late and inclement season of the year, he now abandoned the enterprise and returned to winter quarters at Crown Point, where he arrived on the 21st of October.

While Amherst was at Crown Point he opened a road from that place to " No. 4 " on the Connecticut river, and also planned an expedition against the St.

---

* See Brasrier's Map of Lake Champlain, where the north end of Valcour Island is designated as the place where "the French sunk their vessels in 1759." The schooner carried ten four pounders and the three smaller crafts carried each eight guns of small calibre and a crew of fifty men. M. Bourlemaque says the schooner was run aground and the three smaller vessels were sunk at nightfall. [Dispatch to Marshal de Belle Isle] Lieut. Hadden, in a map made in 1776, designates the place in the little bay opposite Crab Island.

Francis Indians, who lived on the east side of the St. Lawrence, near Three Rivers. The command of this expedition was entrusted to Major Rodgers of the New Hampshire troops, who, in October, left Crown Point in bateaux, with two hundred men. This number was afterwards, by an accident, reduced to one hundred and forty-two, with whom Rodgers proceeded to Missisco Bay, where he concealed his boats and a portion of his provisions and started by land for the Indian village. The expedition was successful. After reducing the village to ashes, Rodgers and his men returned to Crown Point by the way of the Connecticut River. In May, 1760, General Amherst ordered Major Rodgers to proceed down the lake with 275 Rangers and twenty-five light infantry, and attempt the surprise of the French forts at St. Johns and Chambly. On the 4th June, Rodgers landed with 200 men on the west shore of the lake, twelve miles south of Isle Aux Noix (Rouse's Point), the rest of his party remaining on board the sloops, which, under command of Capt. Grant, had been sent back to Isle La Motte. Rodgers was attacked on the 6th, while encamped near the place of landing, by 350 French troops sent from the fort at Isle Aux Noix, under command of M. La Force, and, after a short but severe engagement, defeated the French, who returned to Isle Aux Noix. In this engagement Ensign Wood of the 17th regiment and sixteen Rangers were killed and Capt. Johnson and ten men were wounded. Capt. Johnson died a few days after the battle. On the part of the French forty were killed and several wounded, including M. La Force.

After the action Rodgers retired to Isle La Motte, where he remained until the 9th, when he landed at the mouth of the Great Chazy river, and passing around Isle Aux Noix attacked and destroyed a small stockade fort below St. Johns and returned to the lake with twenty-five prisoners, reaching Crown Point on the 23d day of June.*

* Rodger's Journal.

Major Robert Rogers

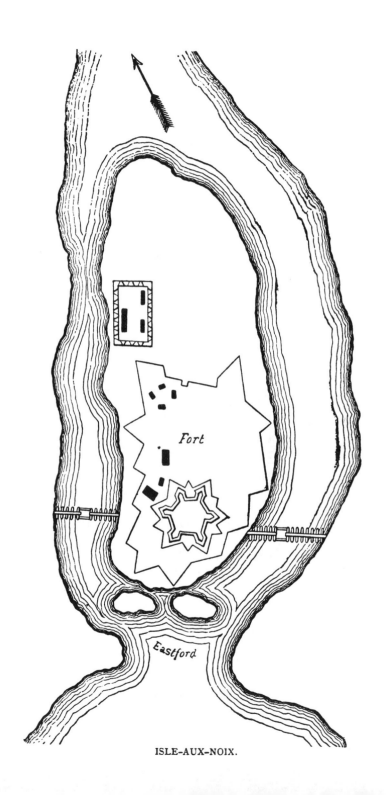

Fort

Eastford

ISLE-AUX-NOIX.

In August 1760, Colonel Haviland left Crown Point at the head of fifteen hundred regular troops, eighteen hundred Provincials and some Indians, and on the 16th of that month, encamped opposite the French post at Isle Aux Noix, and by the 24th, opened a fire of mortars upon it. Three days after, M. De Bougain. ville, the Commandant, withdrew from the island leaving a garrison of only thirty men, who immediately surrendered.* On the 8th of September, Colonel Haviland joined Amherst and Murray, under the walls of Montreal. That same day the city was surrendered by Vaudreuil. By this act the French dominion in Canada ceased, and by the treaty of peace signed in Paris on the 10th day of February, 1763, that Province was formally ceded to Great Britain. This, says Mr. Smollet,† "was a conquest the most important of any that ever the British army achieved, whether we consider the safety of the British Colonies in America, now secured from invasion and encroachment; the extent and fertility of the country subdued; or the whole Indian commerce thus transferred to Great Britain."

When the French army retreated to Canada, it was accompanied by the few inhabitants residing upon the borders of the lake. There was, however, at this time, a settlement of French and Indians at Swanton Falls in Vermont, several miles east of the lake, containing a small church, a saw-mill and about fifty huts, which was not abandoned by them until the year 1775.‡

In the course of the year 1760, the New England troops frequently passed over the road opened by Amherst from the lake to the Connecticut, and thus became acquainted with the fertility and value of the lands in that section. These lands were soon sought out and settled upon.

The lands north of Crown Point, although equally fertile, were more remote and did not as early attract the attention of the pioneer or speculator. They, how-

* Conquest of Canada. Williams' History of Vermont.
† History of England.
* Thompson's Gazetteer.

ever, came into notice gradually, so that several permanent settlements were made along the borders of the lake, during the fifteen years which intervened between the expulsion of the French and the commencement of the revolutionary war.

In 1766, Colonel Ephraim Doolittle, Paul Moore, Marshall Newton and others settled in the town of Shoreham, and, in the same year, Donald McIntosh, a native of Scotland, moved into the town of Vergennes. A saw-mill was erected at the lower falls of Otter Creek as early as 1769, and shortly afterwards a grist-mill was built at the same place.

Some years before the commencement of the revolutionary war, two Germans by the name of Logan and Pottier settled upon the points of land, in the town of Shelburne, known as Pottier's Point and Logan's Point. They were engaged in getting out timber for the Canadian market, and are said to have been murdered near the north end of the lake, by a party of soldiers sent out from Montreal to escort them home, on their return with the avails of a raft which they had sold. Soon after their death, about ten families settled in the town, among whom were Thomas and Moses Pierson.

John Strong, Zadock Everest and a Mr. Ward commenced a settlement in the town of Addison, on the opposite side of the lake from Crown Point, in 1769 or 1770. A settlement was also commenced in 1770, in the town of Panton, by John Pangborn and Odle Squires, who were afterwards joined by Timothy Spaulding, Peter Ferris and others. Ferris resided at the bay in which Arnold burned his vessels during the revolutionary war.

The town of Bridport was first settled, in 1768, by Philip Stone, of Groton, Massachusetts. About the same time, two families by the name of Richardson and Smith moved into the township and commenced a settlement, under New York titles, and were followed by Towner, Chipman and Plumer, who held grants from the Governor of New Hampshire. In 1773, Samuel Smith moved his family into the town and was followed during the following winter by Mr. Victory. A settlement was commenced at the lower falls on the Winooski River by Ira Allen and Remember Baker, in 1773.*

These settlements were all on the eastern border of the lake. A few improvements had also been commenced on the New York side, which were principally confined to the grants made, by the colony of New York, to the officers and soldiers who had served in the wars against the French and Indians. The most important of these, lying north of Crown Point, was at the Bouquet River where William Gilliland had erected a saw-mill, and where several persons, including Gilliland, Watson, Scarr, Cross, Blood and McCawley resided.

William Hay and Henry Cross, lived on a tract of land granted, in 1765, to Lieutenant Friswell. Hay's house stood near the shore of the lake opposite Valcour Island. From this house his family watched the progress of the naval engagement between the American and British fleet, 11th Oct. 1776, and witnessed Arnold's masterly retreat during the following night. Before the Revolution, the few inhabitants residing on the north end of the lake received their supplies from Montreal, which they were in the habit of visiting several times in the course of the summer months. About the 1st of June, 1775, Mr. Hay went to Montreal to purchase a supply of flour, and was there arrested and thrown into prison by order of General Carleton. He remained in prison several days, but was at length liberated at the solicitation of the merchants of that city. Mr. Hay, on his return, repaired to Crown Point and gave information to the American commander as to the strength and plans of the Indians, which was considered of great importance at the time. He also brought the first news of Carleton's efforts to enlist the Caughnawagas on the side of the English. For some

---

* For further information in relation to the first settlement of the towns on the eastern border of the lake, see Thompson's Gazetteer of Vermont.

reason he was afterwards suspected of holding communication with the English. In July, 1776, while his wife and children lay sick of the small pox, Hay was arrested and sent to Crown Point, by order of General Sullivan ; Cross accompanied him. " These men are suspected of being inimical to us and have it in their power to give intelligence to the enemy," was the reason assigned for their arrest.

As early as 1763, one John La Frambois, a native of Canada, accompanied by two men named Goude and Swarte, visited the shores of the lake and remained a short time in the present town of Chazy, Clinton County. La Frombois returned to Canada in 1768, and obtained permission from Francis McKay to settle on a tract which McKay pretended to claim by virtue of an assignment of the old French grant to La Gauchetiere.* Under this license La Frombois took possession of what are now lots numbers seventy and seventy-two, in Dean's Patent, and built a house on number seventy-two, where he remained until 1776, when he was driven off by the English and his house burned. He returned in 1784, after the war, rebuilt his house and remained in possession of the lot until his death in 1810. Joseph la Monte (now Monty) moved on to a lot near La Frombois', in 1774, which he abandoned two years afterwards, and reclaimed after the war. His descendants still reside upon the same land.

After La Frombois's first visit, but before his actual location in 1768, Charles de Fredenburgh, a needy German nobleman, who, in 1766, had received from the English Government a warrant for thirty thousand acres of land, lying on the river Saranac, moved on to the tract and built a house and saw-mill there. De Fredenburgh remained on this tract until about the time of the commencement of the Revolution, when he removed his family to Montreal. He soon after re-

* See Chap. 3. Gauchetiere assigned to Estebe, in 1746, who sold to De Pontbriant, Bishop of Quebec, in December, 1757. Pontbriant afterwards conveyed to De Montgolfier, Superior of the Seminary of St. Sulpice, who, in 1768, released to McKay, as one of the heirs at aw of the Bishop, De Pontbriant.

turned to protect his property, and had been back but a short time, when the house and mill were burned down. Fredenburgh disappeared at the same time and was supposed to have been murdered. The saw-mill stood on a fall of the Saranac, two miles above its mouth.

In 1761, Philip K. Skene, an English Major under half pay, who had been with Amherst in 1759, established a large colony near the mouth of Wood Creek. In the autumn, Skene accompanied an expedition against Havana, and on his return, in 1763, found the settlement reduced to fifteen persons. He immediately set about re-establishing the colony, and, in 1765, obtained patents for twenty-five thousand acres of land lying on and near the creek. Here he built a stone mansion forty feet by thirty, and two stories and a half in height. In 1770, he built a large stone building one hundred and thirty feet long, which was used for a military garrison and depot. He also built at this place a stone forge of about the same dimensions as his house, where he commenced the manufacture of iron. This was the first forge erected on the borders of the lake. Skene owned a sloop, with which he kept up a constant communication with Canada, and, at his own expense, cut a road through the wilderness as far as Salem, a distance of about thirty miles, from which point it was continued by others to Bennington. This road was used during the season when the navigation on the lake was closed by ice. In 1773, Skenesborough contained a population of 379.*

The causes which had formerly prevented the occupancy of the fertile lands of the Champlain valley were removed when the whole country came into the possession of the English Government, by the Conquest of Canada in 1760. But other difficulties almost

---

* See a petition to Governor Tryon, praying that Skenesborough might be made the Shiretown of Charlotte County. The petition is signed by thirty-eight "inhabitants of Crown Point district and Ticonderoga." These thirty-eight probably included all the settlers in the vicinity of those posts, on both sides of the lake.—Documentary History of New York, Vol. 4.

immediately sprang up to retard the growth of this section, originating in the conflicting claims of the English colonists to the sovereignty of that portion of the valley lying east of the lake. The colony of New York claimed jurisdiction as far east as the Connecticut River, while New Hampshire asserted her right as far west as the shores of the lake, and south of the lake, to a line running parallel to and twenty miles east of the Hudson River. Both colonies frequently issued grants for the same territory; causing much confusion in the land titles and creating great animosity between the rival claimants.

Prior to the close of the year 1763, the Governor of New Hampshire had granted charters to different persons for fourteen towns lying along and adjoining the east shore of the lake, and, by similar grants, had asserted the right of that colony to the whole territory claimed to be within her jurisdiction. On the other side, the colony of New York issued grants of land on the lake to eighty-one or more reduced officers, who had served in the French and Indian wars; nearly one-half of which were located on the east side of the lake. The colony had also appropriated a large tract, lying between Otter Creek and Mallet's Bay, for the disbanded soldiers of those wars. A county had also been organized by New York, called Charlotte County, which extended, on the north, from Lake Memphremagog to the St. Regis River, and stretched south, on both sides of the lake, far beyond its southern extremity; the county seat was fixed at Skenesborough'.

The efforts of New York to extend its jurisdiction to the east was met, from the first, by a most decided opposition on the part of the people. Conventions were called to devise means to protect the New Hampshire claimants in their rights, committees of safety were organized and the law officers and land surveyors of New York were driven by force from the disputed territory. These disputes were generally confined to the southern part of Vermont. Occasionally, however, they extended as far north as the grants upon the lakes.

In 1761, the Governor of New Hampshire granted a
tract of land, lying around the lower falls of Otter
Creek, (Vergennes,) to several persons, who moved
there and, as early as 1769, had erected a saw-mill at
the falls. Soon after the erection of the mill, Lieutenant-colonel John Reed, who had formerly commanded the Forty-second Royal Highland Regiment,
and who held a claim to the same land under the colony of New York, forcibly drove off the New Hampshire settlers and put about fifteen families, his own
tenants, in possession. These last extended the settlements and had erected several log houses and a grist-
mill, when they were in turn ordered off by a party of
" Green Mountain Boys," who burned the houses, destroyed the grist-mill and put the New Hampshire
claimants again in possession.

In June, 1773, Colonel Reed persuaded a number of
Scotch emigrants who had lately arrived at New York,
including John Cameron, James Henderson, Donald
McIntosh, John Bardans and Angus McBean, to accompany him to Otter Creek for the purpose of retak-
ing possession of these lands. On their arrival they
found Joshua Hyde and several other persons in possession, with whom Reed entered into an arrangement
by which Hyde and his associates were to give up quiet
possession of the lands and to allow Reed's tenants to retain the same, until the dispute as to title should be
decided by the English Government. Colonel Reed
paid £61, 16s, for the crops and improvements, repaired the grist-mill and also purchased a quantity of provisions and some cows for the use of his tenants. He
then left them and returned to New York.

This arrangement, although made with the consent
of the New Hampshire claimants, was disapproved by
the committee of safety, who sent Ethan Allen, Seth
Warner and Remember Baker, with a party of about
one hundred " Green Mountain Boys " to Otter Creek
for the purpose of driving off the Scotch occupants.
On the 11th of August, Allen's party, attended by
Hyde—the same person who two months before had

sold his claim to Colonel Reed—arrived at the settlements, drove the Scotch from their dwellings, burned
the hay and corn and five houses, and then tore down
the grist-mill, breaking the mill-stones in pieces and
throwing them over the bank into the Creek. Cameron and his companions remained at Otter Creek
about two weeks longer and then returned to New
York. After their departure a small block-house was
erected at the falls, which was garrisoned and afterwards used as a protection to the New Hampshire
claimants. Another block-house was soon after built
near the falls of Winooski River.

During the controversy between the settlers under
the New Hampshire grants and the colony of New
York, a project was started by Major Skene and others
to form that part of New York, lying east of the Hudson River, into a new Province. To effect this object
Skene visited England, and in March, 1775, wrote back
that he had been appointed Governor of Crown Point
and Ticonderoga, and should soon call on the people
for an address to show their loyalty to the King. During the absence of Skene the troubles on the grants
had increased to an alarming extent, and it is extremely doubtful what would have been the result of the
contest, had not the commencement of the American
Revolution turned the attention of all parties to the
common cause of the country.

CHAPTER VI.

War of the Revolution—Surprise of Ticonderoga—Arnold at St. Johns—Sentiments of the Canadians—Invasion of Canada—Seige of St. Johns—Death of General Montgomery at Quebec—Retreat of the "Army of Canada."

" WE conjure you by all that is dear, by all that is sacred, that you give all assistance possible in forming an army for our defence," was the appeal of Massachusetts, while the first blood of the Revolution yet moistened the field of Lexington. Every section of the country responded to the call. Liberty poles were raised throughout Massachusetts and the adjoining Provinces, and everywhere the militia took up arms and hastened to the scene of action.

"Putnam was at work in the field when the news came that blood had been shed; he immediately dropped his implements, and started for Cambridge, without waiting to change his apparel. Stark was sawing logs, without his coat; he shut down the gate of his mill, and commenced the journey to Boston in his shirt sleeves." The same spirit was displayed throughout the country. Occasionally, however, a few persons were found who were inimical to the common cause. These were called *Tories*, and were often subjected to the most rigorous discipline. "When a disaffected tory renders himself odious," says Doctor Thacher, "he is seized by a company of armed men, and conducted to the liberty pole, under which he is compelled to sign a recantation, and give bonds for his future good conduct."

Upon one occasion a divine of Long Island pronounced, from his pulpit, a severe philippic against the Patriots, stigmatizing them as rebels, robbers and assassins. Information of the high tory character of the discourse was carried to Captain Nathaniel Platt, a most zealous Patriot, who commanded a company of Long Island Militia. Capt. Platt immediately called out his men, seized the minister and carried him to the liberty pole, around which the company were formed. The minister was there severely reprimanded, and forced to walk up and kiss the pole as a punishment for his political heresy. On the next Sabbath Captain Platt was at the church, to see what effect his "discipline" had produced upon the man of God. For a long time the discourse was unexceptionable, but, while the minister was portraying the enjoyments of heaven to the true Christian, he gave expression to his feelings by turning towards the Captain and exclaiming, "there are no rebels in heaven, my brethren.—No! and you will find no Nathaniel Platts there, nor any accursed liberty poles to kiss."

The great body of the clergy, however, were firm and zealous Patriots, who daily offered the most fervent prayers in behalf of their bleeding and afflicted country. Upon one occasion, a zealous divine, who had been compelled to abandon his congregation in Boston, used the following emphatic language. " Oh! Lord, if our enemies will fight us, let them have fighting enough. If more soldiers are on their way hither, sink them, O Lord, to the bottom of the sea." " Amen," responded his congregation, " Yea, Lord, let them have fighting enough."

Among the men brought out by the Revolution to meet the exigencies of the times, were Ethan Allen and Benedict Arnold. Arnold, a native of Connecticut, was indued with qualities which characterized him at once, as the best of warriors and the meanest of men. In battle he was " the bravest among the brave." No enterprise was too daring for him to undertake, no obstacle too great for him to surmount. Whether among the unexplored forests of Maine, upon the decks of a little vessel on Lake Champlain, before the muskets of a platoon at Danbury, or under the fire of Burgoyne's veterans at Bemis' Heights, he was firm, daring and unterrified. But, in every other respect, the

man was despicable. In early life he had been, by
turns, a half-bred apothecary, a retailer, a skipper and
a jockey, and had marked his course by hypocrisy,
falsehood and crime. To escape the grasp of his
creditors, he committed perjury, and to relieve himself
of pecuniary embarrassments, occasioned by a life of
extravagance and profligacy, he practiced every dirty
act of peculation, and, ultimately, aimed a traitor's
dagger at the bosom of his country.

Ethan Allen was also a native of Connecticut and
possessed all the impetuous daring of Arnold, but without his vices. Associated in early life with the pioneers
of Vermont, he soon became one of the leading men in
that quarter, and by his bold unyielding spirit, repelled
the repeated attempts of New York to extend her jurisdiction over the New Hampshire Grants. As a political writer he was clear and forcible, but uncultivated ;
as a leader, bold and decided, but often rash ; as a man,
frank, generous and unassuming.

Such were the two men who, on the 7th of May, 1775,
met at Castleton to lead an expedition to the surprise
of Ticonderoga. Allen, furnished with funds by Dean,
Wooster and Parsons, in behalf of the Assembly of Connecticut, had collected a band of two hundred and seventy men, all but forty-six of whom were his own well
tried and faithful Green Mountain Boys, led by Brown
and the cool and cautious Warner. Arnold came
attended by a single servant, but bringing with him a
Colonel's commission from the Committee of Safety of
Massachusetts, authorizing him to raise a regiment
of four hundred men. As soon as the two leaders met,
Arnold pompously drew forth his commission and
claimed the right to lead the expedition ; but Allen refused to yield the command. The dispute was at length
referred to a committee of officers, by whom it was decided that Allen should retain the command, while Arnold was to act as his assistant. The main body now
left Castleton to proceed by land to a point opposite Ticonderoga. At the same time Captain Herrick was
sent against Skenesborough, with thirty men, with

orders to seize the small fort at that place, to take the vessels collected there and meet Allen and transport his party across the lake.

The forts at Ticonderoga and Crown Point, had been abandoned soon after the Conquest of Canada, and were now in a ruinous condition. Within the year a garrison had been sent there, at the request of the Governor of New York, to protect the public property, and to secure that section from the threatened encroachments of the New Hampshire claimants. The garrison was, however, small and weak ; Crown Point being held by a sergeant and twelve men, while a company of only forty-eight men, under command of Captain de la Place, was stationed at Ticonderoga.

Early on the evening of the 9th of May, Allen's party reached the shore of the lake opposite Ticonderoga. Herrick not having yet arrived from Skenesborough, it became necessary to procure a supply of boats in the neighborhood, in order to cross to the Fort. This was a work of no small difficulty. Douglass, one of the party, was sent to Bridport for a scow. A large oar boat belonging to Major Skene, which lay at anchor near by, was decoyed ashore and seized by James Wilcox and Joseph Tyler, while several smaller boats were procured from other quarters.

As these boats were not sufficient'to ferry the whole party at once, it was arranged that Allen and Arnold should first cross with eighty-three men, and that the boats should return for the rest of the party, who were to remain behind under command of Warner. The little band, guided by Nathan Beman, a lad of fifteen years, was soon drawn up on the low ground below the fort, where an altercation again commenced between the two leaders ; each claiming the right to lead the advance. Again the subordinate officers interfered, and decided that they should go in together—Allen on the right hand, and Arnold on the left. As the day began to break, it was deemed prudent to make the attack without waiting for the arrival of Warner, who had not yet crossed the lake with his party.

GENERAL BENEDICT ARNOLD

ETHAN ALLEN AND CAPT. DE LA PLACE

Allen now advanced to the front, and addressed his men, as follows: "Friends and fellow Soldiers—You have, for a number of years past, been a scourge and terror to arbitrary power. Your valor has been famed abroad and acknowledged, as appears by the advice and orders to me, from the General Assembly of Connecticut, to surprise and take the garrison now before us. I now propose to advance before you and in person conduct you through the wicket gate; for we must this morning either quit our pretentions to valor, or possess ourselves of this fortress in a few minutes; and inasmuch as it is a desperate attempt, which none but the bravest of men dare undertake, I do not urge it on any contrary to his will. You that will undertake voluntarily, *poise your firelocks.*" "Each man," says Allen, "poised his firelock. I ordered them to face to the right, and, at the head of the centre file, marched them immediately to the wicket gate."*

When they approached, the sentinel snapped his gun, and immediately retreated through the covered way closely followed by the assailants, who were thus guided within the fort. As the Patriots rushed into the parade ground, they formed in the centre, facing the barracks, and gave a loud cheer, while Allen ascended a flight of steps leading to the commandant's quarters, and, in a loud voice, ordered him to appear or the whole garrison would be sacrificed.

In this affair, the Patriots captured forty-eight men, one hundred and twenty pieces of cannon, several swivels and howitzers, together with a large number of small arms and ammunition of every description, and also a warehouse filled with materials for boat building. Colonel Warner arrived, with the remainder of the party, just after the surrender of the fort, and was immediately sent, with one hundred men, to take possession of Crown Point; but a strong headwind drove his boats back, and he returned to Ticonderoga. The next morning a more successful attempt

*Allen's Narrative.

was made, and the fort at Crown Point was captured
without bloodshed. Warner was there met by Captain
Remember Baker, who had left the small fort on the
Winooski to join Allen's party, and who, on his way
up the lake, had intercepted two boats, which had been
sent from Crown Point to carry intelligence of the reduction of Ticonderoga to St. Johns and Montreal.

It will be remembered that when the Patriots left
Castleton Captain Herrick was sent, with thirty men,
against Skenesborough. Herrick approached the place
unobserved, and captured young Major Skene, twelve
negroes and about fifty dependents or tenants, without
firing a gun. He also took a large schooner and several
small boats belonging to Skene, in which he embarked
his men and prisoners, and, passing down the lake,
joined Allen at Ticonderoga. The history of the surprise of Skenesborough is embellished by an account of
a singular discovery made there by the Patriots. It is
said that some of Herrick's men, while searching
Skene's house, found the dead body of a female deposited in the cellar, where it had been preserved for
many years. This was the body of Mrs. Skene, the
deceased wife of the elder Skene who was then in
Europe, and who was in the receipt of an annuity,
which had been devised to his wife " while she remained above ground." Like a good patriot, Herrick crippled the resources of the enemy, by burying the body
in the garden at the rear of the house.

In order to accomplish their plans, and to obtain
absolute control of the lake, it was now only necessary
that Allen and Arnold should get possession of an
armed sloop, of about seventy tons, which lay at anchor
in the Richelieu River, near the fort of St. Johns.
After consultation and a dispute between the two
officers, who were mutually jealous of each other, it
was agreed that Arnold should fit out and arm the
schooner which Herrick had captured at Skenesborough,
and sail for St. Johns, accompanied by Allen, who was
to take command of several log-boats, which lay at
Crown Point.

The schooner having been brought to Crown Point, Arnold embarked on the evening of the 14th of May, with fifty men under Captains Brown and Oswald, and on the 17th, arrived within thirty miles of St. Johns, where his vessel was becalmed. Leaving the schooner, he manned two small boats with thirty-five men, and started to row down the river. At six o'clock the next morning he arrived at St. Johns, and surprised a sergeant and twelve men who garrisoned the fort. He also seized the sloop, in which he found seven men and two brass six pounders. From the prisoners he learned that the commanding officer of the fort was hourly expected to return from Montreal, with a large detachment of troops for Ticonderoga, and a number of guns and carriages for the sloop. A company of forty men was also momentarily expected from Chambly.

Arnold had at first intended to await the arrival of Allen, who had been left far behind by the schooner, while crossing the lake, but this information caused him to hasten his departure. Having destroyed three row-boats, he immediately set out on his return, taking with him the sloop, four boats loaded with stores and twenty prisoners. The party had proceeded about fifteen miles when they met Allen, with one hundred men, hastening down the river. Arnold informed Allen of the unexpected arrival of troops at St. Johns, and urged him to return. But this Allen refused to do, declaring that he should push on to St. Johns, and hold possession of it with the men under his command.*

When Allen reached St. Johns, he found the English troops were within two miles of the fort. He therefore crossed to the opposite side of the river, where he encamped for the night. Early the next morning the English commenced a fire upon the party, with six field pieces and two hundred small arms. Allen returned this fire for a short time, but finding he could make no resistance against the superior numbers

* Arnold to Committee of Safety of Massachusetts.

opposed to him, he hastily re-embarked, leaving three of his men behind.*

As soon as Arnold reached Crown Point, on his return, he fitted up the sloop with six cannon and ten swivels, fixed four guns and six swivels on the schooner, and prepared to resist any attack which might be made against that place from Canada. At the same time he wrote to the Committee of Safety of Massachusetts and New York, urging them to send forward a large body of men to rebuild the fort at Ticonderoga.

The fortunate issue of the movement against the British possessions on Lake Champlain was of the utmost importance to the cause of the country, as it created a confidence among the people in the ultimate success of the struggle, and at the same time, placed the colonists in possession of the Key to Canada, effectually preventing any sudden attack from that quarter.

The feelings of the Canadians, in regard to the approaching struggle, were not known, nor could it yet be determined which side of the question they would take. Sir Guy Carleton, Governor of Canada, used every exertion to enlist them on the side of the Government, while the American Congress, on its part, endeavored to conciliate their friendship and induce them to make common cause with the colonists, or, at least, to stand neutral during the approaching struggle. The efforts of Congress were so far successful as to secure their neutrality.

Disappointed in not receiving the co-operation of the Canadians, Gen. Carleton next attempted to rally the royalists, and for that purpose, organized a corps to which he gave the name of the 'Royal Highland Emigrants." He also entered into negotiations with the Indians. Toward the last of July Colonel Guy Johnson, superintendent of Indian affairs, arrived at Montreal, accompanied by a number of the chiefs and warriors of the Six Nations. Here a solemn council was held, and the assembled Indians swore, in the

* Arnold to General Assembly of Massachusetts.

presence of the Governor, to support the cause of the King against the Colonists. A great number, however, who had not attended the council, declared they would not intermeddle in the dispute, nor would they consent to aid or oppose either party.

The American Congress was informed of these attempts, on the part of General Carleton, to enlist the Canadians and Indians on the side of the King. It was also advised that the Canadians had refused to enter into the contest; but there was no assurance that they would long preserve their neutrality. Carleton had obtained great influence over this class, and might ultimately succeed in drawing them over to his side. To prevent this, and in the hopes that the *habitans* might be persuaded to embrace the opportunity to attempt the vindication of their political rights, Congress determined to fit out an expedition for the invasion of Canada. For this purpose three thousand New York and New England troops were ordered to assemble at Crown Point and Ticonderoga, under the command of Major-general Schuyler and Brigadier-general Montgomery; while an expedition was organized to march against Quebec, by the way of the Kennebec River.

A large number of flat-bottomed boats were built at Skenesborough, Ticonderoga and Crown Point, for the transportation of the army across the lake, and Congress, by great exertions, raised the sum of fifty thousand dollars, in specie, for the support of the army while in Canada. The arrangements for the expedition were conducted by General Montgomery, while General Schuyler remained at Albany, to close negotiations for a treaty of peace with the Mohawk Indians, over whom he had great influence.

General Carleton, in the meantime, was actively engaged in preparations to oppose the advance of the American army. He placed the works at St. Johns in good repair, and directed a large vessel to be constructed there, which he intended to station near the north or lower end of the lake.

The American Generals deemed it important, by an immediate movement, to prevent Carleton from getting possession of the passage down the Richelieu River. Montgomery, therefore, on the 4th of September, embarked what men he had collected at Crown Point, and sailed for Canada, leaving orders for the rest to follow, as soon as they should arrive. Schuyler left Albany in great haste, and following rapidly, joined Montgomery near Isle la Motte. From that place the two Generals moved to Isle Aux Noix, where they issued an address to the Canadians, assuring them that the army was not designed to act against their country, but was directed only against the British garrisons and troops; and exhorting them to join the Americans in order to assert and defend their liberties. Copies of this address were distributed by Colonel Allen and Major Brown, who were sent among the people of the adjacent country for that purpose.

The army, although not over one thousand strong, now moved forward, and soon afterwards landed about one and a half miles above the Fort of St. Johns. At this point the ground was marshy and covered with thick woods, through which the men had to pass, in order to reach the fort. While advancing to reconnoitre the works, the left wing was attacked by a party of Indians, who killed three and wounded eight of the Americans. The Indians were, however, repulsed with some loss. Schuyler then advanced to within sight of the fort, where he commenced a breastwork, but finding the fort strongly fortified and garrisoned, and learning that the armed sloop was preparing to sail from St. Johns towards his boats, which had been left with only a slight guard, he determined to retire to the Isle Aux Noix, and there await the arrival of the artillery and the rest of the troops, who were daily expected. Schuyler fortified Isle Aux Noix, and to prevent the passage of the sloop into the lake, constructed a *chevaux-de-frise* across the channel of the river, which is very narrow at this point. As soon as these arrangements were completed, he returned to

Albany to conclude his treaty with the Indians, where he was attacked with a severe illness which disabled him from duty. The conduct of the Canada expedition then devolved upon General Montgomery, who retained the sole command until he fell under the walls of Quebec.

A small detachment of recruits, with a few pieces of artillery, having arrived at Isle Aux Noix, Montgomery determined again to push forward and undertake the seige of St. Johns. This fort was garrisoned by five or six hundred regulars and two hundred Canadians, under Major Preston, and was well supplied with stores, ammunition and artillery. The American army, on the contrary, was undisciplined and disorderly, the artillery was too light, the mortars were defective, the ammunition scarce and the artillerists unpractised in their duties. Still these difficulties did not abate the ardor or zeal of the commanding officer.

On the 18th of September, Montgomery led a party of five hundred men to the north of the fort, where he met a detachment from the garrison, with which he had a slight skirmish. Proceeding a little further north, he formed an intrenched camp at the junction of the roads leading from Montreal and Chambly, and then hastened back to bring up his artillery. A few days afterwards the camp was moved to higher ground, north-west of the fort, where a breast-work was thrown up.

Although the Americans had now encompassed the fort, they could do but little towards a regular seige for the want of ammunition and heavy guns to breach the works; but fortune soon opened a way through which to remedy this deficiency. A little below St. Johns, and upon the same river, is Fort Chambly, which then contained several pieces of cannon, one hundred and twenty-four barrels of gunpowder and a large quantity of military stores and provisions.—The fort was garrisoned by six officers and eighty-three privates. On the 18th of October, a strong detachment of Americans and Canadians—many of the latter having, by this time, joined the army—were placed under command of Majors Livingston and Brown, and ordered to attack the fort. The detachment passed down the river in boats during a dark night, and surprised the fort, which made but a feeble resistance. The stores and ammunition were sent to Montgomery, who, now supplied with the necessary munitions, pressed the seige of St. Johns with vigor. A strong battery of four guns and six mortars was erected within two hundred and fifty yards of the fort, and a block-house was built on the opposite side of the river, mounting one gun and two mortars.

While Montgomery was thus employed at St. Johns, detachments of his army were scouring the country between the Richelieu and the St. Lawrence. One of these detachments, numbering about eighty men, under command of Colonel Ethan Allen, passed through all the parishes east of the Richelieu, as far as its mouth. From this point, Allen moved up the east bank of the St. Lawrence to Longueuil, where he crossed the river, and, on the morning of the 25th of September, appeared unexpectedly before the city of Montreal. He was there met by General Carleton, and, with his whole party, taken prisoner. A few days later, Carleton left Montreal with one thousand regulars, Canadians and Indians, for the purpose of raising the seige of Fort St. Johns. He embarked upon the St. Lawrence and attempted to land at Longueuil, but was driven back by Colonel Seth Warner, who, with three hundred " Green Mountain Boys," lay secreted on the east bank of the river.

When Montgomery heard of Colonel Warner's success, he sent a flag to Major Preston informing him of Carleton's repulse, and demanding the immediate surrender of the fort. Preston asked for a delay of four days, which was denied, and the demand renewed. The next morning, (Nov. 3d,) the whole garrison surrendered as prisoners of war. Among the spoils found in the fort were seventeen pieces of brass ordnance, two howitzers, seven mortars, twenty-two iron cannon and eight hundred stand of arms, with a quantity of shot and small shells. The prisoners were treated with great kindness, and were conveyed by the way of Ticonderoga, into the interior of New England for safe-keeping.

Montgomery received great praise for the energy and perseverance with which he had, for six weeks, urged the seige against obstacles of the most difficult and embarrassing character. Not only did he lack proper implements and munitions of war, but his army was composed of young and raw troops, unused to the privations of the field, or to military restraint. Indeed his camp at times resembled a great political assembly. Prompt and implicit obedience to orders was unknown. Each man claimed a right to canvass, debate and decide upon all the plans and movements of the campaign. This insubordination extended through all the grades of the army. The Colonels would dispute with the General, to be themselves opposed by their Captains; and when these last were convinced, the whole subject must again be debated with the rank and file, who claimed an equal right of judging for themselves whether the proposed plan was expedient. It required the kind temper, patriotic zeal and winning eloquence of Montgomery to restrain such turbulent and disaffected spirits from acts of open mutiny.

After the capitulation of Fort St. Johns, Montgomery marched against Montreal, and entered that city on the 13th of November. He then moved down the St. Lawrence, and on the 1st of December arrived at Point Aux Trembles, about twenty miles above Quebec, where he found Colonel Benedict Arnold, who had crossed to the St. Lawrence, through the thick forest and the almost impassible mountains of Maine. On the 5th, the united forces, even yet less in number than the British, arrived within sight of the walls of Quebec, and at two o'clock on the morning of the 31st, advanced to the assault of the city.

Captains Brown and Livingston, with ninety-four men, were directed to lead a feint against the upper

town, while Montgomery was to advance by the way
of Cape Diamond, and Arnold through St. Roche, to
assault the lower town, on opposite sides. The morning was cold and stormy; the snow fell fast, and was
piled in heavy drifts by a furious north-west wind.
Cautiously Montgomery led his men in the dark from
the Plains of Abraham to Wolfe's Cove, and along the
margin of the river to a point under Cape Diamond,
where the British had erected a strong stockade, extending from the precipice to the brink of the river.
On the approach of the Americans, the men posted
behind the stockade retreated to a block-house, which
stood a short distance to the north, and which was
pierced with loop-holes for musketry and cannon. In
the second story of the block-house were some cannon
charged with grape and canister shot, and so pointed
as to sweep the narrow cartway above.

As the assailants advanced, and when they were
within forty paces of the block-house, a single gun
loaded with grape was discharged, which killed Montgomery, his two aids, Captains McPherson and Cheese-
man, and every man in front except Captain Aaron
Burr and a French guide. The brave and gallant
Montgomery fell into Burr's arms and expired. The
rest of the party, appalled at the fearful havoc and the
death of their general, retired in confusion.

The attack upon the opposite side of the town was
equally unsuccessful. The detachment passed through
St. Roche towards a two gun battery, which was captured by Morgan's riflemen, after an hour's severe
struggle. At the commencement of the attack Arnold
received a severe wound in the leg, and was carried
helpless from the field. Morgan continued the fight,
until one half of his men were killed, and the rest were
benumbed and helpless from cold, when he surrendered.

Montgomery was endeared to the army and to his
country, by the possession of every noble virtue.
With intrepid bravery he led his little band of half
clothed and undisciplined men under the walls of
Quebec, and fell upon a soil already hallowed by the

General Knox's troops haul the cannon from Fort Ticonderoga
to Boston. Painting by Tom Lovell

GENERAL HENRY KNOX

blood of a Wolfe and a Montcalm. His death was a great public calamity. America acknowledged his worth and paid public honors to his memory, while the eloquence of England's purest statesmen proclaimed his praise upon the floor of the British Parliament. "Happy would it have been for Arnold," exclaims a celebrated American,* "if instead of being wounded, he too had died, since by his subsequent treason at West Point, he blasted forever the glory of his gallant conduct on that occasion."

After the death of Montgomery, the remains of the little army retired to a point about three miles up the river, where they remained during the winter. On the 1st of May, General Thomas arrived and took command of the troops, which, by reinforcements from time to time, now numbered about nineteen hundred men. The army was soon afterwards increased to three thousand, but the small-pox breaking out in the ranks, with great severity, not over nine hundred were fit for duty. General Thomas in a few days retired as far as the mouth of the Richelieu, where he was taken down with the small-pox. He was removed to Chambly, and died there on the 2d of June. About the time of Thomas' death, General Sullivan arrived in Canada with a reinforcement of several battalions, and assumed the chief command.

Early in the spring of 1776, the British force in Canada was augmented by the arrival from England of thirteen thousand men, a large portion of whom were sent into camp at Three Rivers. Against this place an unsuccessful attack was made, in which General Thompson and two hundred men were taken prisoners. Other reverses followed, until General Sullivan, finding his numbers greatly diminished by sickness, desertion and death, determined to evacuate Canada. He therefore, on the 14th of June, abandoned his position at the mouth of the Richelieu and leisurely moved up its banks towards St. Johns. Arnold, who had been promoted to the rank of Brigadier-general, and who then

* Colonel Trumbull.

commanded at Montreal, withdrew from that city on the 15th, and marching across the country, joined Sullivan's division at Chambly.

The American General conducted the retreat in good order, and saved all the baggage, artillery and military stores, which were dragged up the rapids of the Richelieu in boats. The army reached St. Johns towards the last of June. The sick were immediately sent to Isle Aux Noix, Point au Fer and Isle La Mott, when the boats returned and took the remainder of the troops to Isle Aux Noix.—Here the men fit for duty remained for eight days, waiting for the boats to take the sick to Crown Point and to return. It is difficult to conceive a degree of misery greater than that suffered by the invalids during their voyage through the lake. The boats were leaky and without awnings, and the men, lying upon the bottom, were drenched with water, and, at the same time, exposed to the burning sun. Their only sustenance was raw and rancid pork and hard biscuit or unbaked flour. "The sight of so much misery, privation and distress," says Doctor Meyrick, "broke my heart, and I wept till I had no more power to weep."

When the boats returned to Isle Aux Noix they were loaded with the baggage, while the men were sent by land to Point Au Fer, which had been fortified by order of General Sullivan. At that place they found a supply of boats awaiting them, in which they embarked, and, on the 3d of July, reached Crown Point.

The broken fragments of "the army of Canada" presented one of the most distressing sights witnessed during the whole war. Of the five thousand two hundred men collected at Crown Point, twenty-eight hundred were so sick as to require the attentions of the hospital, while those reported as "fit for duty," were half naked, emaciated and entirely broken down in strength, spirits and discipline. Some few lay in tents, others in half-built sheds, but by far the greater number occupied miserable bush huts, which afforded a slight shelter from the burning sun, but were no protection against the damp and unhealthy night air.

Among these tents and huts the men were scattered in indiscriminate confusion, without regard to comfort or health or to the distinction of companies, regiments or corps. " I found the troops totally disorganized by the death or sickness of officers," says Colonel Trumbull ; " and I can truly say, that I did not look into tent or hut in which I did not find either a dead or dying man." The troops remained about ten days at Crown Point, and when they left for Ticonderoga, over three hundred new made graves attested the frightful ravages that death had made among their broken ranks.*

* Botta's American Revolution—American Archives, Fifth Series —Trumbull's Reminiscences of his own Times—Thacher's Military Journal—Davis' Memoirs of A. Burr—Journal of the New York Provincial Congress—Allen's Narrative.

CHAPTER VII.

1776—The Americans and British Build Armed Vessels on Lake
Champlain—Arnold's Cruise on the Lake—Battle of Valcour Isl-
and—Defeat of the American Fleet near Split Rock—The British
occupy Crown Point—Condition of the American Army at Ticonderoga.

THE plan of the campaign of 1776, as formed by
the British Ministry, contemplated a separate movement against Ticonderoga and New York, and the
conjunction of the two armies at Albany. General and
Lord Howe were sent with a large military and naval
force against New York, while the thirteen thousand
troops collected in Canada were placed under the command of Sir Guy Carleton, who had under him Generals Burgoyne, Phillips, Fraser, Nesbit and Reidesel;
all men of acknowledged skill and ability. Several
vessels were built in England, and sent over to be used
on Lake Champlain.

During the summer of 1776, the English were busily engaged in preparing a fleet for the lake service.
Seamen, ship carpenters and laborers were collected at
St. Johns in numbers. The vessels built in England
were taken to pieces, carried over the rapids of the
Richelieu and reconstructed. Several other vessels
were brought up from the St. Lawrence, and a great
number of transports were framed and launched at St.
Johns. The fort at St. Johns was repaired and
strengthened, and garrisoned with three thousand men ;
an equal number was stationed at Isle Aux Noix. The
rest of the troops were reserved to man the armed vessels and transports, and to form the army of invasion.
Six hundred and ninety-seven seamen were also drafted
from the Isis and the other ships of war lying at Quebec, and sent forward to Lake Champlain.*

* The number of seaman detached for this service, were as follows:

While the English were thus engaged, the Americans were actively employed, at the other extremity of the lake, in preparations to repel the threatened invasion. On the 17th of June, Congress appointed Major-General Gates to the command at Ticonderoga and Crown Point. Gates found those posts in a very reduced condition. The small-pox was still prevalent among the troops, not a cannon was mounted, nor were any preparations made for defense. The first efforts of the Commander-in-chief were directed to recruiting the ranks, restoring the men to health, and providing them with clothing and necessary accommodations. Those sick of the small-pox were sent to a general hospital established at the head of Lake George. Reinforcements were earnestly solicited from the Eastern States, and requisitions made for ship carpenters to be employed at Skenesborough in building the hulls of galleys and boats. Crown Point was reduced to a mere post of observation, while the most active efforts were made to enlarge and strengthen the defenses at Ticonderoga. Mount Independence was carefully examined by Colonels Wayne and Trumbull, who reported that the ground was finely adapted for a military post. A portion of the troops were ordered to clear away the wood and to encamp upon this eminence. The Pennsylvania regiments, the *elite* of the army, were posted at the " French lines," which they were ordered to repair ; and the old works were strengthened at all points.

The small fort at Skenesborough was also repaired, and that place selected as the point of rendezvous for the expected reinforcements. The lake above Ticonderoga soon presented a scene of busy activity, as boats were constantly passing and repassing, loaded with men, provisions and munitions of war. By the month of September an army of from eight to ten thousand

From the Isis, 100; Blood, 70; Triton, 60; Garland, 30; Canceaux, 40; Magdalen, Brunswick and Gasper, 18; Treasury and several armed Brigs, 90; Fell, 30; Charlotte, 9; from Transports, 214; Volunteers, 9; besides 8 Officers and 19 Petty Officers.

men were assembled at Ticonderoga. Each regiment had its alarm post assigned, to which it was ordered to repair at daylight every morning, and every means was taken by the officers to bring the whole body to a state of high discipline.*

The superintendence of the construction of the fleet was confided to General Arnold, who entered upon the work with his characteristic energy, but, in its progress, found himself surrounded by great and complicated difficulties, occasioned by the want or limited supply of nearly all the materials necessary for boat building, or for a naval equipment. But these embarrassments only excited the men to greater exertions. By the middle of August, Arnold was prepared to take the lake with a naval force, carrying fifty-five guns and seventy-eight swivels and manned by three hundred and ninety-five men. His fleet consisted of the sloop *Enterprise*, Captain Dickson; the schooner *Royal Savage*, Captain Wynkoop; schooner *Revenge*, Captain Seaman; schooner *Liberty*, Captain Premier; and the gondolas *New Haven*, *Providence*, *Boston*, *Spitfire* and *Philadelphia*.†

With this force Arnold sailed from Crown Point on the 20th of August, and cruised between that place and the mouth of the Bouquet River, until the 2d of September. On the evening of the 2d he proceeded north as far as Schuyler Island, and, the next day, reached Windmill Point, eight miles below Isle la Motte. It was his first intention to have gone as far down as Isle Aux Tetes, but finding that island already occupied by the British, he anchored off Windmill Point, in a line from shore to shore, and sent his lookout-boats about one mile below, with orders to keep a sharp eye upon the movements of the enemy.

On the morning of the 6th, several boats were sent on shore for fascines to fix on the bows and sides of the

---

* Trumbull's Reminiscences of his own Times.

† The Enterprise had been captured by Arnold at St. Johns; the Liberty by Herrick at Skenesborough. The other vessels were built at Skenesborough and then taken to Ticonderoga and Crown Point, where they received their sails, military stores, and equipment.

gondolas, to prevent the enemy from boarding, and to protect the men from the fire of musketry. One of the boats reached the shore before the others, and was attacked by a party of Indians, who occupied the adjoining woods. Before the men could row off, three of their number were killed and six wounded. Arnold immediately ordered his vessels to discharge their broadsides towards the woods, when the Indians precipitately retreated.* The same morning the fleet was reinforced by the arrival of the galley *Lee*, of six guns, and the gondola *Connecticut*, of three guns.

The noise of the firing on the morning of the 6th, was distinctly heard at Crown Point, fifty miles distant Lieutenant-Colonel Hartley, the commanding officer there, immediately wrote to General Gates, at Ticonderoga, that an engagement had undoubtedly taken place between Arnold and the enemy. Gates sent the letter, by express, to General Schuyler, then at Albany, who ordered out the Ulster and Dutchess County, and a portion of the New England militia. This order was revoked on the 18th, when the true account of the affair reached Albany.†

On the night of the 7th, the English sent strong parties up the river, and commenced preparations to erect batteries on both sides of Arnold's position. This movement induced Arnold to retire as far back as the Isle La Motte, where he came to anchor about two o'clock on the afternoon of the 6th. Here the fleet remained until the 19th, when it removed to Bay St. Amand, which lies on the west side of the lake, a few miles north of Cumberland Head. As the schooner Liberty was on her way to this anchorage, she was hailed by a Canadian, who came down to the water's edge and requested to be taken on board. Captain Premier sent a boat towards the shore, with orders to approach with caution and to keep her swivels pointed and the matches ready to fire in case everything was not right. The man on shore waded about a rod into the water and

* Arnold to Major-general Gates, Sept. 7, 1776.
† American Archives, Fifth Series.

stopped, entreating the boat's crew to come to him. Finding he could not decoy them into shallow water, he made a signal, when about three hundred Canadians and Indians, who were secreted in the woods near the shore, uncovered and fired into the boat, wounding three of the crew. The boat returned the fire with her swivels and small arms, and the schooner discharged several broadsides of grape, when the party retreated, having apparently suffered some loss.*

While Arnold lay at Bay St. Amand he sent two boats to sound the channel between Valcour Island and the main shore, who reported that they found the anchorage there exceedingly fine and secure. To this harbor the fleet moved on the 23d of September. A few days afterwards the galley *Trumbull*, Captain Warner, arrived, and on the 6th of October, Brigadier General Waterbury came up with the galleys *Washington*, Captain Thacher, and *Congress*, Captain Arnold. The entire naval force of the Americans was now collected at Valcour Island, with the exception of an eight gun galley, then receiving her armament at Ticonderoga, and the schooner Liberty, which had been sent to Crown Point for supplies. The fleet consisted of the sloop Enterprise, mounting ten guns and ten swivels; the schooner Royal Savage, twelve guns and ten swivels; the schooner Revenge, eight guns and ten swivels; the galley Lee, six guns and ten swivels; the galleys Trumbull, Congress, and Washington, each eight guns and sixteen swivels; and the gondolas New Haven, Providence, Boston, Spitfire, Philadelphia, Connecticut, Jersey, and New York, each mounting three guns and eight swivels. There were therefore fifteen vessels in all, mounting eighty-four guns and one hundred and fifty-two swivels. The number of men and sailors detached to serve on these vessels was eight hundred and eleven, but of this number at least one hundred had not yet joined the fleet. Arnold daily trained his men at the guns and used his best endeavors to reduce them to the proper discipline. He, however,

*Arnold to Gates, Sept. 21, 1776.

complained frequently of their inefficiency. "The drafts from the regiments at Ticonderoga," he writes General Gates, "are a miserable set; indeed the men on board the fleet in general are not equal to half their number of good men." Again he says, "we have a wretched motley crew in the fleet; the marines, the refuse of every regiment, and the seamen, few of them ever wet with salt water; and we are upwards of one hundred men short of our complement."

At this time the British naval force in the Richelieu consisted of the ship *Inflexible*, Lieutenant Schank, of eighteen guns; the schooner *Maria*, Lieutenant Starke, fourteen guns; schooner *Carleton*, Lieutenant Dacres, twelve guns; radeau *Thunderer*, Lieutenant Scott, twelve guns and two howitzers; the gondola *Loyal Convert*, Lieutenant Longcraft, seven guns; twenty gun-boats, mounting one gun each, and four long boats, with one carriage gun each. There were also twenty-four long-boats loaded with the baggage and provisions.* The whole force was twenty-nine vessels, mounting eighty-nine guns, and manned by six hundred and ninety-seven picked seamen, besides a number of soldiers and artillerists. A party of Indians accompanied the fleet, in canoes. On their way the British erected a block-house at Point Au Fer and left four companies to defend it. †

The route taken by vessels passing up the lake from Canada, lies along and nearly parallel to the west shore of Grand Isle. Opposite Cumberland Head the lake is two miles wide, but, as soon as that point is passed, it increases in width to five miles, and does not again contract until you approach the mouth of the Bouquet. On the western side of the lake, about four miles southwest of Cumberland Head, and nearly two miles to the right of the track of vessels sailing directly up the lake, is the island of Valcour, which is separated from

* Letter of Captain Douglass of the Isis. The Inflexible, Maria and Carleton, were brought from England and reconstructed at St. Johns.

† Hadden's Journal.

the main shore by a channel about one-half mile in width. This channel is deep enough for the largest vessels, and is hid from the view of boats sailing up the lake, until they have passed some distance south of the island. Midway of this channel, and where it is most contracted, Arnold anchored his vessels in a line extending from shore to shore. "We are moored," he writes to General Gates, "in a small bay on the west side of the island, as near together as possible, and in such form that few vessels can attack us at the same time, and those will be exposed to the fire of the whole fleet."

At eight o'clock on Friday morning, October 11th, the English were discovered passing Cumberland Head with a strong north or north-west wind, and bearing in the direction of Crown Point, towards which it was supposed Arnold had retired. The fleet at this time was under the command of Capt. Thomas Pringle, of the Lord Howe, who made the schooner Maria his flag ship. General Carleton was also on board the Maria, but took no command of the fleet. As the English appeared in sight, oft Cumberland Head, General Waterbury went on board the Congress galley, and urged that they should immediately set sail and fight the enemy on the retreat in the broad lake ; but Arnold declined, at that late hour, to change his plan of defense.

Capt. Pringle was some distance ahead of Valcour when he first discovered the American vessels. He immediately changed his course towards the island, with a view to engage, but found great difficulty in bringing any of his vessels into action. About eleven o'clock, however, the gun-boats were enabled to sweep to windward and take a position to the south of the American fleet, when they opened a fire upon the Royal Savage, which, with the galleys, had advanced a short distance in front of the line. The British schooner Carleton soon after came to the assistance of the gun-boats. The Royal Savage sustained the fire of the British vessels for some time, during which her

BATTLE OF VALCOUR ISLAND, 1776

GENERAL RICHARD MONTGOMERY

mast was crippled and much of her rigging shot away. She then attempted to return to the line, but, running too far to the leeward, grounded near the south-west point of the island, and was abandoned by her men, who succeeded in reaching the other boats in safety. At night the British boarded the schooner, and set fire to her.*

At half-past twelve o'clock the Carleton and the gun-boats had approached within musket shot of the American line, when the action became general, and continued without cessation until about five in the afternoon. During the engagement Arnold was on board the Congress, Waterbury on the Washington and Colonel Wigglesworth on the Trumbull. The Congress and Washington suffered severely. The latter was hulled in several places, her main-mast shot though, and her sails torn to pieces. Waterbury fought bravely on the quarter-deck of his vessel, and towards the close of the action was the only active officer on board; the captain and master being severely wounded, and the first lieutenant killed. The gondola New York lost all her officers except Captain Lee, and the gondola Philadelphia, Captain Grant, was so badly injured that she sank about one hour after the engagement. Arnold fought the Congress like a lion at bay, pointing almost every gun with his own hands, and cheering his men with voice and gesture. His vessel was hulled twelve times and received seven shot between wind and water; the main-mast was injured in two places, the rigging cut to pieces, and many of the men were killed and wounded.

On the side of the English, the battle was sustained by the gun-boats and the schooner Carleton, and by a party of Indians who were landed on the island and main shore, and kept up an incessant fire of musketry during the engagement. The English ves-

---

* Arnold's account of the engagement. The hull of the schooner lies on the spot where she was sunk, and her upper timbers can yet be seen at low water in the lake. Arnold's papers were on board the schooner and were lost.

sels suffered considerably. On board the Carleton eight men were killed and six wounded. Two of the gun-boats were sunk, and one was blown up, with a number of men on board.* About five o'clock in the afternoon, Captain Pringle, who had made several unsuccessful attempts to bring his larger vessels into action, called off those engaged, and anchored his whole fleet just out of reach of the American guns. The Thunderer lay at the right of the line, a little south of Garden Island,† the schooner Maria on the left near the main shore, while the Loyal Convert and the Inflexible occupied intermediate positions. The Carleton and gun-boats were anchored near and among the other vessels. By this arrangement, Captain Pringle hoped to prevent the escape of the American fleet during the night.‡

Arnold was well satisfied that he could not successfully resist the superior force, with which the English were prepared to attack him on the following morning. His men had fought with the most daring bravery and resolution, but he had only succeeded in retaining his position, by the direction of the wind, which had prevented the larger vessels of the British fleet from joining in the action. Even under equally favorable circumstances, he could not resist a renewed attack, for his boats were already badly crippled, sixty of his men, including several officers, killed or wounded, and nearly three-fourths of each vessel's ammunition spent. A council of war was immediately called, when it was determined that the fleet should retire during the night towards Crown Point

---

* Arnold states the loss, by the blowing up of the gun-boat, at sixty men.—*Letter to Gen. Schuyler, Oct.* 15. Lieut. Haddon, who was in command of one of the gun-boats, states the loss at twenty.—*Journal.*

† This is a small island about six hundred yards south of Valcour.

‡ Had the gun-boats retained the position occupied by them immediately after the action, the engagement would probably have been renewed the next day and would have resulted in the surrender or destruction of Arnold's vessels, but, about sundown, after the gun-boats had received a supply of ammunition, they were ordered to anchor under cover of Garden Island, thus leaving the passage along the west shore of the lake unguarded.—*Hadden's Journal.*

At seven o'clock in the evening* Colonel Wigglesworth got the Trumbull under way, and directed his course towards the upper end of the lake. The Trumbull was soon followed by the Enterprise and Lee, with the gondolas ; and about ten o'clock, Waterbury started in the Washington galley, followed closely by Arnold, in the Congress. In this order, with a light at the stern of each vessel, the fleet passed to Schuyler Island, about nine miles distant, where they arrived early next morning. On examination Arnold found two of the gondolas too badly injured to repair. These he sank near the island, and, having fitted up the other vessels as well as his limited time and means would permit, again set sail for Crown Point.

While Arnold was repairing his vessels, the British fleet weighed anchor and commenced beating up the lake in pursuit; the wind blowing gently from the south. Early on the morning of the 13th, the American fleet was off the Bouquet, and the English lay a little above Schuyler Island. Arnold now had the wind in the south, while a fresh north-east wind, blowing in the broader part of the lake, favored the English commander, who brought up his leading vessels soon after the former had passed Split Rock. On this occasion Captain Pringle led in the person in the Maria, closely followed by the Inflexible and Carleton. The Maria and Inflexible at first attacked the Washington galley, which was too much shattered to keep up with the rest. The galley struck after receiving a few shots. The two vessels then joined the Carleton, and, for several hours† poured an incessant fire into the Congress galley, which was briskly returned. Arnold kept up a running fight until he arrived within ten miles of Crown Point, when he ran the Congress and four gondolas into a small bay

* Arnold's account of the Battle. Mr. Cooper, in his Naval History, erroneously states that Arnold got under way at 2 o'clock, P. M. He also states that the American fleet, on the morning of the 11th, "was lying off Cumberland Head," and includes in the fleet the schooner Liberty, which was then at Crown Point.

† Captain Pringle says the action commenced at twelve and lasted two hours. Arnold says it continued "for about five glasses."

in Panton, on the east side of the lake, and, having re-moved the small arms, burned the vessels to the water's edge. In this action the Congress lost her first lieu-tenant and three men.

As soon as the boats were consumed, Arnold led his party through the woods to Crown Point, where he ar-rived at four o'clock the next morning. The sloop Enterprise, the schooner Revenge and the galley Trum-bull, with one gondola, had reached that place the day before, in safety. The galley Lee, Captain Davis, was run into a bay on the east side of the lake above Split Rock, where she was blown up. The only vessels taken by the enemy were the Washington galley and the gondola Jersey. The loss of the Americans in both en-gagements was between eighty and ninety, including the wounded. The English stated their loss in killed and wounded at forty.

Immediately after the action of the 13th, Sir Guy Carleton gave orders for his surgeons to treat the wounded prisoners with the same care they did his own men. He then directed all the other prisoners to be brought on board his ship, where he treated them to a drink of grog, praised the bravery of their conduct, re-gretted that it had not been displayed in the service of their lawful sovereign, and offered to send them home to their friends, on their giving their parole that they would not again bear arms against Great Britain until they should be exchanged. On the 14th, Captain, after-wards Sir James Craig, accompanied the prisoners to Ticonderoga, where he dismissed them on parole. The generous manner in which they had been treated, filled the prisoners with the highest emotions of gratitude, and they returned proclaiming the praise of the British General. The feelings and sentiments expressed by these men were such, that it was not considered safe to allow them to land, or to converse with the American troops. They were therefore sent forward to Skenes-borough the same night.*

The humanity of Governor Carleton's course was

*Trumbull's Reminiscences of his own Times.

tinctured with policy. He well knew the great dissatisfaction which had prevailed among the American troops, and, with a profound sagacity, that distinguished his whole administration, took advantage of every opportunity to direct this feeling into a channel favorable to the British cause, and to impress upon the minds of the half clothed and destitute troops, a high opinion of the generosity, kindness, and liberality of their opponents.

Although the results of the two naval engagements of the 11th and 13th, had been so disastrous, yet the Americans gained great credit for the obstinacy of their resistance. Even the English acknowledged that no man ever manœuvred with more dexterity, fought with more bravery or retreated with more firmness, than Arnold did on both of these occasions. Such gallantry converted the disasters of defeat into a species of triumph. Several American officers, however, were found ready to censure Arnold, whom they called "our evil genius to the north,* but General Gates, who understood perfectly all the details of the affair, always speaks of him in the highest terms of praise. "It would have been happy for the United States," he writes to Governor Trumbull, " had the gallant behavior and steady good conduct of that excellent officer been supported by a fleet in any way equal to the enemy's. As the case stands, though they boast a victory, they must respect the vanquished."

On the 14th of October, the works at Crown Point were destroyed and the troops and military stores removed to Ticonderoga. As soon as the Americans left, Carleton landed his army, and occupied the shores on both sides of the lake. It had been his intention to march immediately against Ticonderoga, but, on the 15th, the wind commenced blowing so hard from the south that, for eight days, the English vessels could not sail up the lake. This delay was of great importance to the Americans, as it afforded them time to receive reinforcements of militia, and to prepare for a vigorous

* General Maxwell to Governor Livingston.

defense. In that short interval they made carriages for, and mounted forty-seven pieces of cannon; they also surrounded the works with a strong abattis. General Gates had about twelve thousand men under his command, all of whom were now full of activity and vigilance, and desirous of an opportunity to display their prowess before the enemy.

General Carleton, finding he could not advance immediately, proceeded to establish himself at Crown Point, and to repair the fort at that place. He also occupied Chimney Point with a portion of his army, and placed three of his largest vessels at anchor near Putnam's point, a little below which the Light Infantry, Grenadiers, and a body of Canadians, and Indians were encamped. Reconnoitering parties filled the woods in every direction, and frequently penetrated as far south as Lake George, where one or two slight skirmishes occurred with struggling parties of the militia, who were passing from Fort George to Ticonderoga. Boats were also sent to sound the channel of the lake above Crown Point. On one occasion, one of these boats approached within shot of the lower battery of Ticondeoga, when it was fired into, and two men killed and one wounded.

On Monday the 27th of October, between eight and nine o'clock in the morning, the advance guard-boat, lying below Ticonderoga, made signal that the English fleet was approaching, and about an hour afterwards, five of the largest transport boats appeared in sight of the fort, and landed a number of troops upon Three Mile Point. Soon afterwards, two armed boats stood over to the east side of the lake and appeared to be reconnoitering. As soon as they approached near enough, they were fired upon from the lower battery, and from a row-galley stationed in the river near by, when they retired. In the mean time other British troops were landed upon the point, and a body of men were sent across the lake into a small bay about four miles below the works.

As these movements indicated an attack upon Ti-

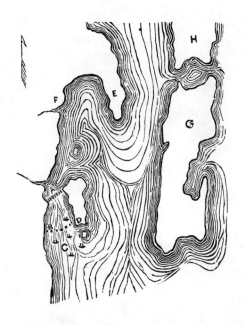

MAP OF BATTLE AT VALCOUR ISLAND.

REFERENCES.—A, American Fleet drawn across the Channel. —B, British Gun-Boats and Schooner Carleton.—C, Anchorage of British Vessels after the Battle.—D, Point where the Royal Savage was lost.—E, Cumberland Head.—F, Saranac River.—G, Grand Island.—H, Island of North Hero.

Major-General Horatio Gates

conderoga, General Gates ordered the lines and re-doubts to be manned, and brought three regiments from Mt. Independence to reinforce those on the western side. " Nothing," says General Gates, "could exceed the spirit and alertness which was shown by all the officers and soldiers in executing every order that was given." The display made on this occasion convinced Carleton that Gates' means of defence were sufficient to resist an assault. At four o'clock in the afternoon, he withdrew his forces and returned to Crown Point, where he made immediate preparations to retire into winter quarters, in Canada. The rear-guard of the English army left Crown Point on the morning of the 3d of November, and the place was, the same day, oc-cupied by a detachment sent forward from Ticonderoga. As soon as it was ascertained that the English had retired to Canada, Gates dismissed the Militia and soon afterwards left with the greater part of the regular troops to join Washington, who was then in New Jersey.

CHAPTER VIII.

1777—1783.—Burgoyne invades the United States— Evacuation of Ticonderoga by General St. Clair—Battle of Hubbardton—Surprise and Indignation of the People—Vindication of St. Clair and Schuyler—Lincoln's Expedition against Ticonderoga—Surrender of Burgoyne—Retreat to Canada—Operations on Lake Champlain from 1778 to 1783.

THE British Ministry still adhered to the scheme of opening a communication between Canada and the City of New York, by way of Lake Champlain. This project had acquired new favor at the English Court from the representations and sanguine promises of General Burgoyne, who had visited England in the winter of 1776-7, and urged upon the government its importance, and the certainty of its success. Dissatisfied, without just cause, with the proceedings of Governor Carleton, the Ministry formed their arrangements for the new campaign, without his counsel or advice, and assigned to General Burgoyne the command of the army in Canada, and the direction of all its operations.

The regular force allotted to Burgoyne numbered seven thousand one hundred and thirteen men, among whom were three thousand two hundred and seventeen Brunswick troops, commonly known as Hessians. A large and complete train of brass artillery was sent to Canada, together with a full supply of arms, ammunition and military accoutrements of every description. Major-general Phillips and Brigadier-generals Fraser, Powell and Hamilton served under Burgoyne. The Brunswick troops were commanded by Major-general Reidesel, and Brigadier General Specht.

Burgoyne arrived at Quebec in the month of May, 1777, and immediately commenced preparations for the prosecution of the campaign. Two thousand Canadians were employed upon the fortifications at Sorel, Chambly,

St. Johns and Isle Aux Noix, and boats were constructed in great numbers, on the Richelieu, for the convey-
ance of the troops and supplies through the lake.

To favor the operations of the army, Colonel. St. Leger
was sent against the American posts on the Mohawk
River, with a force of about eight hundred men, and a
large body of Indians under Sir John Johnson. St.
Leger was to proceed by the way of Oswego, and,
having reduced the posts on that route, was to rejoin
the main army at Albany.

Early in the month of June, the army left St. Johns,
in boats, and after several delays occasioned by contrary winds, reached Cumberland Head, where it
halted to await the arrival of the ammunition and
stores. The naval part of the expedition was under
the command of Captain Lutwidge, and consisted of
the armed vessels built during the preceding year.
Seven hundred carts were brought on with the army,
to be used in transporting baggage and provisions
across the portages between the lakes and the Hudson
River, and fifteen hundred Canadian horses were sent
by land up the west side of the lake, under a strong
escort.

As soon as the supplies arrived, Burgoyne left Cumberland Head and advanced as far as the Bouquet
River, where he again halted. He was there joined by
four hundred Iroquois, Algonquin, Abenaouis and
Ottawa Indians, to whom he gave a war-feast on the
21st of June, at their encampment near the falls of the
Bouquet. On this occasion he made a speech to the
assembled Indians, in which he humanely endeavored
to soften their ferocity and restrain their thirst for
blood. He spoke of the abused clemency of the King
towards the colonies, and explained to them that the
present war was carried on against a country, where
the faithful were intermixed with rebels, and traitors
with friends. He released them from restraint, but
cautioned them not to violate the rules of civilized warfare or disregard the dictates of religion and humanity.
" Be it our task," he said, " from the dictates of our

religion, the laws of our warfare, and the principles and interest of our policy, to regulate your passions when you overbear, to point out where it is nobler to spare than to revenge, to discriminate degrees of guilt, to suspend the uplifted stroke, to chastise, and not destroy." He then called their attention to the rules which they should observe during the campaign. " I positively forbid bloodshed where you are not opposed in arms. Aged men and women, children, and prisoners must be held sacred from the knife or hatchet, even in the time of actual conflict. You shall receive compensation for the prisoners you take, but you shall be called to account for scalps." The Indians pledged obedience to his orders, and Burgoyne had the credulity to believe them. Little did he understand the unappeasable appetite for blood, of those by whom these fine promises were made.

While the English were slowly approaching Ticonderoga, the Americans were busily engaged in strengthening its defenses. The northern department, including Albany, Ticonderoga, Fort Stanwix and their dependencies, was now under the charge of Major-General Schuyler, while the immediate command of the works on Lake Champlain was confided to Major-general St. Clair, an officer of great military experience and reputation.* Both generals were advised of the plans of the British government for the present campaign, and used every exertion to prevent its success. The old French lines, to the west of the fort, had been repaired and were guarded by a strong block-house; an

---

*Arthur St. Clair, was born in Scotland in 1734, and was a grandson of the Earl of Roslyn. He entered the army as an ensign and served under Amherst at Louisburg and under Wolfe at Quebec. He resigned in 1762, and settled in Pennsylvania. In 1776 he was created a Colonel in the Continental Army and in August a Brigadier-general, and was in the battle of Trenton and Princeton; was made a Major-general in 1777. After the Evacution of Ticonderoga he was tried by court-martial and acquitted. He was with the army at the surrender of Cornwallis. Was elected to Congress in 1786 and became President of that body in 1787. In 1789 he was made the first Governor of the Northwest Territory and held that position until 1802. He died near Greensburgh, Pa,, August 31, 1818.

outpost was established at the saw-mills, on the falls of the outlet, and another just above that point, and a block-house and hospital were erected at the foot of Lake George. Redoubts and batteries were established upon the low lands, below the fort, and the extreme left was protected by a small fort on Mount Hope, an eminence about half a mile in advance of the old French lines.

A star-fort, in the centre of which was a convenient square of barracks, had been built on the summit of Mount Independence, which was well supplied with artillery, strongly picketed, and its approaches guarded with batteries. The foot of the hill, towards the lake, was protected by a breast-work which had been strengthened by an abattis and a strong battery standing on the shore of the lake near the mouth of East Creek. A floating bridge connected the works of Mount Independence and Ticonderoga, and served as an obstruction to the passage of vessels up the lake. This bridge was supported on twenty-two sunken piers formed of very large timber; the spaces between the piers were filled with floats, each about fifty feet long and twelve feet wide, strongly fastened together with iron chains and rivets. A boom made of large pieces of timber, well secured together by riveted bolts, was placed on the north side of the bridge, and by the side of this was a double iron chain, the links of which were one and a half inches square.

Opposite Mount Independence is the lofty eminence of Mount Defiance, which rises abruptly from the water to the height of about seven hundred and fifty feet, and is separated from Ticonderoga by the mouth of the outlet of Lake George. The American works formed an extensive crescent, of which this eminence was the centre. The entire line required at least ten thousand men, and one hundred pieces of artillery, for its defence. At the time of Burgoyne's approach, St. Clair's whole force did not exceed two thousand five hundred and fifty-six continental troops and nine hundred militia; the latter badly equipped, worse armed, and most of them raw and

undisciplined. They, however, were zealous and determined, and were ready to oppose any force that might be
brought against them.

The works about Ticonderoga were, by many, considered impregnable ; but in fact they were weak and unten-
able, for every position, whether at the old French lines,
at the fort or on Mount Independence, was commanded
by the summit of Mount Defiance, which had hitherto
been neglected by the engineers of all parties. In 1776,
Colonel John Trumbull, Adjutant-general under Gates,
made several experiments which proved the controlling
position of the eminence, and he afterwards, in company
with General Arnold, Colonel Wayne, and others ascended its rocky sides. "The ascent," says Trumbull,
"was difficult and laborious, but not impracticable, and
when we looked down upon the outlet of Lake George
it was obvious to all that there could be no difficulty in
driving up a loaded carriage."

While Ticonderoga was thus poorly garrisoned and its
defences exposed, Burgoyne was moving against it at
the head of a well disciplined army, numbering seven
thousand nine hundred men. On the 30th of June, the
whole force reached Crown Point, where the English
General halted to issue a proclamation, by which he expected to intimidate the Patriots and to strengthen the
hopes of the disaffected. In this paper he extolled the
strength and number of the British forces, and portrayed
in vivid language, the horrors which would result from an
opposition to their arms. He offered encouragement and
employment to those who should assist the King in-
redeeming the colonies, and restoring to them the blessings of British liberty," while against those who should
disregard his offers of mercy and forgiveness, he threatened the merciless vengeance of the whole Indian force
under his command. Of the Patriots, he says, " The messengers of justice and of wrath await them in the field ;
and devastation and famine and every concomitant
horror, that are luctant but indispensable prosecution
of military duty must occasion, will bar the way to their
return," These thundering anathemas were received, in

every quarter, with derision and ridicule. Their only effect was to call forth a reply, written by a young officer which created much amusement in the ranks of the American army, by its admirable imitation of the pompous style of the proclamation.

Burgoyne's army moved from Crown Point on the 1st of July, in three divisions; the Germans under Reidesel, taking position on the east shore of the lake, at Richardson's opposite Putnam Creek; the right wing under Fraser, advanced as far as Three Mile Creek, and the centre commanded by Burgoyne in person, moved up the lake in transports, accompanied by the ships Royal George and Inflexible, and anchored in a position just out of reach of the American guns. The following day, a party of Indians approached the outposts at Lake George and were soon followed by a large detachment under Major-general Phillips. On the approach of this column, the Americans evacuated and burned the blockhouses, and, abandoning the saw-mills, retired within the lines. In the course of the night, General Phillips. took possession of Mount Hope, which, the next morning was occupied in force by Fraser's corps, consisting of the First British brigade and two brigades of Artillery. Phillips now held the ground west of Mount Hope, and Fraser's camp, at Three Mile Creek, was occupied by a body of men drawn from the opposite side of the lake. The column under Reidesel, was pushed forward as far as East Creek, from which it could easily stretch behind Mount Independence.

During all these movements, the American troops kept up a warm fire against Mount Hope, and against Reidesel's column, but without effect. On the 4th, the British were employed in bringing up their artillery, tents, baggage and provisions, while the Americans, at intervals, continued the cannonade. The same evening the radeau Thunderer arrived from Crown Point, with the battering train.

The British line now encircled the American works on the north, east and west. The possession of Mount Defiance would complete the investment, and effectually control the water communication in the direction of Skenesborough.—Burgoyne's attention had, from the first, been attracted towards this eminence, and he had directed Lieutenant Twiss, his chief engineer, to ascertain whether its summit was accessible. On the 4th, Lieutenant Twiss reported that Mount Defiance held the entire command of Ticonderoga and Mt. Independence, at the distance of about fourteen hundred yards from the former, and fifteen hundred yards from the latter, and that a practicable road could be made to the summit in twenty-four hours. On receiving this report, Burgoyne ordered the road opened and a battery constructed for light twenty-four pounders, medium twelves and eight-inch howitzers. This arduous task was pushed with such activity, that, during the succeeding night, the road was completed, and eight pieces of cannon were dragged to the top of the hill.

On the morning of the 5th, the summit of Mount Defiance glowed with scarlet uniforms, and the guns of its batteries stood threateningly over the American forts. "It is with astonishment," says Doctor Thacher, in his Military Journal, "that we find the enemy have taken possession of an eminence called Sugar-Loaf Hill or Mount Defiance, which, from its height and proximity, completely overlooks and commands all our works. The situation of our garrison is viewed as critical and alarming; a few days will decide our fate. We have reason to apprehend the most fatal effects from their battery on Sugar-Loaf Hill." General St. Clair immediately called a council of war, by whom it was decided to evacuate the works, before Reidesel should block up the narrow passage south of East Creek, which, with the lake to Skenesborough, presented the only possible way of escape.

The decision of the council was concealed from the troops until the evening order was given. About twelve o'clock at night, directions were issued to place the sick and wounded and the women on board two hundred long-boats, which had been collected for this purpose.

The boats were then loaded deep with cannon, tents
and provisions, and, at three o'clock in the morning,
started for Skenesborough, accompanied by five armed
galleys and a guard of six hundred men, under command of Colonel Long of the New Hampshire troops.
The boats reached Skenesborough about three o'clock
on the afternoon of the same day, where the fugitives
landed to enjoy, as they fancied, a temporary repose,
but in less than two hours, they were startled by the
reports of the cannon of the British gun-boats, which
were firing at the galleys lying at the wharf.   By uncommon effort and industry, Burgoyne had broken
through the chain, boom, and bridge at Ticonderoga,
and had followed in pursuit with the Royal George
and Inflexible, and a detachment of the gun-boats under Captain Carter.   The pursuit had been pressed
with such vigor that, at the very moment when the
Americans were landing at Skenesborough, three regiments disembarked at the head of South Bay, with the
intention of occupying the road to Fort Edward.   Had
Burgoyne delayed the attack upon the galleys until
these regiments had reached the Fort Edward road, the
whole party at Skenesborough would have been taken
prisoners.   Alarmed, however, by the approach of the
gun-boats, the latter blew up three of the galleys, set
fire to the fort, mill, and store-house and retired in
great confusion towards Fort Ann.   Occasionally the
overburdened party would falter on their retreat, when
the startling cry of "march on, the Indians are at our
heels," would revive their drooping energies and give
new strength to their weakened limbs.   At five o'clock
in the morning they reached Fort Ann, where they
were joined by many of the invalids, who had been
carried up Wood Creek in boats.   A number of the
sick, with the cannon, provisions, and most of the baggage were left behind at Skenesborough.

On the 7th, a small reinforcement sent from Fort
Edward, by Schuyler, arrived at Fort Ann.   About
the same time, a detachment of British troops approached within the sight of the fort.   This detachment

was attacked from the fort, and repulsed with some loss; a surgeon, a wounded captain and twelve privates were taken prisoners by the Americans. The next day Fort Ann was burned, and the garrison retreated to Fort Edward, which was then occupied by General Schuyler.

As soon as Colonel Long had started for Skenesborough, St. Clair with the main army retired by land, towards Castleton. The garrison of Ticonderoga crossed the bridge, about three o'clock in the morning, and, at four o'clock, the rear guard, under Colonel Francis, left Mount Independence. Up to this time a continued connonade from one of the batteries was kept up, in the direction of Mount Hope, in order to allay any suspicions of the movement, on the part of the enemy. The whole army would have departed unobserved, had not General De Fermoy, who commanded on Mount Independence, foolishly and regardless of express orders, set fire to the house he had occupied. The light of this conflagration revealed the whole scene to the British, and, at the same time, threw the Americans into great disorder; many of them now pushing forward without any regard to discipline or regularity. At Hubbardton the stragglers were collected, and the ranks again organized. After a halt of two hours at this place, the main army proceeded toward Castleton, leaving Colonels Francis, Warner, and Hale behind with a rear-guard of about thirteen hundred men.

As soon as the retreat from Ticonderoga was discovered by the British, General Fraser started in pursuit with his brigade, and was soon followed by Reidesel. The British troops continued the pursuit during the day, and, at night, lay on their arms near the position occupied by the American rear-guard, at Hubbardton. Early on the following morning, Fraser, with eight hundred men, advanced to the attack, without waiting for the arrival of Reidesel, who was approaching with his column. The attack was resisted by seven hundred under the command of Colonels Francis and Warner. Colonel Hale, who had charge of a body of invalids belonging to different regiments, continued his retreat towards Castleton. Hale's conduct on this occasion was severely censured by many, but not more so than was St. Clair for the abandonment of Ticonderoga. Colonel Hale's retreat and his subsequent surrender appear to have been influenced by the dictates of humanity, for his men were in no condition to enter into the fight. He unfortunately died before he had an opportunity to justify his conduct.

The battle between the two parties was severe and bloody, and at one time the British Grenadiers recoiled before the galling fire of Francis' and Warner's men, but Reidesel coming up at that moment, the Grenadiers rallied, and, sustained by the whole Britih sline, returned to the charge with fixed bayonets. The American troops now broke and fled in every direction. In this action the Americans lost three hundred and twenty-four men, in killed, wounded and prisoners. Among the killed was the gallant Colonel Francis, who fell at the head of his regiment. On the part of the English, the loss was one hundred and eighty-three, including Major Pratt and about twenty inferior officers. Hale was intercepted on the road to Castleton, and surrendered. St. Clair, as soon as he had been joined by the remnant of Warner's men, retreated to Fort Edward, where he arrived on the 12th of July.

The loss to the Americans, by the evacuation of Ticonderoga, was very great ; no less than one hundred and twenty-eight pieces of cannon, together with all the boats, provisions, stores, and magazines were either destroyed or fell into the hands of the British. Among the trophies of the day was the Continental Standard, which the Americans had neglected to take with them on their retreat.

The evacuation of Ticonderoga and Mount Independence was condemned throughout the country. The people were surprised and alarmed. They were not prepared for so disastrous an event, for it was generally believed that the works on Lake Champlain were in a condition to resist any attack of the enemy. Both

Schuyler and St. Clair were severely and unjustly censured; the former for not sending on reinforcements, when he had none to send, and the latter for omitting to fortify Mount Hope and Mount Defiance, when his whole force was insufficient to man the defenses of the forts themselves. That a great error was committed, in relying too much upon the supposed strength of the positions at Ticonderoga, cannot be denied; but there were no just grounds for attaching blame to either of the officers in command.

The attention of the Government had been directed to the exposed situation of this post, and St. Clair had repeatedly called for more troops for its defence. As late as the 25th of June, he addressed a letter to General Schuyler, in which he vividly portrayed his want of men, and his fears that he might not be able to resist Burgoyne, who was known to be approaching with a large force. In that letter, he says: " I cannot help *repeating* to you the disagreeable situation we are in, nor can I see the least prospect of our being able to defend the post, unless the militia come in; and should the enemy protract their operations, or invest us and content themselves with a single blockade, we are infallibly ruined."

On the 28th of June, General Schuyler writes to General Washington, at the same time enclosing St. Clair's letter of the 25th, and says, " Should an accident happen to the garrison of Ticonderoga, and General Burgoyne makes a push to gain the south part of the lake, I know of no obstacle to prevent him : comparatively speaking, I have not a man to oppose him; the whole number at the different posts at and on this side of the lake, including the garrisons of Fort George and Skenesborough, not exceeding seven hundred men, and these I cannot draw away from their several stations, in every one of which they are already too weak."

These letters show the real state of the frontier at the time. Burgoyne was approaching with an army of over seven thousand veterans, besides Canadians and Indians, while St. Clair had three thousand four hun-

dred men to defend a circle of works which could not
be properly manned with less than ten thousand, and
Schuyler had not troops enough with him to defend the
posts in the rear.   It has been said that, considering his
want of men, St. Clair should have evacuated the
works before the approach of the British army.   Such
a course would have received as great censure as did
the retreat.   It would have been considered inexcus-
able.   Besides the question, whether all or even a part
of these works should be abandoned, had already been
presented to the consideration of the Provincial Congress of New York, and that body, on the 6th of May
preceding, had passed a resolution declaring that, in
their opinion, the abandoning of any part of the works
of Ticonderoga, would be productive of great evils.   A
copy of this resolution was at the time forwarded to
General Gates, who replied that he saw no reason for
abandoning any part of the post at Ticonderoga, and
that he had good ground to hope there would never be
any necessity of evacuating or surrendering any portion
of the position, if the body of the eastern troops arrive
in any reasonable time.

When Burgoyne placed his batteries upon the summit of Mount Defiance, he effectually destroyed all
hopes of resistance, on the part of the Americans.   The
only alternative was to surrender or evacuate the works.
By adopting the latter course, St. Clair saved the greater
portion of his garrison, and preserved the nucleus of
an army, which ultimately baffled Burgoyne, and compelled him to surrender.   At the moment, however, all
classes of people were astonished at the unexpected
result.   It is "an event of chagrin and surprise," says
Washington, "not apprehended nor within the compass
of my reasoning."   The Council of Safety of New York
stigmatized it as a measure "highly reprehensible," and
"probably criminal."*   Among the people, the most

---

* "The evacuation of Tionderoga appears to the council highly reprehensible, and it gives them great pain to find that a measure so
absurd and probably criminal should be imputed to the direction of
General Schuyler, in whose zeal, vigilance and integrity the council

violent charges were made against both St. Clair and Schuyler. It was even asserted they had both been bribed by Burgoyne, who, it was said, had fired *silver bullets* into the fort, which were gathered by order of St. Clair, and divided between him and Schuyler.

This report would seem too ridiculous to gain credit with any one, and yet we have the authority of Wilkinson, who was Adjutant-general to Gates, that respectable men questioned him, with much gravity, as to its truth.* Time softened the disappointment of the people, and when the true condition of the case was known, both officers were fully reinstated in the confidence of the nation.

When St. Clair joined Schuyler at Fort Edward, their whole force, including recent arrivals, did not exceed four thousand four hundred men, who were immediately employed in obstructing the roads leading to Lake Champlain, and in placing impediments to the navigation of Wood Creek. So thoroughly was this work accomplished that, when Burgoyne afterwards ..d his army on this route, he was often unable to advance more than one mile in twenty-four hours. Schuyler remained at Fort Edward until the latter part of the month of July, when he fell back as far as Saratoga, and subsequently retired to Stillwater. While at Fort Edward, he removed the provisions, stores, boats and arms from Fort George, and on the 17th of July, destroyed the fort itself.

We left Burgoyne at Skenesborough and Fraser and Reidesel at Hubbardton, on the 7th of July. After the retreat of St. Clair towards Fort Edward, these two columns occupied the ground between Castleton and Skenesborough ; the English right wing occupying the heights at Skenesborough, in two lines, the right flank

repose the highest confidence"— *Letter to Major-general Putnam, July* 11, 1777. To this letter from the Council of Safety General Putnam replied, " I am greatly astonished at the evacuation of Ticonderoga in the manner it is represented : Think there is great fault somewhere."

* See also Doctor Thacher's Military Journal, where he gravely denies the truth of the absurd report.

to the mountain and the left to Wood Creek; the German troops were stationed at Castleton, with detachments on the roads leading to Rutland and Poultney; the centre was occupied by Fraser's corps.—A third column of the English army, under General Phillips, was engaged in getting the gun-boats, transports and provisions, over the falls of the outlet, into Lake George. This was accomplished after great labor and fatigue. Phillips then advanced as far as Fort George, where he established a depot and erected magazines for the army.

While Burgoyne was at Skenesborough, he issued a proclamation addressed to the inhabitants on the New Hampshire Grants, in which he directed them under pain of military execution, to send deputations, consisting of ten persons or more from each township, to meet Colonel Skene at Castleton, " who," adds the proclamation, " will have instructions not only to give further encouragement to those who complied with the terms of my late manifesto, but also to communicate conditions upon which the persons and property of the disobedient may yet be spared." As soon as General Schuyler saw this proclamation, he issued an order that every person, who had taken or might take a protection from Burgoyne, should be secured and sent to jail; at the same time he gave notice, by a counter proclamation, that all who should join with, or in any manner assist or hold correspondence with the English, should be considered and dealt with as traitors.

Burgoyne had placed great reliance upon the discontent of the inhabitants on the New Hampshire Grants, and supposed that large numbers, if not the whole population, would join his army. But in this he was most sorely disappointed, for, not more than four hundred royalists or disaffected joined him, and at least half of these he represented as " trimmers, merely actuated by interest," in whom he could place no dependence. He also declared, in a letter to Lord George Germain, that the New Hampshire Grants abounded in the most active and most rebellious race on the continent, who

9

hung like a gathering storm upon his left.—This opinion had not been formed without good reasons, as we shall now see.

When the column under General Phillips moved up Lake George, the posts at Ticonderoga and Mount Independence were left with a guard of nine hundred and ten men, composed of the 53d British regiment, four hundred and sixty-two strong, and a German regiment, numbering four hundred and forty-eight men, rank and file. About the time that Burgoyne had collected his troops at Fort Edward, General Lincoln, who commanded a strong detachment of militia, stationed at Manchester, Vt., determined to make a diversion in the rear of the British line, in the hopes of recovering the Fort of Ticonderoga, and thus cutting off Burgoyne's communication with Canada.

General Lincoln ordered Colonel Warner, with a detachment of the Massachusetts militia, to move in the direction of Mount Independence, in order to make a diversion, and an attack in that quarter, if the occasion should favor one. Another detachment was sent, under Colonel Woodbridge, against Skenesborough and Fort Ann, while Colonel Brown, with Herrick's regiment of Rangers, and some Militia and Volunteers, was to cross the lake at the narrows, pass through the woods and take the outposts of Ticonderoga, and the works at the landing of Lake George. These places were to be attacked at the same time. Captain Ebenezer Allen, with his rangers, was to leave Brown and Herrick at a certain point and take Mount Defiance, and then rejoin them to attack Ticonderoga, in conjunction with General Warner. The plan thus arranged, they set out for Pawlet for their different places of destination. Brown had to cross the lake in the night and to pass, for fourteen miles, over rugged mountains, which he accomplished, reaching the head of Lake George the day before the attack. Before it became dark, sentinels were placed at different points on Mount Defiance and in the direction of the other British posts, with directions, from time to time, to give " *three hoots*

of an owl," as a signal, to guide the main party on their
way, through the darkness of night. Colonel Brown
took possession of Mount Hope and of a block-house
near the old French lines. He also seized two hundred
long-boats, an armed sloop, and several gun-boats, stationed to defend the carrying-place, and captured two
hundred and ninety-three soldiers, at the same time re-
leasing one hundred American prisoners.

But the most difficult task was the capture of the
British works on the summit of Mount Defiance; which
could be reached only by a cut way well defended and
guarded. Captain Allen and his men had, after great
difficulty and labor, nearly reached the top of the
mountain, when they found a cliff they could not climb
in the ordinary way. Allen therefore ordered one of
his men to stoop, and stepping on his back, clambered
to the top, which was only large enough to hold eight
men without their being discovered by the enemy. As
soon as the men had reached the top, he rushed upon
the garrison, already alarmed by the firing at the landing, closely followed by his little party, who, says Allen,
"came after me like a stream of hornets to the charge."
The garrison immediately fled, with the exception of
one man who attempted to fire a cannon at the assailants. " Kill the gunner," cried Allen, at the same
time discharging his musket. At this the man ran
away with the match in his hand, leaving the Americans in full possession of the works. The terrified soldiers rushed down the cut way and were captured by
Major Waite, who had been stationed on the bridge to
intercept their retreat. The only resistance offered,
during the night, was by Lieutenant Lord of the 53d
regiment, who commanded at the block-house, and
who did not yield until several pieces of ordinance,
taken from the sloop, had been brought against it.

Colonel Warner did not arrive near Mount Independence until early the next morning. " He moved so extremely slow," says Ira Allen.* " that he saved his own

* History of Vermont—London, 1798.

men and hurt none of the enemy." When he came up, his force was united with Colonel Brown's and the fortress of Ticonderoga summoned, but Brigadier-general Powel, who commanded there, refused to surrender, declaring that he was resolved to defend himself to the last. Brown and Warner continued a cannonade against the fort for four days, when finding the guns made no impression upon the walls, they abandoned the siege and withdrew their forces to the lower Lake George. Here they embarked on the gun-boats which they had captured, and on the 24th sailed against and attacked Diamond Island. On this island a large quantity of public property had been stored, which was guarded by two companies of the 47th regiment, under Captain Aubrey. In this attack the Americans were repulsed with a small loss, and retreated to the east shore of the lake, pursued by several gun-boats which were stationed at the island. As soon as the Americans landed, they burned their boats, crossed over the mountains to Lake Champlain and returned to Lincoln's camp at Pawlet.*

The fate of Burgoyne's army, after it left the lake, is well known. On the 30th of July, the three divisions were united at Fort Edward. On the 16th of August, Colonel Baum was defeated at Bennington, by a body of New England Militia, under General Stark. St. Leger raised the siege of Fort Stanwix on the 28th of that month, and passing through Canada and Lake Champlain, soon after joined Burgoyne, between whom and General Gates a battle had been fought at Stillwater, on the 18th of September, in which the advantages were decidedly in favor of the latter. After the action Burgoyne retired as far as Saratoga, where another severe action was fought on the 7th of October. On the 17th of that month " articles of capitulation " were signed and five thousand seven hundred and

* In this expedition the American recovered the Continental standard which had been left behind when St. Clair's army evacuated the fort in July.

ninety-one British and German troops were surrendered as prisoners of war.*

As soon as the news of Burgoyne's surrender reached Ticonderoga, the troops stationed in that vicinity prepared for an immediate retreat to Canada. A few open boats now held what remained of the proud host, who three months before had ascended the lake with all the pomp and panoply of war. Then, their banners floated gayly in the breeze, and the clear notes of the bugle startled the echoes of the surrounding hills; now, with watchful eyes they hurried silently along, and carefully avoided the shores, lest the thick and tangled forest might contain some bold and unseen foe. Nor were their fears without foundation; for, as they passed the mouth of the Bouquet, they were suddenly attacked by a party of "Green Mountain Boys," led by Captain Ebenezer Allen, who cut off the rear division of boats and captured fifty men, besides a large quantity of baggage and military stores.

Thus closed the military operations of the year on Lake Champlain. The works at Ticonderoga were not reoccupied by the Americans, nor was this section of country the scene of any important military movement during the remainder of the war. In the fall of 1777, Gates, who had been placed at the head of the Board of War, conceived the project of directing a descent upon Canada, in mid-winter, by the way of Lake Champlain, for the purpose of destroying the stores and shipping at St. Johns on the Richelieu. The conduct of the expedition was entrusted to the Marquis de Lafayette, who repaired to Albany, full of high hopes and panting for an opportunity to distinguish himself in a separate command. But the project failed from the

* After his exchange, which took place in 1781 or 1782, Burgoyne was commissioned as Colonel of the 4th or King's Own regiment of foot and soon afterward was appointed commander-in-chief of the forces in Ireland and was also one of the privy counsellors there. After resigning his position in Ireland he was in constant attendance as a member of the House of Commons, and was one of the managers on the impeachment of Warrer Hastings. He died August 4, 1792, of gout and was buried in the cloister of Westminster Abbey.

want of troops. Scarcely twelve hundred men could be mustered, and the greater part of these were half naked and unarmed. "The Generals only," says Marshall, "were got in readiness." Lafayette was much annoyed, but the obstacles were insuperable.

In 1780, Sir John Johnson made a descent upon Johnstown, near the Mohawk, for the purpose of recovering his silver plate, which he had secreted in the cellar of his house, at the time of his flight in 1776. Having accomplished this object, Johnson retired to Canada by the way of Lake Champlain, taking with him about forty prisoners. He was pursued by Governor Clinton at the head of a body of militia, as far as Ticonderoga. Here Clinton was joined by a party of "Green Mountain Boys," but from a want of boats the pursuit was discontinued. In the fall of the same year, a party of two hundred and three Indians, led by seven tories and refugees, passed up the Winooski and attacked the flourishing settlement of Royalton, Vt., burning twenty-one houses and taking fourteen of the principal inhabitants prisoners.

In October, Major Carleton was sent up the lake from St. Johns, with a fleet of eight large vessels and twenty-six long-boats, containing upwards of one thousand men, in order to create a diversion in favor of Sir John Johnson, who directed an attack upon the Schoharie and Mohawk county. On the 10th and 11th, Major Carleton surprised Fort George and Fort Ann, and took the garrisons prisoners. In the two assaults the British lost four officers and twenty-three privates killed; while the loss of the Americans, in killed and prisoners, was two captains, two lieutenants and one hundred and fourteen privates. Carleton remained at Ticonderoga until the first of November, when he returned with the boats and shipping to St. Johns.

In the spring of 1781, the Iroquois Chief, Thayendanegea, (Brant), meditated an expedition against the Oneidas, who had been driven for safety to a position about fifteen miles west of Saratoga. This enterprise received the sanction of Sir Frederick Haldimand, then Governor of Canada, who proposed to send a party of sixty loyalists under Major Jessup, the commandant at Point Au Fer, towards Fort Edward, to co-operate with Brant's Indians, who were to rendezvous on Carleton* Island, in Lake Champlain. For some cause now unknown, the project was never executed.

In the course of the summer, the British, upon several occasions, entered the lake with their whole fleet, but attempted nothing beyond landing at Crown Point and Ticonderoga. The mysterious and, at the time, inexplicable movements of the enemy, in this quarter, kept the northern frontier in a state of ceaseless inquietude and alarm. The army about Albany was small and weak, and the American Generals were greatly perplexed at these strange manœuvres of the fleet. Whenever it ascended the lake, an attack was expected in the direction of Fort Edward, but when, a few weeks afterwards, the fleet would withdraw without making any hostile demonstration, the idea prevailed that the movement was intended to create a diversion, while the actual blow was to be struck in another quarter. The mystery of these singular proceedings was not fully explained until several years afterwards, when it became publicly known that the leaders of the people on the New Hampshire Grants had been, during the years 1780 and 1781, in frequent and secret correspondence with the authorities of Canada in relation to the political destiny of the Grants.

It is not my purpose to enter into an investigation as to the character or effect of this correspondence. The subject properly belongs to the History of Vermont, and has already been ably reviewed by her historians. It is enough here to say, that on the part of the British, the negotiation consisted of repeated endeavors to persuade the leaders on the Grants to abandon the American cause, and to declare the country a British Province, and on the other side, of evasive and am-

* This is a small island near the south end of Grant Isle. It is now called Stave Island.

biguous answers, calculated to keep alive the hopes of the British authorities, but not intended to pledge the leaders or the people to any certain action.

When the remnant of Burgoyne's army retreated to Canada in 1777, the British retained possession of Point Au Fer, which they occupied as a military post. They also held a small block-house on the west side of the island of North Hero. These places were not given up until some time after the close of the war.

Batta—Burgoyne's Narrative—Thacher's Military Journal—Thumbull's Reminiscences of his own Times—Stone's Life of Joseph Brant—Journal of the New York Provincial Congress—Lossing's Field Book of the Revolution, etc., etc.

CHAPTER IX.

From 1783 to 1800—Progress and extent of Settlements on the borders
of Lake Champlain—Personal Sketches—Trade and Commerce of
the Country—Population, etc., etc.

We have now traced the history of Lake Champlain,
from its first exploration by the Europeans, in 1609,
to the close of the war of the Revolution, a period of
one hundred and seventy-five years. This history, thus
far, has been little more than a narrative of continued
strife and contention. Champlain was guided to the
lake by a war party of Indians, who were seeking their
enemies upon the well known battle ground of that
early day. He wrote the name of the lake upon its sands
with the blood of the Iroquois, and proclaimed it, for
the first time, amid the cries of tortured and dying
prisoners. For many years afterwards the French and
English colonists crimsoned its waters with each other's
blood, and when, after a short interval of comparative
quiet, the war of the Revolution broke forth, the tide
of battle almost instinctively returned to its old channel. It is not surprising that, under such circumstances, but little progress had yet been made towards
the settlement and improvement of the country.

In 1783, the settlements near the lake were principally confined to the few towns in Vermont opposite
and south of Crown Point. In that year the whole
population upon the borders of the lake, on both
sides, did not exceed six hundred.

For several years after the declaration of Peace,
emigration to the north-eastern part of Vermont was
retarded by the still pending dispute between the
claimants under the New Hampshire Grants and the
state of New York, in regard to land titles. This controversy had, however, lost much of its acrimony, and
all parties were prepared for his final adjustment, which
took place in 1790. On the 4th of March, 1791,

Vermont was admitted into the Union as a separate and independent State. In this year the population of the lake towns was six thousand seven hundred and seventy-three.

In 1782, a party of royalists emigrated from St. Johns on the Richelieu, and commenced several improvements in the town of Alburgh. Soon afterwards Ira Allen obtained a grant of the town, from the authorities of Vermont, and brought actions of ejectment against the royalists, which however terminated in their favor. A claim to the township was afterwards advanced by Sir George Young, under color of a grant from the Duke of York, which was also successfully resisted by the settlers.

Isle La Motte was settled in 1785, by Ebenezer Hyde, Enoch Hall and William Blanchard, and was organized as a town in 1790. In 1802, the name of the town was changed to Vineyard, which it retained until 1830, when the original name of Isle La Motte was again resumed. The islands of North Hero and Grand Isle were chartered as a town in 1779, but no settlement was commenced there until 1783. In March of that year Ebenezer Allen,* Alexander Gordon and Enos Wood visited the township for the purpose of locating their respective claims. Wood, who, by agreement between the parties was entitled to the first choice, located upon the south end of the north island; Gordon took the north end of the south island, and Allen the south end. In August, all three brought on their families and commenced permanent improvements. For the first few years the inhabitants of these islands, in common with those of the neighboring towns, suffered great inconvenience from the want of grist-mills,

* Ebenezer Allen was a native of Massachusetts. At the age of twenty-four, he moved into Poultney, and in company with his brother-in-law, Thomas Ashley, commenced the first settlement in that town. He was soon afterwards appointed Captain of a company of Minute Men, and served in Colonel Herrick's regiment of Rangers during the Revolution. He led the attack against the British post on Mount Defiance in September, 1777, and afterwards captured about fifty of the rear-guard of Burgoyne's army on their retreat to Canada.

the most accessible being at Whitehall and Granville, from eighty to one hundred miles distant.

The town of Milton was first settled in 1783, Georgia in 1784, and St. Albans in 1785. In 1782 McClain, Low and Boardman moved on to Colchester Point, and in the same year Ira Allen returned to the lower falls of the Winooski, where he soon after erected mills, a forge and a shop for making anchors.*

The first residents in the town of Burlington abandoned their improvements at the time of Burgoyne's invasion in 1777, Stephen Lawrence, Frederick Saxton, Simeon Tubbs and John Collins moved into the town and renewed the settlement in 1783. The first town meeting was held in March, 1787, when Samuel Lane was chosen town clerk. In 1789 Stephen Keyes built a store in the village, which was opened in the fall of that year under the charge of Orange Smith. Another store was soon afterwards started by Zacheus Peaslee.

In the year 1787, there were about twenty families in the town of Shelburne. Charlotte was first permanently settled in 1784, by Derick Webb and Elijah Woolcut. John McNeil soon afterwards moved into the town. He was elected its first town clerk and representative. In 1790 he removed to the lake shore and established a ferry between that place and the town of Willsborough (now Essex), N. Y. Ferrisburgh was settled, after the war, by Abel Thompson, Gideon Hawley, Timothy Rogers, and others. In 1783 Amos Spafford, Shadrack Hathway, Eben Murray and Ephraim and Wm. Fisher and John Charter commenced a settlement at Mt. Independence, in the town of Orwell, and the next year Pliny Smith and others moved into the town with their families. The same year, Barber, Durfee and Noble moved into the town of Benson.*

* Ira Allen was the first Secretary of Vermont. Subsequently he was State Treasurer, Member of the Council, and Surveyor-General. He rose to the rank of Major-General of Militia, and, in 1795, was sent to Europe to purchase a supply of arms for the State.

† For further information, in regard to the first settlement of Vermont, see Zadock Thompson's Gazetteer of Vermont—a most able and elaborate work.

Let us now cross to the western or New York side of the lake. In 1784 the County of Washington was organized, and originally included all the territory lying west of and adjoining the lake. In 1788 that portion, contained in the present counties of Clinton, Essex and Franklin, was taken from Washington and formed into a new county, which was called Clinton. Essex was taken from Clinton in 1799, and Franklin in 1808. The town of Plattsburgh was organized as a part of Washington County in 1785, and included all the territory within the limits of the present towns of Beekmantown, Saranac, Schuyler's Falls, and also portions of Old Peru and Old Chateaugay. It was the only town on the west side of the lake until 1788, when Champlain, Willsborough and Crown Point were organized. Willsborough originally included the present towns of Chesterfield, Essex, Lewis and a part of Old Peru. Crown Point embraced all the territory lying between Willsborough and Lake George.

When Burgoyne entered the United States, all the persons residing on the west side of the lake abandoned their habitations, and either joined the American army, or retired to the neighborhood of Albany. They returned immediately after the Peace, and were soon followed by others; but the progress of the settlement of the county was very slow for the first ten years. In 1790 the population of Clinton County, which then embraced the whole territory west of the lake, was to be found in the vicinity of the Saranac and the Bouquet rivers, and did not then exceed sixteen hundred and fourteen.

Prior to the revolution William Gilliland had commenced a settlement at the falls of the Bouquet river, from which he was taken and sent to Albany by order of General Gates, in 1776. After the war he returned, accompanied or soon followed by Aaron Fairchild, Jonathan Lynde, Joseph Sheldon, Abram Aiken, Martin Pope, Melchor and John Hoffnagle, John Morehouse and others, who in 1784 settled at or near the mouth of the Bouquet. In 1783 Jacque Rous emigrated

from Canada and settled at Rouses Point. John La
Frombois and Francis La Monte returned to their
farms on the lake shore in Chazy, in 1784. Prisque
Ashline lived on the Corbeau river in 1786, and Pliny
Moore in Champlain in 1785. In 1787 Robert Cochran
and Nathaniel Mallory resided on the lake shore, near
the mouths of the Ausable rivers; Moses Dickson,
Jabez Allen and Lot and John Elmore on the rich lands
lying between those rivers, and Edward Everett and
John Stanton in what is now called the " Union," in the
town of Peru. In August, 1783, Benjamin Mooers
commenced the first permanent settlement within the
limits of the present town of Beekmantown. Mr.
Mooers was a native of Haverhill, Massachusetts. At
the age of eighteen he entered the army as a volunteer,
and in 1777 was appointed Ensign in Hazen's regiment,
and was afterwards promoted to the rank of Lieutenant
and Adjutant. On the 26th of July, 1783, Mr. Mooers
left Poughkeepsie in a bateau, accompanied by Francis
Monty and son, Zacheus Peaslee, Pierre Boilan, Charles
Cloutier, Antoine Lavan, Joseph Latournau, Antoine
Lasambert, P. Aboir and John Fessie. The party arrived at Albany on the 29th, where Mr. Mooers was
joined by John La Frombois, who was returning to his
farm on the lake shore in Chazy. On the 31st they
left Albany and proceeded up the Hudson about five
miles, where the boat was partially unloaded and taken
over the rapids to Stillwater. On the 2d August they
reached Fort Miller, and at noon of the 3d arrived at
Fort Edward. The baggage and boat were drawn
across the country to Fort George, where the party
procured another boat, and the same evening sailed
nine miles down the lake and encamped on a small
island near its eastern shore. The next day they
reached the lower end of Lake George, and on the 6th
drew the boats around the falls at Ticonderoga into
Lake Champlain, and sailed down the lake with a fair
wind, passing Crown Point about sundown. On the 8th
the party landed on Valcour Island, where they were
delayed by head winds until Sunday morning, the 10th

of August, when they set sail, and the same day arrived at Point Au Roche. The next day, the whole party, except La Frombois, who had gone on to visit his old place a few miles below, commenced work, and in ten days completed a log house and cleared a small patch of land for turnips. One of the first labor of the new settlers, after building the house, was to cut a quantity of grass for the support of the oxen during the winter. This grass grew wild in many places upon the low lands near the shore of the lake and for several years was the only fodder used in the country. By the 11th September Mr. Mooers had cleared up a small field near his house, which he sowed to wheat and turnips.

He subsequently removed to Plattsburgh, where he resided until his death in February, 1838, in the 80th year of his age. He was the first Sheriff of Clinton County, was four times elected Member of the Assembly and once of the State Senate, and was County Treasurer for forty-eight years. During the war of 1812 he held the office of Major-general of Militia and co-operated with and materially aided the United States military officers in the defense of the northeastern frontier of the State.

In 1781, the Legislature of the State of New York, in order to encourage the raising of troops for the defence of the State, passed certain acts offering bounties of unappropriated lands to such officers and soldiers as should enlist within a specified time. These bounties were divided into rights of five hundred acres each, and there was a provision in the act, that whenever any number of persons entitled collectively to sixty-one rights, or 30,500 acres, should join in a location, the lands so located should be laid out in a township of seven miles square, and that the remaining 860 acres, in such township, should be reserved for Gospel and School purposes. These rights were sometimes retained by the soldiers, but, more frequently, a company of land speculators would furnish money to the recruiting officers, to be paid as a bounty to those who on enlistment should transfer their certificates to the company. In this way a large portion of the un-appropriated lands of the State, subject to location, passed into the hands of a few individuals.

Judge Zephaniah Platt, of Poughkeepsie, and thirty-two other persons, having united in the purchase of the number of rights requisite to entitle the holders to a township, located them, in 1784, upon the lands which had formerly been embraced in the warrant is-sued by the English Government to Charles De Fre-denburgh. A survey of the land was made in the same year by Captain Nathaniel Platt and Captain Simon R. Reeves, two of the proprietors, and a patent issued by the State to Zephaniah Platt in 1785.*

The proprietors were active in their efforts to secure the immediate settlement of the tract. Ten "gift lots" were set apart for the first ten persons who should move into the town with their families, and arrange-ments were made, at an early day, for the building of Mills, &c.

On the 30th of December, 1784, twelve of the pro-prietors met at the house of Judge Platt, in Pough-keepsie, where they agreed to become jointly interest-ed in building a saw-mill, a grist-mill and a forge on the Saranac, near its mouth. They also agreed to fur-nish twine for a seine, and to build a piragua "of a moderate size." Attached to the agreement was an estimate of the probable cost of the mills, from which it appears that three hundred and sixteen dollars were

---

* The following is a list of the original proprietors of Plattsburgh Old Patent, and of the number of acres allotted to each. Thomas Treadwell, Nehemiah Benedict and Thomas Benedict, 1120 acres; Nathaniel Platt, 950; Nathaniel Tom, 480; Burnet Miller, 480; Ezra L. Hommedieu, 320; Peter Tappan, 480; John Miller, 640; Benjamin Walker, 320; John Berrien, 480; Jonathan Lawrence, 480; Benjamin Smith, 480; Israel Smith, 960; Melancton Smith, 1120; Zephaniah Platt, 900; William Floyd, 320; Benjamin Conklin, 500; Andrew Billings, 400; John Adams, 1600; Thomas Stone, 1000; Lewis Barton, 200; Ebenezer Mott, 200; Zacheus Newcomb, 1200; Platt Rogers, 1500; General Schuyler, 950; Benjamin Titus, 400; Charles Platt, 800; John Smith, 400; Albert Adriance, 200; Samuel Smith, 200; Jacobus S. Swartout, 200; Simon R. Reeves, 2800; Zephaniah and Nathaniel Platt, 4050; Zephaniah and Nathaniel Platt and S. R. Reeves, 4300.

appropriated for mill-stones, irons, nails, bolting-cloth and saw, and sixty-five dollars for flour and bread. One hundred and sixty dollars were divided equally between pork and New England rum—a pint of rum to a pound of pork being a workman's requisite in those roistering days.

Among those who received the "gift lots" were Jacob Ferris, Thomas Allen, John B. Hartwick, Derrick Webb, Jabez Pettit, Moses Soper, and Kinner Newcomb. Ferris received a deed for one hundred and twenty acres lying on the south side of the river Saranac, at its mouth, which covered all that part of the present village of Plattsburgh lying east of the river. In 1785, Charles McCreedy, Melancton L. Woolsey and several others moved into the town. Cumberland Head was then supposed to present the most eligible point for business, and the first stores established in the town were located there. After a few years, the stores were removed to the present village, but "the Head" still continued to be a place of some importance. It had a direct communication with Vermont, by ferry, and for a long time was the usual landing place for vessels navigating the lake.

Probably few towns in the State of New York can claim among their first inhabitants and proprietors, a greater number of men of talent than Plattsburgh. Conspicuous in this class were Melancton Smith, Zephaniah Platt, Thomas Tredwell and Peter Sailly.

MELANCTON SMITH, one of the proprietors, was a native of Jamaica, Queen's County, L. I., where he was born in 1744. While a boy he was placed in a retail store in Poughkeepsie, and resided in that town until his removal to the city of New York in 1784. At the early age of thirty-one, he was chosen one of the delegates to represent the county of Dutchess in the first Provincial Congress of New York, which met in May 1775, and soon became a leading and distinguished member of that body. He was one of the committee who prepared the celebrated address to the Canadians, at the commencement of the revolutionary struggle.

On the 22d of June, 1776, he was appointed captain
commandant of three companies of Militia raised in
Dutchess and West Chester, and the next year was
placed on the commission to prevent and subdue insurrection and dissatisfaction in those counties. He was
in the same year appointed the first sheriff of Dutchess
county, which office he held for four years and was
afterwards made a Judge of the Common Pleas.*

In 1778, though then a resident of the city of New
York, Mr. Smith was chosen by the people of Dutchess
County, to the convention which met in June of that
year to consider the Constitution of the United States,
as prepared by the Convention at Philadelphia in May
of the preceding year. In the discussions and deliber-
ations of this body, he exhibited talents and information of the highest order, and was ranked as one of
the ablest opponents of Hamilton and Livingston on
the floor of the Convention. When it was ascertained
that a sufficient number of States had so decided as to
render the adoption of the Constitution certain, Mr.
Smith gave up his objections. "This was deemed at
the time," says Chancellor Kent, "a magnanimous sacrifice of preconceived principles and party discipline
for the national welfare, and the effort was the greater
inasmuch as he had to desert his friend, Governor Clinton, who persevered to the end in his hostility to the
Constitution."†

On 6th March, 1790, he was appointed by the legislature of the State of New York one of the commissioners on the part of the state to agree with the commissioners of Vermont as to the boundary between that
State and New York.

Mr. Smith was twice married. His first wife was
Sarah Smith, of New Jersey, who died in 1770; his second, Margaret, daughter of Richbill Motte of Long Isl-
and, whom he married in 1771, and by whom he had
four children, Richbill, Melancton, Sidney and Phœbe,

* Journal of the New York Provincial Congress.
† Chancellor Kent, as quoted in Appendix to Thompson's History
of Long Island.

all of whom afterwards resided in Plattsburgh. He died in the city of New York on the 29th of July, 1798, in the 55th year of his age.

"Melancton Smith," says Mr. Dunlap, "was a man of rough exterior, powerful in bodily appearance, and undaunted in expressing his mind, which he did in plain language, but with a sarcasm that was cutting and a humor correct and playful." "He was," says Chancellor Kent, "very amiable in his temper and disposition, of a religious cast, and very fond of metaphysical and logical discussions, in which he was a master. In private life he was kind, affectionate and communicative, and as benevolent as amiable; indeed his charity knew no limits. While the army was encamped near his residence in Dutchess County, the females of the family were constantly employed in making clothing for the soldiers. "I could only make up my bedding by stealth," Mrs. Smith afterwards used to say, "for if the Judge came in and found me sewing upon a pair of sheets, he would request the cloth cut into shirts for the half naked soldiers of Washington's army."

ZAPHANIAH PLATT was possessed of a clear, sound and discriminating mind, and was classed among the first men of the State. In 1776, when forty-one years of age, he was chosen a delegate from Dutchess county to the first Provincial Congress, and occupied a prominent position in that body; he was a member of the Committee of Safety and took an active part in the convention called for forming a constitution for the State. He was for a short time commissary for the troops under command of Brigadier-general Clinton. In June, 1777, he was appointed a Judge of the Dutchess Common Pleas, and the same year was elected one of the State Senators for the middle district, then composed of the counties of Dutchess, Ulster and Orange. He was also a member of the State Convention which assembled at Poughkeepsie, in June, 1788, to deliberate on the adoption of the Constitution of the United States.

In the Spring of 1777, the counties of Dutchess and

West Chester were filled with disaffected persons, who, it was feared, upon the first advance of the British troops out of New York city, would attack those friendly to the American cause. To prevent this, the Provincial Convention appointed Mr. Platt and two other members of their body a committee to clear those counties of all dangerous and disaffected persons. " You are," were the instructions to the committee, " on every occasion, by every means in your power, (torture excepted,) to compel the discovery and delivery of all spies and emissaries of the enemy, who you may have reason to believe are concealed in any part of the country through which you may make your progress, and upon due proof immediately execute them *in terrorem*."* The committee executed the delicate and responsible duty confided to them with firmness, and with the most impartial justice.

After the war Mr. Platt engaged largely in the purchase of military land warrants and located them principally upon Lake Champlain. He removed from Poughkeepsie to Plattsburgh about the year 1801, where he resided until his death, in September, 1807.

THOMAS TREADWELL, another of the original proprietors of Plattsburgh, was born in Smithtown, Long Island, in 1742, and graduated at Princeton in 1764. He was well educated, and highly distinguished for his good sense, prudence and firmness. In 1755, he was a member of the Provincial Convention. He was also a member of the Convention that framed the State Constitution, and was one of the Senators under that constitution. In 1788, he was a member of the Convention which assembled to consider the Constitution of the United States, in which he co-operated with Clinton, Melancton Smith, Yates and Lansing. He was made Judge of Probate of Suffolk county in 1783, and held the office until surrogates were appointed, when he received the appoinment of surrogate, which he held until 1791.† Soon after the organization of

* Journal of the New York Provincial Congress.
† Thompson's History of Long Island.

Clinton county, he removed to Plattsburgh and was chosen a Senator for the northern District. In 1807, he was appointed Surrogatecof Clinton County, which office he held until the spring of 1831. He was for many years the last surviving member of the venerable assembly that framed the first Constitution of the State ; and died on the 30th of January, 1832, enjoying to the last the respect and confidence of his fellowmen.

PETER SAILLY was a native of Loraine, France. He first visited the United States in 1783, and made a tour of exploration through the valley of the Mohawk and the country bordering on Lake Champlain. In 1785, he returned to France for his family, with whom he arrived at the city of New York in the summer of that year, and, having passed the winter in Albany, settled the following spring in the town of Plattsburgh. Mr. Sailly was a man of great probity, possessing strong powers of mind and a clear discernment of character. He was active, enterprising and firm ; a master of order and method and scrupulously exact in his business transactions. Although educated in a foreign land, he brought to the country of his adoption a mind deeply imbued with the principles of liberty, which he carefully cherished and enlarged in after life. He held several offices of public trust, and to the hour of his death enjoyed the unlimited confidence of his fellowmen. In 1804, he was elected a member of Congress from the Saratoga, Clinton and Essex district, and by his strict attention to business and a judicious and unostentatious course, won the confidence of Mr. Jefferson, by whom he was soon after appointed Collector of Customs for the district of Champlain—an office he held through the successive administrations of Madison and Monroe until his death in 1826; a period of over eighteen years.

The duties of Collector, during a portion of this time, were most delicate and responsible, as upon the revenue officers devolved the arduous and unpopular service of putting in execution the embargo and non-intercourse laws. In the discharge of this duty Mr. Sailly never hesitated, but, upon all occasions, enforced the laws with promptness and strict impartiality. Kind and affable in his intercourse with his fellow-citizens, he wounded the feelings of none by a rough or unnecessary display of power, while his firmness and determination of character were too well understood, for any one to hope, by the strongest opposition, to deter him from the prompt discharge of his public duties.

The first Court of Common Pleas and General Sessions for Clinton County was held at Plattsburgh, on the 28th of October, 1788. Judge Charles Platt presided. Peter Sailly, Theodorus Platt, William McAuley, Pliny Moore, and Robert Cochran, were the associate justices; Benjamin Mooers was sheriff: Melancton L. Woolsey, clerk; John Frontfreyde, coroner; and Robert Paul, Jonathan Stephenson, Lewis Lizotte, and Jonathan Lynde, constables. One attorney, only, was in attendance, who appeared in behalf of the people; the prisoners were defended by the clerk.* The first Circuit and Oyer and Terminer, for the northern part of the State, was held by Judge Benson, at the Court-house in Plattsburgh, on the 18th of August, 1796. The next year Judge Lansing held a circuit court at the "Block-house" in Willsborough, where the court also convened in 1798.

In 1789 George Clinton and Robert Yates were opposing candidates for Governor. The canvass was so warmly contested that the supporters of Governor Clinton secured his re-election by the small majority of

---

* CHARLES PLATT was a native of Long Island and a brother of Zephaniah Platt. He removed to Plattsburgh soon after the organization of the town, was elected its first supervisor, and for several years was town clerk. He was first judge of the Clinton Common Pleas until the year 1804, and in 1808 was appointed to the office of county clerk, which he held until 1822. MELANCTON L. WOOLSEY was the youngest son of Melancton T. Woolsey of Long Island, and in early life had served as an officer in the army and as aid to Governor Clinton. He removed to Plattsburgh in 1785, was soon after appointed Clerk of Clinton County and was, for several years, Collector of Customs for the Champlain District.

four hundred and twenty-nine votes. The entire vote of Clinton County, at this election, was forty-five, which was thus divided between the two candidates.

	CLINTON.	YATES.
Crown Point,	10	
Willsborough,	15	3
Plattsburgh,	17*	

In 1793 the vote of the County was increased to one hundred and thirty-four. George Clinton was elected Governor over Stephen Van Rensselaer, in 1801, by a majority of three thousand nine hundred and sixty-five. At this time Essex, had been set off from Clinton, and several new towns had been organized in both counties. This year the vote was as follows:

CLINTON COUNTY:

	CLINTON.	VAN RENSSELAER.
Champlain,	42	45
Lisbon,	21	71
Plattsburgh,	107	21
Chateaugay,	11	52
Peru,	90	24
	271	213

ESSEX COUNTY:

	CLINTON.	VAN RENSSELAER.
Willsborough,	50	82
Crown Point,	10	6
Elizabethtown,	69	9
Jay,	46	13
	175	110

The vote of both counties in 1803 was 749, which

* The poll list of this election was not preserved, but it can be conjectured who cast these seventeen votes, when it is known that the following *seventeen* persons were elected to town offices in Plattsburgh, at that election. Charles Platt, Kinner Newcomb, Theodorus Platt, Melancton L. Woolsey, Abraham Beeman, John Stephenson, John Cochran, Jr., Nathan Averill, Cyrenus Newcomb, Edward Everett, Peter Sailly, John B. Hardwick, Jonas Allen, Moses Soper, Titus Andrews, Benjamin Mooers, and Lucius Reynolds.

was increased to 929, in 1804. Two years later the number of votes polled in both counties was 1,247.

The increase of population on both sides of the lake, from 1790 to 1800, was nearly two hundred per cent. During this decade considerable progress was made in agriculture ; particularly on the Vermont side, where the attention of the great body of the inhabitants was directed to the cultivation of the soil, the raising of sheep and the production of flax. The manufacture of pot and pearl ash was also carried on to a considerable extent. Some attention had likewise been given to the manufacture of iron. As early as 1792, four forges were erected in Addison County and two in Chittenden, and prior to the year 1800, several other forges had been erected at other points, upon both sides of the lake. These forges were principally supplied from a bed near Crown Point, which is yet celebrated for the quality and quantity of its ore.* The country abounded with maple trees from which large quantities of sugar were annually made. Many of the maples were of very large size and it was not unusual for the farmers to make from twelve to fifteen pounds of sugar, in the course of the season, from a single tree.†

The first settlers were generally hunters and derived considerable profit from the sale of peltry, as the country then abounded with moose, deer, bears, beavers, foxes, wolves, rabbits, martins, etc. The lake was also celebrated for the abundance, variety and delicate flavor of its fish. Salmon, maskinonge, bass, shad, pike, pickerel, and perch were caught in great abundance in all parts of the lake, and in the mouths of the principal streams. The lower part of the lake near Wind-mill Point, and the Big Chazy river at the foot of the first rapids, were especially celebrated for their salmon fisheries. Cham-

* When Kalm was at Crown Point, in 1749, he noticed black sand upon the shores of the lake, but he says it was not then known whether there were iron mines in the neighborhood or not. Iron ore was first found within the present limits of Clinton County, in 1800, when the "Winter Bed" was discovered by Mr. George Shaffer. The "Arnold Bed" was first opened in 1809.
† Williams' History of Vermont.

plain, in the account of his expedition in 1609, describes a large fish found in the lake, which the Indians called *chaousarou*, and which grew to the length of eight or ten feet. He saw one five feet long, "as thick as a thigh, with a head as big as two fists, with jaws two feet and a half long and a double set of very sharp and dangerous teeth." "The form of the body," says Champlain, "resembles that of the pike, and it is armed with scales that a thrust of a poniard cannot pierce; and is of a silver gray color. The point of the head is like that of a hog."* This fish made war upon all others in the lake, who fled in terror at its approach. It was probably the *esox longirostris* or the *esox osseus* of Mitchell. The species, of smaller size, still exists in the lake, and is occasionally caught near Isle La Motte..†

A large quantity of pine and oak timber was annually cut on the borders of the lake, which was rafted, through the Richelieu and St. Lawrence, to Quebec, from whence it was shipped to England. The timber trade had furnished employment for the early settlers before the Revolution. After the war, it greatly increased, and, for many years, formed an important traffic for the inhabitants residing on the west side of the lake. The amount of sawed lumber exported at that early day was inconsiderable, for although there were sawmills upon all the principal streams on both sides of the lake, they were generally rude buildings, erected and used solely to supply the wants of their immediate neighborhood.

The commerce of the lake was principally limited to a small export and import trade with Canada. Vermont imported rum, wines, brandy, gin, coarse linens and woolens, tea, coffee, chocolate, and many articles necessary for building. Her exports were grain of all kinds, bar iron, wrought nails, pot and pearl ashes, beef, pork, lumber, peltry, maple sugar and some flax.‡

---

* Voyages de la Nouv. France, 1609.
† See DE KAY's description of the Gar Fish and of the Buffalo Bony Pike, in the Natural History of New York.
‡ Williams' History of Vermont.

The exports on the New York side were lumber, pot and pearl ashes, peltry and iron. Large quantities of grain and provisions were brought from Vermont and Canada, to supply the inhabitants of Clinton and Essex counties, who, from the first, had been allured from the pursuits of agriculture, by the attractions of the lumber trade.

Large tracts of land, lying in Clinton county, were set apart in 1784 and 1786 for Canadian and Nova Scotia refugees, and for such of the inhabitants of the State as had served in the United States Army and were entitled to land bounties, under the act of 1782. These tracts were surveyed and subdivided, and many of the lots were occupied under the State Grants. The greater portion, however, was forfeited for want of actual occupation, and the lands were afterwards patented by the State to other persons. Among those acquiring title by patents was William Bailey, who purchased an extensive tract in the present town of Chateaugay. He moved there in the year 1800, and cleared and cultivated a large farm near the " Four Corners." At an early day he built a forge on the Chateaugay River, near the falls, which he intended to supply with ore from a bed at the south end of the Upper Chateaugay Lake. This bed, when first opened, presented every indication of containing a large supply of ore, but it soon became apparently exhausted, and the forge was abandoned. Mr. Bailey also erected a paper-mill at Chateaugay, which continued in operation for several years. This was the first paper-mill in northern New York.*

* WILLIAM BAILEY was a son of Colonel John Bailey of Dutchess county. At the age of eighteen, he was drafted into the Dutchess county militia, and was sent to join the army at West Point. He first visited Lake Champlain in 1786, and aided in the survey of the lands belonging to Zephaniah Platt and his associates. He was one of the Associate Justices of the Clinton Common Pleas in 1779, and was appointed First Judge of the County in 1806. In 1800, he was appointed First Major in Lt. Col. Benjamin Mooers' regiment of Militia, and was elected a member of the Assembly in 1802, and again in 1806. He removed to Plattsburgh in 1811, where he resided until his death, in the year 1840. About eighty years after the ore bed was abandoned by Judge Bailey, it was re-opened by the Chateau-

Before Mr. Bailey settled in Chateaugay, he was employed by the State to survey the lands set apart for the Canadian and Nova Scotia refugees. At this time the British occupied Point au Fer as a military post, and the commanding officer there refused to allow the surveying party to approach or to continue their survey to the Point. The claim of the British commandant seems to have included all the territory north of the Big Chazy River, for after Judge Pliny Moore settled in Champlain in 1785, he was visited, on the first of each month, by a corporal and file of men, sent from Point au Fer to notify him that his claim of title from the state of New York would not be recognized. No attention was paid to these repeated warnings, which continued until the British gave up possession of Point au Fer, about the year 1788.

I have already had occasion to refer to the conflicting claims set up by various parties, and at different times, to the title and sovereignty of the country bordering on Lake Champlain. The last of these claims had been adjusted in the year preceding the admission of Vermont into the Union. In the year 1792, the Caughnawaga and St. Regis Indians, calling themselves the Seven Nations of Canada, sent a deputation to the Government of the State of New York, claiming a tract of land covering a large portion of the northern part of the State. A commission, consisting of Egbert Benson, Richard Varick and James Watson, was appointed to treat with the Indian Chiefs upon the subject, and in the summer of 1796, an arrangement was effected, by virtue of which the Seven Nations relinquished their claim, with the exception of the St. Regis reservation, for a small sum in hand paid, and a yet smaller perpetual annuity.

As soon as the Seven Nations had completed their negotiations with the State of New York, they advanced a similar claim against Vermont, for lands lying on the east side of Lake Champlain.

gay Iron & Ore Company and proved to be a very large deposit of rich and valuable ore.

The subject was carefully examined by the Legislature of Vermont, but no decision was had until the next year, when the Governor of the State was requested to inform the claimants that the Legislature was of the opinion that their claim, if it ever existed, had long since been done away and become extinct, in consequence of the treaty of Peace, in 1763, between the King of Great Britain and the French King, and the treaty of Peace between the King of Great Britain and the United States, in the year 1783; and that the Indians had now no real claim either in justice or equity. This decision was communicated to the Indians and the subject was dropped, without any further negotiations by either party.

The Caughnawagas resided on the south bank of the St. Lawrence, near the Island of Montreal, in Canada. The St. Regis Indians lived above and upon the same bank of that river. The latter still occupy the lands reserved to them by their agreement with the State, in 1796. These Indians were quiet and peaceable, and endeavored not only to preserve order within their own territory, but to prevent the violation of the laws of New York.

CHAPTER X.

Difficulties between Great Britain and the United States—Henry's Mission to New England—President Madison's Message to Congress —Report of Committee on Foreign Affairs—Declaration of War in June, 1812—Troops ordered to the Champlain Frontier—General Dearborn's " Morning Visit " in Canada—His Army go into Winter Quarters—Affairs at St. Regis—Operations on the Ontario Frontier during the Summer of 1813—British and American Naval force on Lake Champlain—Loss of the Growler and Eagle—Colonel Murray burns the Barracks and Public Buildings at Plattsburgh.

ALTHOUGH Great Britain acknowledged the Independence of the United States by the Treaty of 1783, she could not forget that they had once formed the largest and most important of her colonial possessions. A feeling of dissatisfaction pervaded the British nation, and led to many acts of oppression towards the infant confederacy. Vessels, sailing upon the high seas under the American flag, were boarded by her ships of war; American seamen were impressed; trade with neutral nations was forbidden, and the territory of the United States invaded.

In June, 1807, the British ship of war Leopard fired into and boarded the U. S. Frigate Chesapeake, while the latter vessel was yet within sight of the American coast. Ten days after this attack, Mr. Jefferson issued a proclamation interdicting all intercourse with the British armed vessels then within the waters of the United States. This proclamation was followed, on the 22d of December, of the same year, by an Act of Congress declaring an unlimited embargo on every port in the Union.*

---

* Troops were sent to the northern frontier of New York to aid the customs officers in enforcing the embargo. These troops numbered about 200 men, and consisted of a portion of Capt. Delaney's and Capt. Stephenson's companies of militia, a company of U. S. Infantry under Capt. Brooks, and a company of U. S. Artillery, under Capt. Townsend. The militia was soon mustered out of service, but

During the year 1808, negotiations were conducted between the two countries in a temper that promised a pacific termination of the dispute: but no definite arrangement was concluded. The United States, in the meantime, was making preparations for defense. A large number of gunboats were constructed for the protection of the sea coast, and, in January, 1809, the President was directed to equip four new vessels of war. About the same time, Lieutenant Melancton T. Woolsey was sent north to build two gun-boats on Lake Champlain, and a brig of sixteen guns on Lake Ontario.

When the news of the attack upon the Chesapeake first reached the people, there was a general cry of indignation throughout the country. Politics, however, ran high at the time, and this natural and national sentiment was soon consumed, in many quarters, by the fire of party strife. As the dispute with Great Britain progressed, the opposition of the anti-administration party developed itself more and more against the policy and measures of the Government, until, at length, the authorities of Canada were induced to believe that a portion of the States were anxious to secede from the Union.* To encourage this feeling of discontent, Sir John Craig, Governor of Canada, sent the notorious John Henry as an emissary among the federalists of the New England States, with directions to ascertain how far, in case of their separation from the Union, they "would look to England for assistance or be disposed to enter into a connection with Great Britain."

Mr. Henry reached Burlington on the 12th of February, 1809, and at first was much pleased with the evidences of discontent among the people. "On the

the two companies of regulars were stationed in the county until after the declaration of war with Great Britain; the artillery generally occupying a position on the lake shore, near Rouse's Point, and the infantry at Champlain, or in the vicinity of Plattsburgh.

* This opposition was the most violent in the Eastern States, the inhabitants of which were more commercial, and had suffered more from the effects of the embargo, than those of any other section of the Union.

subject of the embargo laws," he writes Governor Craig, "there seems but one opinion; namely: that they are unnecessary, oppressive and unconstitutional. It must also be observed that the execution of them is so invidious as to attract towards the officers of Government, the enmity of the people, which is of course transferred to the Government itself; so that, in case the State of Massachusetts should take any bold step towards resisting the execution of these laws, it is highly probable that it may calculate upon the hearty cooperation of the people of Vermont." A few days later Mr. Henry expresses some doubts as to the correctness of his first opinions. "The federal party," he again writes Governor Craig, "declare that in the event of war, the State of Vermont will treat separately for itself with Great Britain, and support to the utmost the stipulations in which it may enter, without any regard to the policy of the general Government. The democrats on the other hand assert that, in such a case as that contemplated, the people would be nearly divided into equal numbers; one of which would support the Government, if it could be done without involving the people in a civil war; but at all events would risk everything, in preference to a coalition with Great Britain."

Henry's investigations were not very satisfactory, and before he left for Boston, he evidently became convinced that in the event of a dispute among the States, the citizens of Vermont could not be relied upon to join the seceders, or to unite in a strong opposition to the war. He had at first been led astray by the loud clamor of politicians, and by the complaints of those who had suffered most from the operation of the embargo. These laws had severely injured the commerce of the lake, and had broken up the direct communication with the Canada markets, upon which the inhabitants of the lake counties depended for a sale of their products, and for a supply of foreign commodities.

The country was filled with smugglers, who frequently came in collision with the revenue officers. In some of these encounters blood had been shed and lives lost. The first serious affray occurred on the Winooski River, in 1808, between a party of Government officers and a smuggling vessel called the Black Snake, in which two of the Government officers were killed. Attempts were frequently made to seize the Collectors and Revenue officers, stationed on both sides of the lake. These attempts always failed, but, on one occasion, two of the assailants were severely, although not mortally wounded. The feeling of opposition to the embargo was strong at the time of Henry's visit, in 1809, and induced him to attach greater importance to the representations of a few persons, as to the sentiments of the inhabitants of Western Vermont, than was warranted by the real inclinations of the people themselves. It is well known that when war was declared, the Vermontese were not only ready to repel an invasion of that State, but that many of them volunteered to cross the lake, and oppose the advance of the British into the State of New York

The difficulties between the United States and Great Britan continued to increase, in number and importance, until the year 1812. On the 1st of June of that year, Mr. Madison sent a message to Congress, in which he reviewed the various grounds of complaint against Great Britain, and set forth, at length, the unsatisfactory manner in which that power had received and treated the frequent remonstrances made on the part of the United States. This message was referred to the Committee on Foreign Affairs, who, a few days afterwards, made a report in which they fully concurred in the sentiments expressed in the President's message.

In this report the Committee declare that more than seven years had elapsed, since the commencement of a system of hostile aggressions, by the British Government, on the rights and interests of the United States. That the United States had done everything in their power to preserve the relations of friendship with Great Britain, and had given proof of this disposition at the moment when they were made the victims of an opposite policy. The committee then referred to the attack made by Great Britain upon the commerce between the United States and the Colonies of France and Spain. A commerce which, they declared, was just in itself, sanctioned by the example of Great Britain in regard to the trade with her own colonies ; sanctioned by a solemn act between the two Governments in the last war, and by the practice of the British Government in the then existing European War.

They refer, at length, to the different attacks made by great Britain upon the rights and sovereignty of the United States ; the interference with her neutral trade ; the pretended blockade of the whole coast of Europe, from the Elbe to Brest, inclusive ; the order of Council of January 1807, by which neutral powers were prohibited from trading from one port to another of France, or of her allies, or to any country with which Great Britain might not freely trade ; the order of Council of November of the same year ; the claim of right to search vessels sailing under the American flag; the impressment of American citizens into the British naval service, and the attempt to dismember the Union, by a secret mission to foment discontent and excite insurrection against the constituted authorities and laws of the nation.

Having clearly and plainly stated the facts upon which these charges were based, and reviewed the whole course of Great Britain against the United States, since 1804, the Committee recommended an immediate appeal to arms, and introduced a bill declaring war between the United States and Great Britain. This bill passed the Senate by a vote of nineteen to thirteen, and the House of Representatives by a vote of seventy-nine to forty-nine, and was promulgated by the proclamation of President Madison, on the 17th day of June, 1812.

Active measures were immediately taken by many of the States to second the action of the general government. The State of New York approved warmly of the course of the administration, and prepared to proecute the war with vigor. Vermont was at the time under the control of the democrats, and both the Governor and Legislature pledged themselves to support the country in the approaching contest. A law was immediately passed by the Legislature of the latter State, prohibiting all intercourse with Canada without a permit from the Governor, and measures were taken for calling out the militia whenever their services might. be required.

The effective force in Canada, at the time of the declaration of war, was about ten thousand men. These troops were principally concentrated around Quebec, but the greater part were soon afterwards removed to Upper Canada, which was threatened on the west by an army under General Hull. In the summer of 1812, General Bloomfield was ordered to the Champlain frontier, with several regiments. By the 1st of September, he had about eight thousand men, including regulars, volunteers and militia, under his command. This force was stationed at Plattsburgh, with small advance parties thrown forward as far as Chazy and Champlain. The troops remained in quarters until the 16th of November, when they advanced north, under the immediate command of Major General Dearborn, and, on the 18th, encamped about half a mile south of the Canada line. The army collected at this point numbered three thousand regulars and two thousand militia.

The entire British force on the northern frontier did not exceed three thousand men, and of these not more than one thousand were within striking distance of the American army. When Dearborn had concentrated his troops near the lines, he prepared to cross into Canada. As he approached Odelltown, Major Salaberry, who commanded in that quarter, sent forward two companies of voltigeurs and three hundred Indians to support the two companies of embodied militia, who formed the British outposts on the Lacolle.—Major Salaberry followed, the next day, with the remainder of the voltigeurs and four companies of chasseurs.

Before day-break on the morning of the 20th, a detachment of Dearborn's army forded the Lacolle, and surrounded the guard-house which was occupied by the Canadian militia and a few Indians, who rushed out, broke through the American lines, and escaped unhurt. In the mean time a second party of the Americans had advanced, and commenced a sharp fire upon those in possession of the ground mistaking them for the British picket. This fire continued for nearly half an hour, when being undeceived, the two parties united and hastily retreated, leaving behind them five killed and as many wounded.* The troops immediately afterwards returned to Champlain. The designs of the American General were so completely obscured, that no one discovered the particular advantages intended to be gained by this singular and inefficient movement. It was a prelude to many similar operations on the Champlain frontier, during the war.

On the 23d of September, the army returned to Plattsburgh, where the 6th, 15th, and 16th regiments went into winter quarters. The militia were disbanded; the 9th, 11th, 21st and 25th regiments were sent to Burlington, and the light artillery and dragoons returned to Greenbush. Brigadier-general Chandler commanded the troops left at Burlington, and Colonel Pike those stationed at Plattsburgh. †

On the 23d of October, a gallant affair took place at St. Regis, where Major Young surprised a party of

---

* Christie's History of the War in Canada. Genearal Aarmstrong then U. S. Secretary of War, says this account does not differ materially from those given by the American officers.

† Zebulon Montgomery Pike was born in Lamberton, N. J., January 5, 1789. He joined the army when young, and soon rose to the rank of lieutenant. In August, 1805, he left St. Louis at the head of twenty men to explore the country west of the Mississippi river, and, during his explorations, discovered Pike's Peak, the summit of the Rocky Mountains. On his return he was made successively captain, major; and in 1810, colonel of infantry. In 1813 he was appointed brigadier-general and placed in command of the land forces in the expedition against York. He arrived at York (then the capital of Upper Canada) on the 27th April, 1813, and, after landing and carrying the battery, was mortally wounded from the British magazine.

British and took forty prisoners. But the campaign of 1812 did not add to the lustre of the American Arms On the Champlain frontier, nothing was achieved beyond the little affair at St. Regis. The operations on the Ontario frontier were confined to a few skirmishes, the defence of Fort Niagara, and an unsuccessful and most disastrous assault upon Queenstown; while the incompetent and timid Hull surrendered Detroit and the North western Army, without a battle, or any effort to maintain the honor of the country.

In the course of the winter preparations were made for the invasion of Upper Canada. The two brigades stationed on Lake Champlain, moved for the Ontario frontier in February, leaving a small detachment at Burlington to protect the magazines and provisions collected there. The west side of the lake was left wholly unprotected, and remained so until the month of September following.

During the year 1811 a very active trade had been carried on between the United States and Canada. The value of exports for that year from the District of Champlain, which included the New York side of the lake only, exceeded half a million of dollars, of which four hundred and fifty thousand dollars was of property of American growth and manufacture. Among the articles exported were 1,513 barrels of beef, 2,678 barrels of pork, 70,269 pounds of butter, 53,049 pounds of cheese and more than 2,000 head of cattle. The value of masts, spars, timber and sawed lumber exported exceeded two hundred thousand dollars. The number of clearances from the district between the 10th of April and the 10th of December was one hundred and ninety. Of these, forty-two were rafts and the remainder sail vessels, bateaux and row-boats. A steamboat, called the Vermont, made one trip each week to St. Johns.*

---

* The Vermont was the first steamboat on Lake Champlain. She was built at Burlington, by Winans and Lough, in 1808, commenced running in 1809 and continued in service about six years. She was sunk at Isle aux Noix in October, 1815. The following vessels were

The commencement of hostilities between the United States and Canada broke up the trade with Canada and again put in motion a numerous band of old and experienced smugglers, who resided along the frontier from Lake Memphremagog to the St. Lawrence. The collectors used every precaution to put a stop to the illegal practices of these people, but on more than on one occasion the ingenuity of the smuggler was more than a match for the vigilance of the officers. Small row-boats would elude the revenue cutters in the darkness of the night, and pack-horses, loaded with rich and valuable goods, would frequently escape through the thick woods which bounded the settlement on both sides of the lake. The United States troops stationed on or near the frontier occasionally aided the custom-house officers in the discharge of their arduous duties.

Prior to the commencement of the war, the whole naval force on Lake Champlain consisted of two gunboats, which lay at Basin Harbor, on the Vermont side of the lake. In the course of the summer of 1812, two small sloops were fitted up and armed, to which were joined four scows, carrying one long eighteen pounder each. These vessels constituted the whole naval force of the Americans. The British, at that time, had no vessels on the lake, nor any in the Richelieu larger than gun-boats.

Late in the fall of 1812, Lieutenant Thomas Macdonough* was ordered north to take charge of the naval

cleared at the Champlain custom house in 1811 : Schooner Liberty, Capt. T. Babcock ; Sloops Eagle, S. Boardman ; Euretta, John Boynton ; Jupiter, Justin Smith ; Hunter, N. Hinckley ; Independence, Z. Manning ; Juno, A. Ferris ; Champlain, E. Hurlburt ; Essex, A. Rock ; Rising Sun, Elijah Boynton ; Mars, T. Clark ; Enterprise, E. Bellamy ; Lady Washington, R. Johes ; and Richard, Gideon King.

* Thomas Macdonough was born in Newcastle, County Delaware, December 23d, 1783. He entered the navy as a midshipman in 1800, and served in the Mediterranean under Brainbridge and Decatur. In 1807 he was promoted to the rank of lieutenant, and in 1813 to that of master commandant, and was placed in command of the naval forces on Lake Champlain. For his services on that lake he was made captain. His last command was that of the Mediterranean squadron, where he was taken sick and died November 16, 1825, at sea, on board a vessel sent by Government to bring him home.

operations on the lake, which until then had been confided to Lieutenant Sidney Smith.*

Macdonough brought out his vessels in the spring of 1813, as soon as the lake was free from ice. The American flotilla at this time consisted of the sloop President, fitted up during the winter, which was commanded by Macdonough in person; the sloop Growler, Lieutenant Smith, and the sloop Eagle, Mr. Loomis. About the first of June, Macdonough received information of an attack, by several British gun-boats, upon some small craft at the lower end of the lake. In consequence of this intelligence, he ordered Lieutenant Smith to move towards Rouse's Point, with the Growler and Eagle, in order to attack the gun-boats, should they again make their appearance. Lieutenant Smith left Plattsburgh harbor, with his vessels, on the morning of the 2nd of June, and about dark cast anchor within a mile of the lines. The next morning, about day-break, he got under way, and proceeded down the Richelieu as far as Ash Island, (Isle aux Têtes) where he discovered and gave chase to three British gun-boats. The wind was blowing fresh from the south, at the time, and soon brought the sloops, the Growler leading, within sight of the works at Isle Aux Noix. The sloops now tacked and began to beat back towards the open lake, having the wind against them, with a slight adverse current in the river.

As soon as the British were aware of the advantages these circumstances gave them, three of their row-galleys came out from under the works at Isle Aux Noix, and opened a brisk fire upon the sloops. As the galleys carried long twenty-fours, while the largest

* Mr. Smith was 5th lieutenant on board the Chesapeake at the time of the Leopard's attack upon that vessel, in June, 1807, and, on the return of the Chesapeake to Hampton Roads, joined the other officers of that frigate in a letter to the Secretary of the Navy, preferring charges against Commodore Baron, and requesting a court of inquiry upon his conduct. He afterwards served on board the U. S. ship Wasp, and, in March, 1810, was ordered to Lake Champlain, where he remained in command, until the arrival of Lieutenant Macdonough in the fall of 1812. He married a daughter of Judge Bailey, of Plattsburgh, and died a commander in 1827.

guns on the sloops were eighteens, the former were able to select their own distance, nor could the latter come to close quarters without running within range of the fire of the batteries on the island. To render the situation of the sloops still more critical, the British now lined the woods on each side of the river, and opened upon them with musketry. This fire was returned with constant discharges of grape and canister, and, in this manner, the contest was continued for several hours, with great gallantry on both sides. About four hours after the commencement of the action, a shot from one of the galleys struck the Eagle under her starboard quarter and passed out on the other side, ripping off a plank under water. The sloop went down almost immediately, but fortunately in shoal water, and her crew were taken off by boats sent from the shore ; soon after this accident, the Growler had her fore stay and main boom shot away, when she became unmanageable and ran ashore.

In this engagement the Growler had one killed and eight wounded, and the Eagle eleven wounded, including the pilot, Mr. Graves. The whole number of men on board both vessels when they went into action was one hundred and twelve, including Captain Herrick and thirty-three volunteers from his company. The officers and men were taken prisoners and sent to Canada.* The two sloops, having been refitted, were transferred to the British service, their names being changed to the Finch and Chubb, and were subsequently re-captured by Macdonough in September, 1814. The loss to the British in this engagement was never correctly ascertained. It must have been very severe, however, as their forces advanced to the bank of the river, where, destitute of shelter, they received broadside after broadside of canister and grape. A sergeant of the 11th Regiment, who had volunteered on

---

* A court of inquiry was held at Sackett's Harbor in the summer of 1815 on the loss of the Eagle and Growler, when Lieut. Smith was acquitted and his conduct declared to have been "gallant, correct and meritorious."

board one of the sloops, and who was paroled on account of his wounds, reported that he counted thirty of the enemy dead upon one small spot.*

The capture of the Growler and Eagle gave to the British the superiority on the lake. In July Macdonough increased his naval force, which by the loss of the Growler and Eagle had been reduced to one sloop, by the addition of six gun-boats, and, by the 20th of August, had fitted out and armed three small sloops, mounting together 28 guns. This increased the American force on the lake to about fifty guns. In the official returns in the Admiralty office, it is stated that the British had at Isle Aux Noix or St. John, on the 24th of July, two sloops of eleven guns and forty men each, and three gun-boats of twenty men each. Other accounts state their naval force, in August, at three sloops, four gun-boats and three row-galleys, mounting in all about forty-two guns. The efficacy of this arm was, however, less than the number of guns would seem to indicate, for the sloops, on both sides, were originally built and used in the transport service, and were not adapted to war purposes.

Before the American flotilla had been increased by the addition of the three sloops, a party of British, under Colonel Murray, made a descent upon Plattsburgh, and destroyed or took away a large amount of public and private property. Although this was in fact nothing but a predatory incursion, it was treated by the English at the time as a most glorious achievement, and has been so considered by their historians up to the present day. Mr. Alison, in his history of Europe, a work replete with errors in relation to the military operations on this frontier during the war of 1812, refers to the expedition, and says that " the English flotilla, with nine hundred men on board, stretched across the lake, took Plattsburgh, which was evacuated by twelve hundred Americans, without firing a shot,

---

* The current belief, in the neighborhood of the action, was that the British loss exceeded two hundred, but this was probably an exaggeration.

burned part of the naval stores and brought away the rest, and also destroyed the American naval establishments at Champlain and Burlington.

A greater number of errors could not well be collected in so few words. Alison has overrated the number of Americans at Plattsburgh, diminished the actual strength of the British, and misstated every circumstance connected with the transaction. The force under Colonel Murray was embarked on two war sloops, three gun-boats, and forty-seven long-boats, and numbered over fourteen hundred men, including infantry, sailors and marines. With this force Murray crossed the lines on the 30th of July, passed Champlain, where the Americans had not then, nor ever had, a naval establishment, and on the afternoon of Saturday, the 31st, arrived at Plattsburgh, where he landed, without opposition, and began a work of destruction which continued until ten o'clock of the next day, when he re-embarked and stood out of the Bay. At the time the British landed, there were no regular troops on the west side of the lake. Major-General Hampton, it is true, was at Burlington on the opposite side, twenty miles distant, with between three and four thousand men under his command, but, from some unaccountable cause, he made no attempt to cross the lake or to protect the village of Plattsburgh, although he had twenty-four hour's notice of the intended attack.* While the British were at Plattsburgh, about three hundred militia were hastily collected, but they did not approach the village until after the enemy had retired.

When Colonel Murray first entered the village, he assured the civil authorities that private property should

---

* " I could not persuade myself that the American force stationed at Burlington of 4000 effective men, within twenty miles of this place, could be suffered to remain idle spectators of the destruction of the public property and of this village by comparatively a very small British force. Messengers were repeatedly sent to General Hampton with a request that one regiment might be sent here, but to no effect. It is a fact that from the Canada line to the south end of Lake Champlain, on the west side, there is not a military post nor a soldier to be seen."—*Peter Sailly to the Secretary of the Treasury*, August 4, 1813.

be respected, and that citizens, not in arms, should remain unmolested. These promises were, however, most shamefully violated, for the British, not satisfied with destroying the block-house, arsenal, armory and hospital in the village, and the military cantonment near Fredenburgh Falls, two miles above, wantonly burned three private store-houses, took possession of about two thousand dollars' worth of hardware, belonging to merchants of the city of Boston, and plundered several private dwellings, destroying furniture and such articles as they could not use or carry away. The value of the private property plundered exceeded eight thousand dollars. Inventories of this property were prepared and published at the time, and include long lists of furniture, books, clothing, cooking utensils, groceries and dry goods. Soldiers would break into private dwellings and bear off back loads of property to the boats, in the presence of British officers, who, when remonstrated with by the plundered citizens, replied that they could not prevent it, as the men did not belong to their company.* The value of the public property destroyed was estimated at twenty-five thousand dollars.

Colonel Murray, having accomplished the work of destruction, retired in great haste, leaving behind him a picket-guard of twenty-one men, who were made prisoners and sent to Burlington. The long-boats and two of the gun-boats then proceeded to Swanton, Vt., where the men burned some old barracks, and plundered several citizens of the place. On their way, they landed at Cumberland Head and Point Au Roche, and pillaged the houses and farms of Henry W. Brand, Judge Treadwell and Jeremiah Stowe. They also burned a store at Chazy Landing belonging to Judge Saxe. The two sloops and the other gun-boat, after leaving Plattsburgh, stood for the south and sailed ten

---

* It appears by the inventories of plundered property, published at the time, that Judge De Lord lost $1079.18 ; Peter Sailly, Esq., $887.77 ; besides two store-houses burned and valued at $900 ; Judge Palmer, $386.50 ; Doctor Miller, $1200 ; Bostwick Buck, $150 ; Jacob Ferris, $700 ; several smaller amounts were lost by other citizens. A store-house belonging to Major Platt was also burned at the time.

or twelve miles above Burlington, when they returned towards Canada. As the vessels passed Burlington they fired a few shots at the place, but bore away as soon as the batteries on shore began to play upon them. While on the lake, the British took or destroyed eight or ten long-boats engaged in the transportation business, and captured a Durham boat loaded with flour.

While Colonel Murray was at Plattsburgh he dropped a letter from his hat, which was afterwards picked up, and found to contain information as to the best mode of attack on Plattsburgh, together with a map of the encampment and military works at Burlington. A few days afterwards the person who wrote the letter was arrested on a charge of high treason, and sent to Albany for safe-keeping.

CHAPTER XI.

Plan of the Campaign of 1813—Hampton at Lacolle and Chateaugay—
Colonel Clark at Missisquoi Bay—Skirmishes—Operations on the
Lake—Dispute between the Vermont volunteers and Governor Chit-
tenden—Failure of the Campaign of 1813—Battle of Lacolle Mill—
British attack the works near Otter Creek—Operations during the
summer—Death of Colonel Forsyth—Izard ordered to the West—
Condition of Affairs after his departure.

IN July 1813, Major-general James Wilkinson assumed the command of the Northern Department.
About the same time, the American Secretary of War,
Mr. Armstrong, repaired to Sackett's Harbor to super-
vise the military operations on the Ontario frontier.
The plan of the Secretary contemplated " a descent
upon Kingston, and a subsequent movement down the
St. Lawrence." A large force was also collected at
Burlington, on Lake Champlain, which was placed
under the immediate command of Major-general Hampton.

About the 1st of September, Hampton was directed
to move towards the British posts on the Richelieu, in
order to create a diversion in favor of the Western
Army, and to co-operate, if necessary, with Wilkinson
in an attack upon Montreal. The American troops,
numbering about four thousand men, were immediately
concentrated at Cumberland Head, where they were
joined by a body of New York Militia, who had been
called into service by Governor Tompkins. On the
19th, the infantry and light troops moved from Cumberland Head in boats, flanked on the right by Macdonough's flotilla, and at twelve o'clock at night reached
Chazy Landing. The next morning they entered the
Big Chazy river, and disembarked at the foot of the
rapids, near the village of Champlain, where they were

joined by a squadron of horse and two companies of
artillery. The same day the army moved north as far
as Odelltown, in Canada. Hampton remained one day
in Canada, when learning that the springs and streams,
in the direction of the St. Lawrence, had been dried up
by an unusual drought, he determined to change his
route and to approach Montreal by the way of the
Chateaugay.

On the 21st, the army returned to Champlain, and
on the evening of the 24th, reached Chateaugay Four
Corners, where they remained inactive for twenty-six
days. On the 16th of October, Mr. Armstrong was
at Sackett's Harbor, debating whether he should attack
Kingston, or make an immediate descent upon Montreal. Hampton was ordered to advance to the mouth
of the Chateaugay River, or to some other convenient
point on the St. Lawrence, from which an easy and
direct communication could be opened betwen the two
armies. In pursuance of this order, he entered Canada
on the 21st, and the next day encamped on the Chateaugay, at a point about twenty miles below the Four
Corners.—There he remained until the 20th, when he
planned an expedition against a small body of British
troops, who were stationed about six miles below. The
expedition failed, and Hampton returned to the Four
Corners, with a loss of thirty-five men, in killed and
wounded. A few days afterwards be broke up his
camp and returned to Plattsburgh, where the army
was ordered into winter quarters.

While the army lay at Chateaugay, Colonel Isaac
Clark,* who commanded a detachment of troops stationed at Champlain Village, was ordered to " commence a petty war near Lake Champlain." " What
I am aiming at," writes Hampton, "is tranquillity on
the road, by kicking up a dust on the lines."† A better officer than Clark, to accomplish this object, could

---

* Colonel Clark served in the Revolutionary war. He was a lieutenant in Captain Ebenezer Allen's company, and took part in the sur
prise of Mount Defiance, in September, 1777.
† Letter to Secretary of War, October 4th, 1813.

not have been selected.   He had served with Herrick's
Rangers in the Revolution, and was well skilled in
border warfare.

On the evening of the 11th of October, Clark crossed
the lake with one hundred and ten men, a part of whom
belonged to the Rifle corps, and early the next morning reached the village of Missisco Bay, where a small
party of British were stationed, under command of
Major Powell.   Clark placed himself at the head of the
Rifles, and advanced at double quick time until he met
the main body of the enemy, who had been hastily
drawn up near the guard-house.   Directing his men to
halt, he approached the British and ordered them to
lay down their arms.   Major Powell advanced and
attempted to speak, but Clark sternly ordered him to
remain silent, and march "to the rear of the American
line."   The boldness of the order, and the confident
tone in which it was given, induced the Major to
believe that the Rifles were supported by a large force,
and he instantly obeyed.   Clark ordered his men to
advance against the main body, who, under command
of their captain, was preparing to charge.   A volley
from the Riflemen struck down the captain and several
men, when the rest threw down their arms and surrendered themselves as prisoners of war.   Captain
Finch was now sent forward to watch a force of two
hundred British, who were advancing under Colonel
Lock.   Finch proceeded with such promptness and
secrecy, as to surprise an advance guard of cavalry,
except one man who escaped and gave information of
the approach of the Americans, when Colonel Lock
immediately retreated with the rest of his command.
The loss to the British, in these attacks, was nine killed
and fourteen wounded.   One hundred and one prisoners were taken by Clark and sent to Burlington.

During the autumn of this year, a slight skirmishing
war was carried on between the American and British
picket-guards, which kept the frontier 'in a state of
excitement and alarm, without, however, doing much
injury to either party.   Upon one occasion, about the

1st of October, a small party of New York militia crossed the lines and attacked a picket-guard stationed at Odletown, within the district under command of Major Perreault of the Canadian detached Volunteers. The audacity of this act excited the ire of the Canadian officer, who, in retaliation, discharged a gasconade at the whole town of Champlain.

"Citizens of Champlain!" exclaimed the indignant Major, "I am happy that humanity should still have so much power over me as to inform you that, should any of the militia of Champlain be found hovering this side of the line, I will let loose upon your village and inhabitants the Canadian and Indian force under my command. You are probably aware that it has been with the greatest difficulty I have till now withheld them. But your cowardly attack at midnight, of a small picket of our's, has torn asunder the veil which hid you from them—*so beware!*" This message was enclosed in a note to Judge Moore, with a request that he would acquaint the people with "the tenor of the humane advertisement." Judge Moore performed his duty, but the militia were obdurate.

As soon as the army had retired into winter quarters, Hampton repaired to Washington, leaving General Izard in command at Plattsburgh, and General Parker at Burlington. Izard was soon afterwards ordered to join Wilkinson, who, on Hampton's return to Plattsburgh had gone into winter quarters at French Mills. On the departure of Izard's brigade, the frontier on the western side of the lake was again left unprotected. About the middle of December, a strong detachment of British troops, under command of Captain Barker of the frontier light infantry, crossed the lines into Vermont and destroyed some public store-houses and barracks which had been erected at Derby. This attack, and the threatening movements of the British forces stationed along the Richelieu, induced the magistrates of Plattsburgh to address a letter to General Wilkinson, who was then at French Mills, in which they represented the exposed condition of the public property and their apprehension that another invasion might soon be expected, unless a strong force was stationed on the west side of the lake. As soon as Wilkinson received this letter, he ordered a company of dragoons to Plattsburgh from Burlington and a detachment of infantry from Chateaugay Four Corners.—The infantry reached Plattsburgh on the 8th of January, having made a forced march of forty miles that day. Other detachments of troops soon afterwards arrived, and on the 10th Wilkinson repaired to Plattsburgh in person. The camp at French Mills was broken up, and all the magazines and provisions forwarded to Lake Champlain.

The operations on the lake, during the autumn of 1813, were of little importance. The British flotilla remained in the Richelieu, while the American vessels rode quietly at anchor on the lake. About the 1st of December Macdonough moved to King's Bay and anchored under Point Au Fer. A few days after his arrival at that place, Captain Pring entered the lake with six armed galleys, landed at Rouse's Point, and burned a small shed there, which had been used as a public store-house. As soon as Macdonough received information of the approach of the British galleys, he weighed anchor, and it being calm at the time, attempted to work out of the bay with sweeps. At the same time he sent Lieutenant Cassin forward, with four row-galleys, with orders to bring the enemy into action, and thus detain them until the sloops could get up. The British, however, refused to engage, and, Lieutenant Cassin returned after an unavailing pursuit of three miles.*

Sir George Provost gives a different and erroneous account of this trifling affair. In a letter to Earl Bathurst, under date of December 12th, he says "A division of gun-boats with a detachment of troops, which I had ordered, on the 1st of the month, to advance into Lake Champlain, for the purpose of molesting General Hampton's division, succeeded in burning an extensive building lately erected at Plattsburgh, as a depot maga-

* Macdonough to Secretary of Navy, December 5th, 1813.

zine ; some bateaux together with the ammunition, provisions and stores found in it, were either brought
away or destroyed.   The severity of the weather obliged
Captain Pring, of the royal navy, under whose command
I had placed the expedition, to return to Isle Aux Noix
on the 5th.   " Sir George was evidently misinformed as
to the facts, by the officer in command of the expedition
   The " extensive building lately erected at Plattsburgh
as a depot magazine," was a small shed near the lake
shore at Champlain landing, which *had formerly been* in
public use, and the smoke from which gave the first information to Macdonough of the enemy's approach.   A
few days after this affair, the ice blocked up the narrow
channel below Rouse's Point, when Macdonough withdrew his vessels, and laid them up for the winter in
Otter Creek.

   In November of this year, a dispute arose between
Governor Chittenden of Vermont and some of the citizens of that State, involving the right of the militia,
in certain cases, to pass without the territorial limits
of their own State.—The Governor, in his annual
message, had taken strong grounds against the war,
which he considered " doubtful as to its necessity, ex-
pediency or justice."   He also declared that the militia
were exclusively assigned for the service and protection
of the respective States, except in the cases provided
for by the National Constitution.—That it was never
intended that they should, " by any kind of magic," be
at once transformed into a regular army for the purpose
of foreign conquest, and he regretted that a construction
should have been given to the Constitution, " so
peculiarly burdensome and oppressive to that important
class of our fellow citizens."

   In opposition to these friendly suggestions, a portion
of the militia, under Lieutenant-colonel Luther Dixon,
crossed the lake and placed themselves under the orders
of General Hampton.   This movement called forth a
proclamation from the Governor, in which he ordered
the militia to return, and hold themselves in readiness
to act under the orders of Brigadier-General Davis,

who had been appointed to the command of their brigade. " The military strength and resources of the State," says Governor Chittenden, " must be reserved for its own defence and protection, *exclusively*, except in cases provided for by the Constitution of the United States, and then under orders derived *only* from the Commander-in-Chief."

This proclamation was distributed among the volunteers, who were then stationed at Plattsburgh, and created great excitement with both the officers and men. The agent, by whom it had been circulated, was arrested and held to bail, in a large amount, for his appearance before the United States District Court. The officers also published a reply to the proclamation, in which, in very plain terms, they informed the Governor that they should not obey his orders, but should remain in service until regularly discharged. In this reply they say ; " If it is true, as your Excellency states, that we are out of the jurisdiction or control of the Executive of Vermont, we would ask from whence your Excellency derives the right, or presumes to exercise the power of ordering us to return from the service in which we are engaged ? If we are legally ordered into the service of the United States, your Excellency must be sensible that you have no authority to order us out of that service. If we are illegally ordered into the service, our continuance in it is either voluntary or compulsory. If voluntary, it gives no one a right to remonstrate or complain ; if compulsory, we can appeal to the laws of our country for redress against those who illegally restrain us of our liberty. In either case we cannot perceive the right your Excellency has to interfere in the business."

This was pretty sharp firing, and effectually silenced the Governor's batteries. The brigade remained at Plattsburgh, until it became known that the contemplated invasion of Canada had been abandoned for the winter, when the volunteers returned to Vermont, and probably put themselves " under the command of Brigadier-general Davis."

The campaign of 1813 was directed towards the important military posts on Lake Ontario and the St. Lawrence river. It commenced with bright prospects of success, but failed through the imbecility of the officers who had been called to the head of the army. The people were deeply disappointed at the result. They had placed great confidence in their commanding Generals, whose numerous dispatches were written in lofty style, and were filled with predictions of most brilliant victories. " I am destined to and determined on the attack of Montreal, if not prevented by some act of God," 'cries Wilkinson, on the 6th of November, from the head of an army of 8000 men.* " The Rubicon is now passed, and all that remains is to push forward to the Capitol," is the bold declaration of Hampton.† Vain and empty boasting. Two weeks later, the one was quietly settled at Plattsburgh, and the other was building winter quarters at French Mills and Chateaugay.

The campaign of 1813 is closed. General Wilkinson attributed its failure to the refusal of Hampton to join him at St. Regis, on the St. Lawrence. He declared that by a junction of the two armies he could have secured Montreal in eight or ten days. " It is a fact," he writes the Secretary of War, " for which I am authorized to pledge myself on the most confidential authority, that on the 4th of the present month [November,] the British garrison of Montreal consisted solely of four hundred marines and two hundred sailors, which had been sent up from Quebec. What a golden, glorious opportunity has been lost by the caprice of Major General Hampton."‡

General Hampton, on the contrary, censured Wilkinson for desiring a junction of the two armies, with the scanty supply of provisions within reach of St. Regis. He contended that to have moved forward, with the

---

* Letter to General Hampton.
† Letter to Secretary of War, Nov. 12.
‡ A " glorious opportunity " indeed, for two large armies to capture six hundred men !

4000 troops under his command, would have seriously weakened, if it did not destroy both armies. That his true course was to throw himself upon his main depots at Plattsburgh, and from that point to open a communication direct to Caughnawaga ; which would relieve the western army, and at the same time retain all the benefits to be expected from a junction at St. Regis.*

In December General Hampton was withdrawn from the frontier, but General Wilkinson retained his command until after the unsuccessful attack upon a gristmill in Lacolle, when he too was ordered to Head Quarters. The assault on the Lacolle mill was made on the 30th of March, 1814. About the first of that month Major Forsyth had been sent to the lines, near Champlain, with 300 Riflemen and 60 Dragoons to protect the frontier, and to break up an illicit intercourse which had been carried on with the enemy during the winter. Detachments had also been sent to the Vermont frontier, under command of General Macomb and Colonel Clark, for a similar purpose. About the same time General Wilkinson examined the country around Rouse's Point, with a view to the erection of batteries there, which should command the outlet of the lake, and blockade the British flotilla within the Richelieu.

These movements alarmed the British, who hastened to strengthen their military posts in the vicinity of Rouse's Point. Major Hancock, of the 13th, occupied Lacolle with six hundred men, and the forts at St Johns and Isle Aux Noix were garrisoned by about two thousand men, under command of Lieutenant-colonel Williams of the same regiment. When Wilkinson learned that the British force near the lines had been increased, he ordered the troops stationed at Plattsburgh to be advanced to Champlain, where he also directed Macomb and Clark to concentrate their respective

*About one month prior to this time, Hampton attempted this very route, and backed out before he had penetrated four miles into Canada. Referring to the dispatches of the two northern Commanders, Mr. Niles, in his Register, exclaims. " The *cacoethes scribendi* again rages with singular violence in the army. with symptoms fatal to gallons of ink and hundreds of goose quills! "

commands. On the 29th of March, four thousand men were collected at Champlain, of whom 100 were cavalry and 304 artillerists. The latter had with them eleven pieces of cannon of small calibre. Wilkinson now planned an attack against Major Hancock, who occupied a grist-mill on the banks of the Lacolle river, about five miles north of the lines.

On the morning of the 30th, the American army marched out of Champlain, upon the Odelltown road. The advance guard was composed of the Rifles under Major Forsyth, and the 30th and 31st and part of the 11th infantry, under Colonel Clark ; in all about 600 men. They were followed by two corps of infantry, under Brigadier-generals Bissell and Smith. A reserve of 800 men under General Macomb, brought up the rear. The roads at this time were obstructed by fallen trees and by heavy drifts of snow, and were nearly impassable for artillery. The guides, too, were ignorant of the country, and led the army off from the main road into a very narrow and crooked winter path, leading from Odelltown to Lacolle. On the way to Lacolle, Bissell's corps was attacked by and after a short skirmish repulsed a party of Canadian militia, who had been stationed as a picket on the main road at Odelltown.

The Lacolle mill, against which the Americans were now advancing, was a strong stone building. The walls had been braced on the inside with heavy timbers, the windows closed up and port holes made in every direction, for the fire of musketry, A small clearing, of from one to two hundred yards in width on each side of the river, surrounded the mill. The woods adjacent were of small growth but very thick. The river, at the mill was frozen over, but below it was open to its mouth. The Richelieu was also open from the mouth of the Lacolle to Isle Aux Noix,

The American troops did not reach the ground until between one and two o'clock in the afternoon, when a portion of Bissell's brigade took a position to the south of the building and commenced the attack, which, for the first half-hour, was confined to a fire of musketry.

Major McPherson then brought up a twelve-pounder, which he planted about two hundred and fifty yards to the south of the mill. With this gun a brisk but ineffectual fire was directed against the rear of the building, and afterwards against the side wall.

When it was ascertained that the gun was too light to break down the walls, orders were given to bring up an eighteen pounder, but its carriage had broken down, three miles back, and could not be repaired in time to be of service during the day. The cannonade upon the mill was returned by a brisk discharge of musketry, which was kept up during the whole attack, but did little damage, as the American troops were posted out of range of the fire. In the course of the afternoon, an unsuccessful assault was made upon a detachment of Americans who guarded the north banks of the Lacolle, by two companies of the 13th regiment, sent from Isle Aux Noix to reinforce the garrison in the mill. While these companies were engaged a sortie was made against the centre of the American line. The attack was executed with great gallantry but did not succeed, although the artillery were driven from the gun, which would have been captured, had not a portion of General Bissell's brigade been sent to its rescue. A short time afterwards, another attack was made upon the gun by a grenadier company of the Canadian Fencibles and a company of voltigeurs, who had followed the movement of the troops from the Odelltown road. This attack was also unsuccessful. The two companies, however, succeded in gaining a block house which stood below the mill. The loss of the Americans in these attacks was 104 killed and wounded, while that of the British was reported by them at 10 killed and 46 wounded. Among the wounded on the side of the Americans were Captain McPherson and Lieutenant Larabee of the Artillery ; Lieutenants Green and Parker of the Infantry and Lieutenant Kerr of the Rifles. Lieutenant Parker was struck by a random shot. He survived his wounds for several days, and expressed a most sincere regret that he had

not fallen in close action: " Hard is my lot," he exclaimed, " that I should have received this wound at
such a distance from the enemy, and where I was
wholly inactive." Captain McPherson, on the contrary,
was wounded while fighting at the head of his men,
and, at the time, was not expected to recover. As
they were bearing him from the field, several officers
offered their personal services to carry him to Plattsburgh. The gallant captain paused a few moments
and then, thanking them for the interest and regard
they had manifested, added, " I shall be sufficiently honored when you bear me to my grave." The same spirit of
firmness was shown by the other officers, and by the
wounded and bleeding privates. Lieut. Larabee, when
some persons were pitying his misfortune, as he was
passing to the rear of the field, exclaimed, " Have you
never seen a man die!" A private, on receiving similar sympathy, cried, " never mind it, I'll give them
another fight." Another private, when struck down,
cried out, " Give it to them, my boys, never flinch."

At the commencement of the assault a few cannon
shots and several rockets were fired from a sloop, and
from some gun-boats lying in the river below, but the
fire was not continued, as it was soon ascertained
that the American troops were perfectly protected by
the intervening ground.* About sundown Wilkinson
called in the detachments which had been sent to the
north side of the river, and shortly afterwards retired
with the whole army to Odelltown. The next day he
returned to Champlain. From this place General
Macomb was sent to Burlington, while the main army
fell back upon Chazy and Plattsburgh, to protect the
military stores at the latter place.†

---

* Late in the day Lieutenant Creswick, of the Royal Navy, succeeded in landing two field pieces and getting them to the block-
house, but they were not fired during the engagement.

† This account of the affair at Lacolle is derived from the testi-
mony of Bissell, Macomb, Clark, Totten, McPherson and others before
the Court-martial, on the trial of General Wilkinson, in January,
1815, and from the official report of Adjutant-general Baynes of the
British army.

On the 9th of May, Captain Pring of the British navy ascended the Richelieu in the brig Linnet, accompanied by five sloops and thirteen row-galleys, and the next day came to anchor under Providence Island,* where he remained until the evening of the 13th. Macdonough was at this time at Vergennes, on Otter Creek, busily engaged in fitting out the American fleet, which lay at that place. As soon as he was informed that the British flotilla had entered the lake, he ordered Lieutenant Cassin, with a small party of sailors, to reinforce Captain Thornton, who had been sent from Burlington with a detachment of light artillery to man a battery which had been erected at the mouth of Otter Creek. A brigade of the Vermont Militia were also ordered out, and were advantageously posted to oppose the enemy, in case he should attempt to land.

At day-break on the morning of the 14th, eight of the British galleys and a bomb sloop anchored off the mouth of Otter Creek and commenced a warm fire upon the battery, which was promptly returned. A brisk cannonade was kept up by both parties for one hour and a half, when the attack was abandoned.

After this repulse the galleys entered the Bouquet River, and ascended that stream for the purpose of seizing some Government flour, which had been deposited in the grist-mill at the Falls. On their return, the boats were fired into by a company of militia who had hastily collected on the south bank of the river near its mouth. This fire killed or wounded nearly all the men in the rear galley. The boat afterwards drifted into the lake, and was towed off by small boats sent to its assistance. The galleys then joined the brig and the three sloops, which, during the attack on the battery, had remained at anchor near the "Four-Brothers. On the 16th Captain Pring returned to Isle Aux Noix. A few days afterwards Macdonough

---

* This is one of the small islands lying near the south end of Grand Island, opposite Valcour.

brought his fleet out of Otter Creek, and on the 29th cast anchor in Cumberland Bay, off Plattsburgh.

During the summer, the British and Americans were actively engaged in strengthening their positions along the Champlain frontier. Large reinforcements joined the army at Plattsburgh, while the garrisons at Chambly, St. Johns and Isle Aux Noix were increased by detachments of troops drawn from Montreal and Quebec. Major General Izard,* who had succeeded to the command on the withdrawal of Wilkinson, was directed to erect a heavy battery at Rouse's Point, to guard the entrance from the Richelieu into the lake. Considering the occupation of that point hazardous, from its proximity to the enemy's posts at Lacolle and Isle Aux Noix, he objected to erecting works there, and instead, caused a battery of four eighteen pounders and a large redoubt to be constructed on Cumberland Head.†

On the 11th of June, a light brigade, under command of General Smith, Forsyth's regiment of Riflemen, and two companies of Artillery were encamped near the mouth of Dead Creek, about two miles north of the village of Plattsburgh. These troops advanced as far as Chazy on the 17th, and on the 27th occupied the village of Champlain. Smith's brigade was 1400 strong. At the latter date, Colonel Pierce, of the 13th Regiment, was at Chazy with 800 men, and about 1200 men occupied the works on Cumberland Head, at Dead Creek and in the village of Plattsburgh. Macdonough's fleet lay at anchor in King's Bay. The British then held Lacolle with a force of 3600 men. They also had strong garrisons at Isle Aux Noix and St. Johns. Muron's regiment, 1000 strong, was at L'Acadie, two brigades of

* George Izard was born in South Carolina. In 1794 he was appointed lieutenant of artillery and had charge of the fortification in Charleston harbor in 1798. He was appointed colonel of artillery in March, 1812 ; was made a brigadier-general in 1813, and a major-general in 1814. He was Governor of the Territory of Arkansas from 1825 until his death in 1828.

† The works on Cumberland Head were commenced in opposition to the views of Colonel Totten, who considered they would not impede or materially injure a passing fleet. They proved useless, and were abandoned on the first approach of the British.

artillery and 300 cavalry at Chambly, and 2000 regulars at Montreal. Their fleet lay at Isle Aux Tetes.

On the 24th of June, Lieutenant Colonel Forsyth, with 70 of his Riflemen, penetrated into Canada, as far as Odelltown, where he was attacked by a detachment of two hundred British light troops. Forsyth returned to Champlain, with the loss of one killed and five wounded. A few days afterwards, he was ordered again to enter Canada, for the purpose of drawing the British across the lines, into an ambuscade. He advanced a few men on the main road leading to Odelltown, who soon met a party of the enemy, when they retreated, closely pursued by about one hundred and fifty Canadians and Indians, under command of Captain Mahew, until they reached a point about half a mile south of the lines, where the main body of the Rifles lay concealed. As the enemy approached the ambuscade, Colonel Forsyth stepped upon a log to watch their movements. He had scarcely taken this exposed position, when he was shot down by an Indian; the ball passing through his breast. The Rifles immediately uncovered and fired upon the enemy, who retreated in great haste, leaving seventeen of their number dead upon the field.*

A few days afterwards, Captain Nelson, of the 10th Infantry, crossed into Canada with a small detachment surprised a British picket in Odelltown, took some of them prisoners and put the rest to flight. Skirmishes were very frequent along the borders, during the months of July and August, although seldom attended with any considerable loss to either side.

On the 31st of July, Macomb's brigade, consisting of the 6th, 13th, 15th, 16th and 29th regiments, set out in boats from Cumberland Head for Chazy Landing. The same day Bissell's brigade, of the 5th, 14th, 30th, 31st,

---

* Forsyth was the best partisan officer in the army. His men declared that they would avenge his death, and a few days after crossed the lines and shot Captain Mahew, who commanded the Canadians and Indians at the time of Forsyth's death. Captain Mahew was taken to the residence of Judge Moore in Champlain, where he lingered about a week and died.

33d, 34th and 45th regiments, started for Chazy by land. This movement placed three brigades, in all 4,500 strong, at and in rear of the village of Champlain. The invalids and 200 effectives of Macomb's brigade were left behind to finish the works at Cumberland Head, and a working party of about 400 strong, of Bissell's brigade, was left at Plattsburgh under Colonel Fenwick, to complete three redoubts which had been commenced near that village.

In the month of August, Sir George Provost repaired to the Isle Aux Noix, where he had concentrated a large body of men, including several veteran regiments who had lately distinguished themselves on the banks of the Adour and the Garonne. Everything now indicated that a battle was soon to be fought on the Champlain frontier, which would decide the fate of the campaign and the control of the whole country bordering on the lake. It was at this moment that the Government determined to remove the troops from Lake Champlain, and to abandon the large amount of military stores and provisions collected at Plattsburgh, the lives and property of its citizens, and the great military key of the northern and eastern States, to the protection of a few raw, worn-out, sick or disabled men. This strange movement evinced a reckless indifference on the part of the Government as to the result of the war in this quarter.*

General Izard strongly protested against the removal of the troops, and repeatedly represented to the war department the fatal results that might be expected

---

* It has been asserted, in certain quarters, that the authorities at Washington never intended a real invasion of Canada, for fear that the reduction of Montreal and other important points upon the St. Lawrence might ultimately lead to annexation, and to a consequent increase of political power, north of Mason s and Dixon's line. While old and superannuated Generals commanded on this frontier, they were allowed, *ad libitum*, to lead their armies to and fro along the outskirts of Canada, but the moment a fighting man, with the regular snap of war in him, was found to be in command, the army was broken up and its best fragments sent to aid in some distant operations, where the most triumphant success could not endanger the cities of Montreal and Quebec, which were justly considered as the keys of the British Provinces.

from such a movement. As late as the 20th of August, he writes the Secretary of War as follows: "I must not be responsible for the consequences of abandoning my present strong position. I will obey orders and execute them as well as I know how. Major-General Brisbane commands at Odelltown; he is said to have between five and six thousand men with him. Those at Chambly are stated to be about four thousand." On the 23d he again writes that he has decided to move west, by way of Lake George and Schenectady, with 4,000 men, leaving the sick and convalescents and about 1,200 men to garrison Plattsburgh and Cumberland Head, under command of Brigadier-general Macomb.*

Receiving no counter orders, Izard, on the 29th of August, left Champlain and Chazy with the 4th, 5th, 10th, 12th, 13th, 14th, 15th, 16th and 45th Infantry, the light artillery armed as infantry, and the dragoons, and slowly and reluctantly moved towards the west. On the 3d of September his corps reached Lake George, where they remained two days, anxiously expecting orders to return to Plattsburgh. No such orders arrived, and Izard again put his column in motion. On the 7th he reached Schenectady, from which place he urged on more rapidly towards the west.

As soon as Izard left, General Macomb concentrated his whole force at Plattsburgh, where he commenced immediate preparations to resist an attack. From the returns of the 28th of August it appears that on that day he had the following troops within the limits of his command:

* Alexander Macomb was born in Detroit, Michigan, April 13, 1782. He entered the army as a cornet of cavalry in 1799, and at the commencement of the war of 1812 held the rank of lieutenant-colonel of engineers and adjutant-general of the army. In 1813, at his own request, he was appointed colonel of the 3rd regiment of artillery, and in January, 1814, placed in command of the Lake Champlain frontier. For his firmness and courage at the battle of Plattsburgh he was commissioned a major-general. On the disbandment of the army he was retained in the service as colonel of engineers, and, on the death of Major General Brown in 1835, succeeded to the office of commander-in-chief of the army. He died at Washington, June 25, 1841.

Detachments of the regiments and corps that
marched   77
Capt. Leonard's company of Light Artillery. .   100
Capt. McGlassin's company, 15th Regt. . . .   50
The 6th, 29th, 30th, 31st, 33d and 34th regi-
ments, reported from the aggregate present
on the 31st July   1771
Capt. Sproul's detachment of 13th Regt. . .   200
Sick and invalids of the regiments and corps
that left   803

Aggregate   3001

There were two veteran companies of artillery under
Captain Alexander Brooks, which were omitted in the
return.   Two hundred and fifty infantry were also on
board the fleet, doing duty as marines.   This brought
the whole force to about 3400 men, of whom over 1400
were invalids or non combatants.*   With this force
Macomb prepared to resist the advance of fourteen
thousand veteran British soldiers.

---

* General Macomb in his detailed report of the battle of Plattsburgh says, " Except the four companies of the 6th regiment I had
not an organized battalion among those remaining; the garrison was
composed of convalescents and the recruits of the new regiments—
all in the greatest confusion, as well as the ordinance and stores; and
the works in no state of defense."

CHAPTER XII.

Sir George Provost invades the United States—Preparations at Plattsburgh to resist his advance—Description of the American Forts, etc. The British encamp at Chazy—Battle of Beekmantown—Provost's position on the north banks of the Saranac—Captain McGlassin attacks a British battery—American and British force on the lake—Naval engagement off Plattsburgh—Battle of Plattsburgh—Provost retreats to Canada—The Peace.

GENERAL IZARD abandoned the camp at Champlain on the 29th of August, and the next day Major-general Brisbane advanced his division from Odelltown to that place. On the 3d of September, fourteen thousand British troops were collected at Champlain. This force was composed of four troops of the 19th light dragoons, 300 men; two companies Royal Artillery, 400 men; one brigade of rocketeers, twenty-five men; one brigade Royal Sappers and Miners, seventy-five men; the first brigade of infantry, consisting of the first battalion of the 27th regiment, the 58th and 5th, and the 3rd or Buffs, in all 3,700 men, under command of Major-general Robinson; the second brigade, formed by the 88th and 39th, and the 3d battalions of the 27th and 76th, in all 3,600 men, under Major-general Powers; the third brigade, composed of the second battalion of the 8th or King's, and the 18th, 49th and 6th, 3,100 men, under Major-general Brisbane. There was also a light brigade 2,800 strong, composed of Muron's Swiss regiment; the Canadian Chasseurs, the Voltigeurs and the frontier light infantry. The whole was under Sir George Provost, Governor-general of Canada; Lieutenant-general De Rottenburgh being second in command.

On the 4th, the main body reached Chazy village, and the next night, encamped near Sampson's about eight miles from the village of Plattsburgh. At the same time Captain Pring, with a number of gun-boats, moved up the lake as far as Isle La Motte, and erected a battery of three long 18 pounders on the west side of that island, to cover the landing of the supplies for the troops.

Brigadier-general Macomb was now at Plattsburgh actively engaged in preparations to resist the expected attack. On the 3d of September, he issued a general order detailing his plan of defence. " The troops (says this order) will line the parapet in two ranks, leaving intervals for the artillery. A reserve of one fifth of the whole force in infantry, will be detailed and paraded fronting the several angles, which it will be their particular duty to sustain. To each bastion are to be assigned, by the several commanders of forts, a sufficient number of infantry to line all the faces (in single rank) of each tier. Should the enemy gain the ditch, the front rank of the part assailed will mount the parapet and repel him with its fire , and bayonet. If the men of this rank are determined, no human force can dispossess them of that position."

The American works were built upon an elevated plain, lying between the banks of the river Saranac and Lake Champlain. The river descends from the west until it approaches within about one hundred and sixty rods of the lake, and then turns towards the north and runs about one mile, in a northeasterly direction, to the lake. The land between the river and lake, at this point, is nearly in the shape of a right angled triangle ; the perpendicular being formed by the lake shore. About eighty rods above the mouth of the river, and near the centre of the village, is the " lower bridge," and about one mile higher up, following the course of the stream, was another bridge, on the road leading south to Salmon River, called the " upper bridge." One mile and a half above this bridge is a ford of the river.* The stream can also be forded at the bridges, and at

* This ford is near where General Pike encamped in 1812. The buildings were burned by Colonel Murray in 1813.

a point about midway between them. The south bank of
the river, above the village, is from fifty to sixty feet
high, and steep. About sixty rods above the "lower
bridge" is a deep ravine, running back from the
river and extending nearly to the lake shore. The
principal work, called Fort Moreau, stood opposite
the bend of the river, and about half way between it
and the lake. It was three fourths of a mile south of the
lower bridge. A redoubt, called Fort Brown, stood
on the bank of the river, directly opposite the bend,
and about fifty rods west of Fort Moreau. There was
another redoubt to the east of Fort Moreau, near the
bank of the lake, called Fort Scott. On the point, near
the mouth of the river, was a block-house and battery.
Another block-house stood on the south side of the ravine, about half way between the river and the lake.
The defense of Fort Moreau was entrusted to Colonel
Melancton Smith, who had for its garrison the 29th
and 6th Regiments.* Lieutenant-colonel Storrs was
stationed in Fort Brown, with detachments of the 30th
and 31st, and Major Vinson in Fort Scott, with the 33d
and 34th. The block-house, near the ravine, was entrusted to Captain Smith of the Rifles, and had for its defence a part of his company and of the convalescents
of one of the absent regiments. The block-house on
the point was garrisoned by a detachment of artillery,
under Lieutenant Fowler. The light artillery were ordered to take such positions as would best annoy the
enemy. When not employed they were to take post in
the ravine, with the light troops.

As soon as the British had advanced to Chazy village,
Captain Sproul was ordered by General Macomb, with
two hundred men, of the 13th, and two field pieces, to
take position near the Dead Creek bridge, and to abattis

* Colonel Melancton Smith was a son of Judge Melancton Smith,
brother of Captain Sidney Smith, U. S. Navy, and the father of Rear
Admiral Melancton Smith. He was born in 1780. On the increase of
the military establishment during the war, he was appointed a colonel
and assigned to the command of the 29th regiment U. S. Infantry. He
held that rank until the army was reduced after the peace. He died at
Plattsburgh, 28th August, 1818, and was buried at that place with military and masonic honors.

the road beyond, while Lieutenant-colonel Appling was stationed in advance, with one hundred and ten riflemen, and a troop of New York State cavalry, under Captain Safford and Lieutenant M. M. Standish, to watch the movements of the enemy. Macomb also made arrangements with Major-general Mooers for calling out the New York Militia, and addressed a letter to Governor Chittenden, of Vermont, requesting aid from that State. On the 4th, seven hundred of the Clinton and Essex Militia had collected at Plattsburgh.* They were advanced the next day about five miles on the north road, and lay during the night in the vicinity of the present stone church in Beekmantown. The militia were directed to watch the enemy, skirmish with him as he advanced, break up the bridges and obstruct the road with fallen trees.

On the 5th, as we have already stated, the British occupied a possition near Sampson's on the lake road. The troops were there divided into two columns, and moved towards the village of Plattsburgh on the morning of the 6th, before day-light; the right column crossed over to the Beekmantown road; the left followed the road leading to the Dead Creek bridge. The right column was composed of Major-general Powers' brigade, supported by four companies of light infantry and a demi-brigade under Major General Robinson. The left was led by Major General Brisbane's brigade. Information of this contemplated movement having reached General Macomb on the evening of the 5th, he ordered Major Wool, with a detachment of two hundred and fifty men, to advance on the Beekmantown road to the support of the militia. Captain Leonard, of the light artillery, was also directed to be on the ground, before day-light, with two field pieces.

The right column of the British advanced more rapidly than the left, and, at an early hour, met Major Wool's detachment and the militia, who had taken a position near the residence of Ira Howe, in

---

* These belonged to Colonel Thomas Miller's and Colonel Joiner's regiments, Major Sanford's battalion and the 37th regiment.

Beekmantown. Wool's party opened a brisk fire of musketry upon the head of the British column as it approached, severely wounding Lieutenant West of the 3d Buffs, and about twenty privates. Near this place Goodspeed and Jay, two men of Captain Atwood's company of militia, were wounded and taken prisoners. —Wool, with his men, now fell back as far as Culver's Hill, four and a half miles from the village, where he awaited the approach of the British. He was supported by a few of the militia who had been rallied by their officers, but the greater portion had retreated precipitately, after the first fire near Howe's. The resistance at Culver's Hill was intrepid, but momentary, for the British troops pressed firmly forward, occupying the whole road, and only returning their fire by their flanks and leading platoons, the latter of whom were once driven to the base of the hill, after having reached its summit. At this point, Lieutenant Colonel Willington, of the 3d Buffs, fell as he was ascending the hill at the head of his regiment. Ensign Chapman of the same regiment was also killed there, and Captain Westropp, of the 58th, severely wounded. Several of the Americans were killed, including Patridge of the Essex militia.

Learning that a large body of the British were advancing on a parallel road, leading from Beekmantown Corners, to gain his rear, Wool fell back as far as "Halsey's Corners," about one and a half miles from the village bridge. He was there joined, about eight o'clock in the morning, by Captain Leonard with two pieces of light artillery. Leonard placed his guns in battery at an angle in the road, masked by Wool's infantry and a small body of militia, and as the British approached opened a most galling fire upon the head of the column; the balls cutting a narrow and bloody lane through the moving mass. Three times were the guns discharged, but even this terrible fire did not check the progress of the column, for the men, throwing aside their knapsacks, pressed forward, the bugles sounding the charge, and forced Leonard hastily to withdraw towards the village. At this place, a number of the British were killed or wounded. Among the latter was Lieutenant Kingsbury of the 3d Buffs, who was taken into the adjoining farm-house of Isaac C. Platt, Esqr., where he soon afterwards died.*

Finding that the enemy's right column was steadily approaching the village, General Macomb ordered in the detachments at Dead Creek; at the same time directing Lieutenant-colonel Appling to fall on the British flank. The rapid advance of the column on the Beekmantown road had reversed Appling's position, and he had barely time to save his retreat, coming in a few rods ahead, as the British debouched from the woods a little north of the village. Here he poured in a destructive fire from his riflemen at rest, and continued to annoy the enemy, until he formed a junction with Wool, who was slowly retiring towards the lower bridge. The field pieces were taken across the bridge and formed a battery for its protection, and to cover the retreat of Wool's, Appling's, and Sproul's men. These detachments retired alternately, keeping up a brisk fire until they got under cover of the works.

The left column of the British army did not arrive near the village, until after Sproul's and Appling's detachments had been withdrawn; their march having been retarded by the obstructions placed in the road, and by the removal of the bridge at Dead Creek. As this column passed along the beach of the lake, it was much annoyed by a brisk fire from several galleys, which Macdonough had ordered to the head of the bay. After this fire had continued for about two hours, the wind began to blow so heavy from the south as to endanger the safety of the galleys. Mr. Duncan, a midshipman of the Saratoga, was therefore sent in a gig to order them to return. As that officer approached, he received a severe wound from the enemy's fire, which

---

* Lieutenant Kingsbury was buried in Mr. Platt's garden. His remains were removed to the village cemetery in May, 1844, by Captain C. A. Waite, then in command at Plattsburgh barracks.

for a few minutes was concentrated upon his boat.* About this time one of the galleys drifted under the guns of the British and sustained some loss, but was eventually brought off.

As soon as the American troops had crossed the river, the planks were removed from the lower bridge, and were piled up at its east end, to form a breast-work for the infantry. A similar breast-work was made by the militia, at the upper bridge. The British light troops made several attempts, in the course of the day, to cross at the village, but were repulsed by the guards at the bridge, and by the sharp fire of a company of volunteers who had taken possession of a stone grist-mill near by.† An attempt was also made to cross at the upper bridge, which was gallantly resisted by the militia. The loss this day, on both sides, was greater than the whole loss during the rest of the siege ; forty-five of the Americans, and more than two hundred British having been killed or wounded.‡

The configuration of the land, on the north side of the river, differs somewhat from that on the south side. The bank at the mouth of the river is abrupt and about thirty feet high. This bank, with a depression above the lower bridge, opposite the mill pond, follows the margin of the stream, until within about eighty rods of Fort Brown, when the hill recedes from the river, and

---

* On the 26th of May, 1826, Congress passed a resolution of thanks to Midshipman Silas Duncan for his gallant conduct on this occasion.

† This company was called "Aiken's Volunteers" and was composed of the following young men—none of whom were old enough to be liable to perform military duty : Martin J. Aiken, Azariah C. Flagg, Ira A. Wood, Gustavus A. Bird, James Trowbridge, Hazen Mooers, Henry K. Averill, St. John B. L. Skinner, Frederick P. Allen, Hiram Walworth, Ethan Everest, Amos Soper, James Patten, Bartemus Brooks, Smith Batemen, Melancton W. Travis and Flavius Williams. They had been out on the Beekmantown road in the morning, where they behaved with great gallantry. In May, 1826, Congress authorized the President to cause to be delivered to each, "One rifle promised to them by General Macomb, while commanding the Champlain department, for their gallantry and patriotic services as a volunteer corps, during the siege of Plattsburgh in September, 1814."

‡ General Macomb, in his general order of the 7th, estimates the British loss at from two to three hundred. The "Burlington Sentinel" of the 9th states it to have been about three hundred.

is less abrupt. The flat and hill opposite Fort Brown were covered with small trees and bushes. About one mile back from the river is an elevated ridge running to the north. At Allen's farm-house, which stood upon this ridge at the distance of about one and one-fourth mile from the American forts, Sir George Provost established his head-quarters. The army were encamped upon the ridge, and on the high ground north of the village.

From the 7th to the 10th, Provost was busily engaged in bringing up his battering trains and supplies, and in preparing his approaches. He erected a battery on the bank of the lake north of the mouth of the river; another near the edge of the steep bank above the mill-pond; another near the burial ground, and one, supplied with rocket works, on the hill opposite Fort Brown. Besides these, there were three smaller batteries erected at other points within range of the American forts.

While Provost was thus engaged, the American troops were diligently at work, day and night, in strengthening their defences. The barracks and hospitals in the vicinity of the forts were burned, and the sick removed to Crab Island, about two miles distant, where they were protected from the weather by tents. A small battery was erected on that island, mounting two six pounders, which was manned by convalescents. The Americans also, during this time, fired hot shot into and burned some fifteen or sixteen buildings, on the north side of the river, which had afforded protection to the British light troops.*

From the 7th to the 10th, the pickets and militia were engaged in frequent skirmishes with the enemy at the two bridges, and at the different fords along the

---

* The "Burlington Sentinel" says that up to the evening of the 8th, the following buildings had been burned : John Griffin's house and store, Roswell Wait's house and store, Mr. Savage's house, B. Buck's house, Mr. Powers' store, Widow Beaumont's house and store, Charles Backus' house and store, Joseph Thomas' two stores and Mr. Goldsmith's house. The court house and jail were also burned.

river. On the morning of the 7th, a party of British, under Captain Noadie, attempted to cross the river, at a ford about five miles west of the village. They were, however, met by a company of Colonel Miller's regiment of militia, under command of Captain Vaughan, and were repulsed with a loss of two killed and several wounded. The same day Lieutenant Runk, of the 6th, was mortally wounded, as he was passing in the street, near the present dwelling of A. C. Moore, Esq.

On the night of the 9th, while the British were engaged in erecting their rocket battery near Fort Brown, Captain McGlassin of the 15th Infantry, obtained permission from General Macomb to take a party of fifty men and attack a detachment of British troops at work upon the battery. The night was dark and stormy and favored such an enterprise. Ordering his men to take the flints from their muskets, McGlassin crossed the river, and passing through a small clump of dwarf oaks, reached, unobserved, the foot of the hill upon which the enemy were at work. There he divided his force into two parties, one of which was sent, by a circuitous route, to the rear of the battery. As soon as this party had reached its position, McGlassin, in a loud voice, ordered his men to charge "on the front and rear," when they rushed forward, with all the noise it was possible for them to make, and entered the work at both sides on the run. The working party were taken by surprise, and supposing themselves attacked by overwhelming numbers, retreated precipitately towards the main camp. McGlassin spiked the guns and led his party back to the American fort without losing a man. The whole affair was boldly conceived and most gallantly executed. It was long before the British officers would believe that fifty men could make so much noise, or so badly frighten over three hundred of their veteran troops.

When the British army reached Plattsburgh, their gun-boats had advanced as far as the Isle La Motte, where they remained, under command of Captain Pring.

On the 8th Captain Downie reached that place with
the rest of the fleet, and on the morning of the 11th,
the whole weighed anchor and stood south to attack
the Americans, who lay in the Bay, off Plattsburgh.

As the British vessels rounded Cumberland Head,
about eight o'clock in the morning, they found Macdonough at anchor a little south of the mouth of the
Saranac river, and abreast, but out of gunshot, of the
forts. His vessels lay in a line running north from
Crab Island, and nearly parallel with the west shore.
The brig *Eagle*, Captain Henley, lay at the head of
the line, inside the point of the head. This vessel
mounted twenty guns and had on board one hundred
and fifty men. Next to her and on the south lay Macdonough's flag ship, the *Saratoga*, mounting twenty-
six guns, with two hundred and twelve men. Next
south was the schooner *Ticonderoga*, of seventeen guns,
Lieutenant Cassin, with one hundred and ten men,
and next to her, and at the southern extremity of the
line, lay the sloop *Preble*, Lieutenant Charles Budd.
This vessel carried seven guns and was manned by
thirty men. She lay so near the shoal extending north
east from Crab Island, as to prevent the enemy from
turning that end of the line. To the rear of the line
were ten gun-boats, six of which mounted one long
twenty-four pounder and one eighteen pound Columbiad each ; the other four carried one 12 pounder. The
gun-boats had, on an average, thirty-five men each.
Two of the gun-boats lay a little north and in rear of
the Eagle, to sustain the head of the line; the others
were placed opposite the intervals between the different
vessels, and about forty rods to their rear. The larger
vessels were at anchor, while the gun-boats were kept
in position by their sweeps.

The British fleet was composed of the *frigate Confiance*, carrying thirty-seven guns,* with over three
hundred men, commanded by Captain Downie ; the

* There were thirty-nine guns on board the Confiance, but two of
them were not mounted.—*Cooper.*

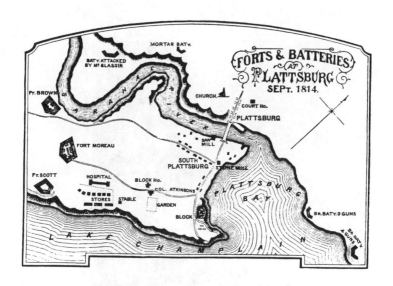

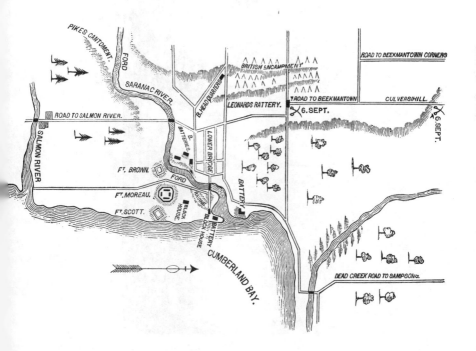

(From painting by Davidson, owned by Hon. Smith M. Weed, Plattsburg.)

The Battle of Plattsburgh.

MACDONOGH'S VICTORY ON LAKE CHAMPLAIN,

September 11, 1814.

Position of the Vessels after the Battle.

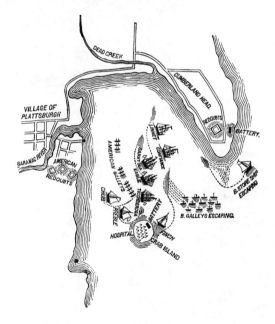

Commodore Thomas MacDonough

General Alexander Macomb

Brig *Linnet*, Captain Pring, of sixteen guns and 120 men; the sloop *Chub*, Lieutenant McGhee, and the sloop *Finch*, Lieutenant Hicks, carrying eleven guns and about forty-five men each. To these vessels were added thirteen gun-boats of about forty-five men each. Five of them carried two guns, and eight one gun each. Thus the force of the Americans consisted of one ship, one brig, one schooner, one sloop, and ten gun-boats, manned by eight hundred and eighty-two men, and carrying in all eighty-six guns. The British had one frigate, one brig, two sloops and thirteen gun-boats, manned by over one thousand men, and carrying in all ninety-five guns. The metal of the vessels on both sides was unusually heavy. The Saratoga mounted eight long twenty-fours, six forty-twos, and twelve thirty-twos, while the Confiance had the gun-deck of a heavy frigate, with thirty long twenty-fours upon it. She also had a spacious top gallant forecastle, and a poop that came no further forward than the mizen mast. On the first were a long twenty-four on a circle, and four heavy carronades; two heavy carronades were mounted on the poop.*

When the British fleet appeared in sight the Finch led and kept in a course toward Crab Island, while the other vessels hove to opposite the point of Cumber-

---

* Cooper's Naval History. Mr. Alison (in his History of England, vol. 4) says: "The relative strength of the squadron on this, as in every other naval action during the war, where the British were defeated, was decidedly in favor of the Americans"—a statement unwarranted by the facts, and unnecessary to sustain the high reputation of the British navy. The following are the number and size of the guns used on both fleets.

AMERICAN.	BRITISH.
14, long 24 pounders.	31, long 24 pounders.
6, 42 pound carronades.	7, 18 "
29, 32 " "	16, 12 "
12, long 18 pounders.	5, 6 "
12, long 12 "	12, 32 pound carronades.
7, long 9 "	6, 24 " "
6, 18 pound Columbiads.	17, 18 " "
	1, 18 pound Columbiad.
86 guns.	95 guns.

land Head, to allow the gun-boats to come up, and to receive final instructions as to the plan of attack. The vessels then filled and headed in towards the American fleet; passing inside of the point of Cumberland Head; the Chub laying her course a little to windward of the Eagle, in order to support the Linnet, which stood directly towards that vessel. Captain Downie had determined to lay the Confiance athwart the Saratoga, but the wind baffling, he was obliged to anchor at about two cables length from that ship. The Finch, which had run about half way to Crab Island, tacked and took her station, with the gun-boats, opposite the Ticonderoga and Preble.

As the British vessels approached they received the fire of the American fleet; the brig Eagle firing first and being soon followed by the Saratoga and the sloop and schooner.* The Linnet poured her broadside into the Saratoga, as she passed that ship to take her position opposite the Eagle Captain Downie brought his vessel into action in the most gallant manner, and did not fire a gun until he was perfectly secured, although his vessel suffered severely from the fire of the Americans. As soon however as the Confiance had been brought into position, she discharged all her larboard guns, at nearly the same instant. The effect of this broadside, thrown from long twenty-four pounders, double shotted, in smooth water, was terrible. The Saratoga trembled to her very keel: about forty of her crew were disabled, including her first Lieutenant, Mr. Gamble, who was killed while sighting the bow gun.

Soon after the commencement of the engagement the

---

* The first gun fired on board the Saratoga was a long twenty-four, which Macdonough himself sighted. The shot is said to have struck the Confiance near the outer hawse-hole, and to have passed the length of her deck, killing and wounding several men, and carrying away the wheel. In clearing the decks of the Saratoga, some hen-coops were thrown overboard and the poultry permitted to run at large. Startled by the report of the opening gun of the Eagle, a young cock flew upon a gun slide, clapped his wings and crowed. The men gave three cheers and considered the little incidence a happy omen.—*Cooper's Naval History and Niles' Register.*

Chub, while manœuvring near the head of the American line, received a broadside from the Eagle, which so crippled her that she drifted down between the opposing vessels and struck. She was taken possession of by Mr. Charles Platt, one of the Saratoga's midshipmen, and was towed in shore and anchored. The Chub had suffered severely; nearly half of her men having been killed or wounded. About an hour later the Finch was driven from her position by the Ticonderoga, and, being badly injured, drifted upon the shoal near Crab Island, where she grounded. After being fired into from the small battery on the Island, she struck and was taken possession of by the invalids who manned the battery.*

After the loss of the Finch, the British gun-boats made several efforts to close, and succeeded in compelling the sloop Preble to cut her cables and to anchor in shore of the line, where she was of no more service during the engagement. The gun-boats, emboldened by this success, now directed their efforts towards the Ticonderoga, against which they made several very gallant assaults, bringing the boats, upon two or three occasions, within a few feet of the schooner's side. They were however as often beaten back, and the schooner, during the remainder of the day, completely covered that extremity of the line.

While these changes were taking place at the lower end of the line, a change was also made at the other ex-

---

* Mr. Alison (History of England, vol. 4), referring to the event, says: "The Finch, a British brig, grounded out of shot and *did not engage;* " and again, "The Finch struck on a reef of rocks and could not get into action." Had Mr. Alison taken the trouble to read Captain Pring's official account of the engagement he would have found in it the following statement : "Lieutenant Hicks, of the Finch, had the mortification to strike on a reef of rocks, to the eastward of Crab Island, about the middle of the engagement, which prevented his rendering that assistance to the squadron, that might from an officer of such ability, have been expected." It is very convenient for the English historian to convert a small sloop of eleven guns and forty men into a brig, and to keep that large vessel out of the action altogether, but, as I have before said, such statements are unnecessary to preserve the well-earned reputation of the British navy for bravery or gallantry in action

tremity. The Eagle, having lost her springs and finding herself exposed to the fire of both the Linnet and Confiance, dropped down and anchored between the Saratoga and Ticonderoga, and a little inshore of both. From this position she opened afresh on the Confiance and the British gun-boats, with her larboard guns. This change relieved the Brig, but left the Saratoga exposed to the whole fire of the Linnet, which sprung her broadsides in such a manner as to rake the ship on her bows.

The fire from the Saratoga and Confiance now began materially to lessen, as gun after gun on both vessels became disabled, until at last the Saratoga had not a single available gun, and the Confiance was but little better off. It therefore became necessary that both vessels should wind, to continue the action with any success. This the Saratoga did after considerable delay; but the Confiance was less fortunate, as the only effect of her efforts was to force the vessel ahead. As soon as the Saratoga came around she poured a fresh broadside from her larboard guns into the Confiance, which stood the fire for a few minutes and then struck. The ship then brought her guns to bear on the Linnet, which surrendered in about fifteen minutes afterwards. At this time the British gun-boats lay half a mile in the rear, where they had been driven by the sharp fire of the Ticonderoga and the Eagle. These boats lowered their colors as soon as they found the larger vessels had submitted, but not being pursued, for the American gun-boats were sent to aid the Confiance and Linnet, which were reported to be in a sinking condition, they escaped, together with a store sloop which lay near the point of Cumberland Head during the battle.

The engagement continued for two hours and a half, and was the most severely fought naval battle of the war. The Saratoga had twenty-eight men killed and twenty-nine wounded; the Eagle, thirteen killed and twenty wounded; the Ticonderoga, six killed and six wounded, and the Preble, two killed. The loss on the gun-boats was three killed and tnree wounded. Total killed and wounded, one hundred and ten, being equal to every eighth man in the fleet. Besides, the Saratoga had been hulled fifty-five times and was twice on fire; the Eagle was hulled thirty-nine times. The carnage and destruction had been as great on the other side. The Confiance had forty-one men killed and eighty-three wounded; the Linnet reported her casualties at ten killed and fourteen wounded, but the killed and wounded probably exceeded fifty; the Chub was reported at six killed and ten wounded, and the Finch at two wounded. No account is given of the loss on the gun-boats, but, from their close and severe contest with the Ticonderoga, it must have been large. The total of killed and wounded on the British side was equal to at least one-fifth of the whole number of men in their fleet. The Confiance had been hulled one hundred and five times. So severe had been the contest, that at the close of the action there was not a mast in either fleet fit for use.*

Among those killed on the side of the British were Captain Downie, who fell soon after the action commenced; Captain Alexander Anderson, of the Marines; Midshipman William Gunn, of the Confiance; and Lieutenant William Paul and Boatswain Charles Jackson of the Linnet. Among the wounded were Midshipman Lee, of the Confiance; Midshipman John Sinclair, of the Linnet; and Lieutenant James McGhee, of the Chub. The American officers killed were Peter Gamble, 1st Lieutenant of the Saratoga; John Stansbury, 1st Lieutenant of the Ticonderoga, and Sailing Master Rogers Carter. Midshipman James M. Baldwin was wounded and died from the effects of the wound in

---

* "I could only look at the enemy's galleys going off, in a shattered condition; for there was not a mast in either squadron that could stand to make sail on; the lower rigging being nearly all shot away, hung down as though it had been just placed over the mast heads."—*Macdonough's Report of the Battle.* "Our masts, yards and sails were so shattered that one looked like so many bunches of matches, and the other like a bundle of rags."—*Letter of Midshipman Lee of the Confiance.*

the city of New York on 23d July, 1816. Referring to
the death of three of these officers, Mr. Cooper, in his
History of the Navy, says :—" Lieutenant Gamble was
on his knees, sighting the bow-gun, when a shot entered
the port, split the quoin, drove a portion of it against
his breast and laid him dead on the quarter-deck without breaking his skin. Fifteen minutes later one of
the American shot struck the muzzle of a twenty-four
on the Confiance, dismounted it, sending it bodily in-
board against the groin of Captain Downie, killing him
also without breaking the skin. Lieutenant Stansbury
suddenly disappeared from the bulwarks forward
while superintending some duty with the springs of
the Ticonderoga. Two days after the action his body
rose to the surface of the water, and it was found that
it had been cut in two with a round shot.

It is said that scarcely an individual escaped on board
of either the Confiance or Saratoga, without some injury.
Macdonough was twice knocked down ; once by the
spanker-boom, which was cut in two by a shot and fell
upon his back, as he was bending his body to sight a
gun ; and again by the head of a gunner, which was
driven against him, and knocked him into the scuppers.
Mr. Brum the sailing-master of the Saratoga, had his
clothes torn off by a splinter, while winding the ship.
Mr. Vallette, acting Lieutenant, had a shot-box, on
which he was standing, knocked from under his feet
and he too was once knocked down by the head of a
seamen. Very few escaped without some accident, and
it appears to have been agreed on both sides, to call no
man wounded who could keep out of the hospital.*
Midshipman Lee of the Confiance, who was wounded
in the action, thus describes the condition of that vessel.
" The havoc on both sides is dreadful. I don't think
there are more than five of our men, out of three hundred, but what are killed or wounded. Never was a
shower of hail so thick, as the shot whistling about our
ears. Were you to see my jacket, waist-coat and trow-

* Cooper's Naval History.

sers, you would be astonished how I escaped as I did,
for they are literally torn all to rags with shot and
splinters; the upper part of my hat was also shot away.
There is one of our marines who was in the Trafalgar
action with Lord Nelson, who says it was a mere *flea-
bite* in comparison with this."*

As soon as the British fleet were observed approaching Cumberland Head, on the morning of the 11th, Sir
George Provost ordered General Power's brigade, and
a part of General Robinson's brigade, consisting of four
companies of light infantry, and the 3d battalions of
the 27th and 76th, to force the fords of the Saranac,
and to assault the American works. The advance was
made, and the batteries were opened, the moment the
action on the lake commenced.

The British attempted to cross the river at three
points; one at the village bridge, where they were repulsed by the artillery and guards under Captains
Brooks, Richards and Smith; one at the upper bridge,
where they were foiled by the pickets and Riflemen,
under Captain Grovener and Lieutenants Hamilton
and Smith, supported by a detachment of militia; and
the third at the ford near "Pike's cantonment," where
they were resisted by the New York Militia, under
Major-general Mooers and Brigadier-general Wright.
At this latter point, several companies succeeded in
crossing, driving the militia before them towards Salmon River. The British advanced, firing by platoons, but
with such carelessness of aim as to do but little injury.†
At Salmon River, the militia were joined by a large
detachment of the Vermont volunteers, and were soon

---

* Letter to his brother, published in Niles' Register, vol. 8. The result of the engagement depended, from the first, upon the Saratoga and
Confiance. When Macdonough anchored his vessel he not only attached
springs to the cables, but also laid a kedge broad off on each bow of the
Saratoga, and brought the hawsers in upon the two quarters. To this
timely precaution he was indebted for the victory, for without the larboard hawser he could not have brought his fresh broadside into action.

† I have conversed with several who boast of their *activity* during this
retreat, and who felt a personal interest in the subject at the time, and
they all state that the balls, at each volley, struck the pine trees at least
fifteen feet from the ground.

afterwards reinforced by Lieutenant Sumpter, with a party of artillery and a field-piece. Here they rallied and were drawn up to meet the attack of the British troops, who were rapidly approaching. Just at this moment an officer* rode up to the ranks, proclaiming the welcome intelligence that the British fleet had surrendered. With three hearty cheers the militia immediately pressed forward against the enemy, who, having been at the same moment recalled, were now rapidly retiring towards the ford. In their retreat, a company of the 76th lost their way among the thick pines, where they were surrounded and attacked by several companies of militia and Vermont volunteers. Three Lieutenants and twenty-seven men were made prisoners, and Captain Purchase and the rest of the company killed.† The rest of the British detachment regained the north bank of the Saranac without much loss.‡

Although no further attempt was made to cross the river, the British batteries continued their fire upon the American works until sundown. This fire was returned by the guns of Fort Brown, which were managed during the day with great skill, by Captain Alexander Brooks and the corps of veteran artillery under his command.

Sir George Provost had now under his command over thirteen thousand troops, more than half of whom had served with distinction under Wellington, while the American force did not exceed fifteen hundred regulars, fit for duty, two thousand five hundred Vermont volunteers, under Major-general Strong, six hundred of whom had just arrived, and General Wright's brigade

---

* Chancellor Walworth, then Adjutant-general of Major-general Mooers' division.

† It is said Captain Purchase was shot down, while waving a white hadkerchief over his head, as a notice that he had surrendered.

‡ Sir George Provost, in his account of the battle, says: "Scarcely had his Majesty's troops forced a passage across the Saranac *and ascended the heights on which stand the American works.*" &c.—This would imply that the British had gained ground near the forts, bnt such was not the case. They crossed nearly two miles above the forts, and followed the militia *from,* instead of towards the American works.

of Clinton and Essex Militia, seven hundred strong, under command of Major-general Mooers. With his superior force, Provost could have forced the passage of the Saranac, and have crushed Macomb by the mere weight of numbers. But the victory would have been attended with great sacrifice of life, and would have led to no permanent advantage to the British. Macdonough was in command of the lake; reinforcements of regulars were hastening to the support of Macomb; the militia were rising *en masse*, in every quarter, and within two weeks Provost would have been surrounded, his supplies from Canada cut off, and an only alternative left to force his way back with the loss of half his army, or to have surrendered. In a dispatch to Earl Bathurst, after referring to the loss of the fleet, he says : " This unlooked-for event depriving me of the co-operation of the fleet, without which the further prosecution of the service was become impracticable, I did not hesitate to arrest the course of the troops advancing to the attack, because the most complete success would have been unavailing; and the possession of the enemy's works offered no advantage to compensate for the loss we must have sustained in acquiring possession of them."

This was a just and merited compliment to the skill and bravery of the American regulars and militia. The former were few in number, but resolute and unflinching. Among the latter the greatest enthusiasm now prevailed. They had become accustomed to the " smell of powder," and animated by the recollection of Macdonough's victory, were ready to oppose any force that might attempt the passage of the Saranac. It is due to the patriotism of the citizens of Vermont, to mention the fact that as soon as Governor Chittenden received information from General Macomb of the invasion by the enemy, he issued a spirited address calling on the Vermont militia to rally to the aid of their countrymen on the opposite side of the lake. This address was most nobly responded to, for when the requisition of the President for a reinforcement of two thousand militia to aid General Macomb, reached the Governor, he replied that the order had not only been anticipated, but far exceeded, by the voluntary enrollment of his fellow-citizens. The same enthusiasm pervaded the militia on the New York side. When Major-general Mooers' orders were received for the Militia of Warren and Washington Counties to assemble, *en masse*, and march to the frontier, there appeared, under arms, two hundred and fifty men *more* than had ever mustered at an inspection or review.

Acting upon the considerations stated in his dispatch to Earl Bathurst, Sir George Provost prepared for an instant and hasty retreat. As soon as the sun went down, he dismantled his batteries, and, at 9 o'clock at night, sent off his heavy baggage and artillery, which were quickly followed by the main army; the rear guard, consisting of a light brigade, started a little before day-break, leaving behind them vast quantities of provisions, tents, camp equipage, ammunition, etc. The sick and wounded were also left behind, consigned to the generosity and humane care of General Macomb. So silent and rapid was the retreat, that the main army had passed through Beekmantown before its absence was known in the American camp. The light troops, volunteers and militia were immediately sent in pursuit. They followed the retiring column as far as Chazy, and took a few prisoners. The roads were muddy, and very heavy at the time, which not only prevented further pursuit, but delayed Provost's retreat. The last of the British army did not leave Champlain until the 24th.*

General Macomb, in his returns, states the number of killed, wounded and missing of the regular force under his command, during the skirmishes and bombardment, at one hundred and twenty-three. The only commissioned officer killed was Lieutenant George W.

---

* Provost was recalled to England soon after his return to Canada, when charges were preferred against him. He died in December 1815, before his trial had commenced.

Runk, of the 6th Regiment, who was severely wounded on the 7th and died the next day.* The loss among the volunteers and militia was small. The loss of the British has never been correctly ascertained. Their accounts fix the casualities of the expedition at under two hundred killed and wounded, and four hundred lost by desertion. This, however, is far below the true number. At the time, the American officers believed the total loss of the British, from the time they first crossed the lines until they again entered Canada, in killed, wounded and prisoners, and by desertion, was over two thousand men.—Seventy-five prisoners were taken.*

On the 12th the Vermont volunteers returned home, and on the 13th the New York Militia were disbanded by General Macomb, and orders issued countermanding the march of thousands, who were flocking to the frontier.

On the morning of the 13th of September, the remains of the lamented Gamble, Stansbury, Carter and Barron were placed in separate boats, which, manned by crews from their respective vessels, proceeded to the Confiance, where they were joined by the British officers, with the bodies of Downie, Anderson, Paul, Gunn, and Jackson. At the shore of the lake, the procession was joined by a large concourse of the military and citizens of Plattsburgh, who accompanied the bodies to the village burial-ground. Near the centre of the graveyard,

---

* Lieut. Rusk was buried on Crab Island. His remains were removed to the burial-ground in the village of Plattsburgh on the 19th September 1816.

† The following list of British officers killed or wounded during the invasion was published in the London Gazette of the 19th and 26th November, 1814,

KILLED.—Captain (Brevet Lieut.-Col.) James Willington and Ensign John Chapman, of the 3d Buffs. Captain John Purchase, 76th Regiment, foot.

WOUNDED.—Captain T. Crosse, A. D. C., (slightly); Lieut. R. Kingsbury, severely, (since dead); Lieut. John West, (severely); Lieutenants Benson and Holmes, (slightly); all of the 3d Buffs. Captain L. Westropp, (severely,); Lieut. C. Brohier and Adjutant Lewis, (slightly); of the 58th regiment, foot.

beneath the shade of two pines, now rest the ashes of those gallant officers. The sailors and marines, who fell in the engagement, were buried on Crab Island, side by side, in one common grave.

With the battle of Plattsburgh closed all active operations upon the Champlain frontier. For several months, however, the inhabitants were kept in a state of alarm, as it was rumored that the British authorities contemplated another campaign. Major-general. Mooers, New York, and Major-general Strong, of Vermont, ordered their respective divisions of militia to hold themselves in readiness for active service. General Macomb remained at Plattsburgh with a small force, and caused two redoubts to be thrown up a short distance to the south of Fort Moreau, which he named Fort Tompkins and Fort Gaines.

The Treaty of Ghent was signed on the 24th of December, 1814, and on the 17th of February following, was ratified by the United States Senate. With the publication of this treaty all fears of further hostilities ceased.

Architect's rendering of the restoration of Fort Ticonderoga

The Ruins of Ticonderoga, 1820

APPENDIX.

AN ACCOUNT OF THE CELEBRATION OF THE ANNI-
VERSARY OF THE BATTLE OF PLATTSBURGH, BY
THE CITIZENS OF PLATTSBURGH AND THE CLINTON
COUNTY MILITARY ASSOCIATION, SEPTEMBER 11th,
1843.

At a meeting of the CLINTON COUNTY MILITARY
ASSOCIATION, held on the 21st of August, 1843, it was,
on motion of Mayor A. A. Prescott,

Resolved, That this Association do celebrate, in some
appropriate manner, the Anniversary of the Battle of
Plattsburgh, on the eleventh of September next.

Resolved, That a committee of three be appointed to
confer with the Trustees of the Village, and make arrangements for the Celebration.

Maj. Gen. Skinner, Brig. Gen. Halsey and Col. Moore,
were appointed said committee.

The following named gentlemen were duly appointed
a committee on the part of the citizens to confer with
the committee of the Military Association in making
the necessary arrangements for the proper celebration
of the day:—

William F. Haile, Moss K. Platt, D. B. McNeil, C. S.
Mooers, R. A. Gilman, G. M. Beckwith, G. W. Palmer,
S. Couch, Benj. Ketchum, R. A. Weed, J. Bailey, Peter
S. Palmer, T. DeForris, William H. Morgan, J. W.
Tuttle.

At a meeting of the Joint Committee of Arrangements, Col. D. B. McNeil, (who was Acting Assistant
Adjutant-general of the Militia forces at Plattsburgh,

in September 1814,) was designated to act as President of the day, and the following resolutions were adopted :

Resolved, That the citizens of Plattsburgh, in connection with such other persons as may unite with them, will on the 11th of September, instant, proceed to the erection of plain marble monuments to mark the several spots where rest the mortal remains of the American and British officers who fell at the memorable " Battle of Plattsburgh."

Resolved, That R. A. Gilman, George Moore, and Roby G. Stone be a committee to procure the monuments and make the necessary arrangements to carry out the foregoing resolution.

Resolved, That Brig.-Gen. Wool, and Lt.-Col. B. Riley, of the U. S. Army, be requested to unite with the citizens and military of this place in the proposed celebration, and the erection of the monuments above-mentioned.

Resolved, That Gen. Skinner, Gen. Halsey, and Col. R. G. Stone be the committee of invitation.

Resolutions were also passed inviting the U. S. Officers and troops stationed at this post, the surviving officers and soldiers of the regular army, the Clinton and Essex Militia, and the Vermont volunteers who participated in the events of that time, to unite with us in the proposed celebration.

In accordance with the above arrangements, the Anniversary of the Battle of Plattsburgh was celebrated in an appropriate manner by the Clinton County Military Association and the citizens of Plattsburgh and its vicinity generally, on Monday last. General Wool and suite, and several other gentlemen who were in the battle of the 11th, were present by special invitation.

The procession was formed at Fouquet's hotel at 10 o'clock, under the direction of Gen. C. Halsey, Chief Marshal, assisted by Messrs. C. S. Mooers, G. W. Palmer, and R. G. Stone, escorted by the U. S. Troops at this post under the command of Capt. C. A. Waite, and moved to the Park in front of the Court House, where an able and patriotic address was delivered by Col. A. C. Moore, to a large and attentive audience of ladies and gentlemen.

After the address, the procession was again formed and moved to the burying-ground, where a square was formed by the U. S. Troops and the Military Association around the unmarked graves of those who fell in the battle of Plattsburgh.

After a prayer by the Rev. Mr. Witherspoon, and an address by Gen. Skinner, the president of the day (Col. McNeil) said :

" FELLOW-CITIZENS :—The President of the day has designated our distinguished guest, Brigadier-General Wool, of the United States Army, who commanded the detachment of American regular troops opposed to that division of the British Army which advanced upon Plattsburgh by the Beekmantown road on the 6th of September, 1814, to erect a monument at the head of the grave of Col. Willington, of the 3d Regiment of British Buffs, who gallantly fell at the head of his regiment at Culver's Hill, on the Beekmantown road, in the memorable battle of the 6th of September, 1814.

" The division of the British Army in which the brave and lamented Willington fell was not less than 4,000 strong ; and when we take into view the fact that General Wool (then a Major), with a light corps of but 250 regular troops, all told, contested every inch of ground with this formidable force in their descent upon Plattsburgh, the selection of General Wool to perform the melancholy duty assigned to him cannot fail to give deep interest to the solemn occasion which brought us together upon this hallowed spot. Nothing can be more appropriate than that the monument about to be erected should be raised by the hand of an officer who bore an honorable and conspicuous part in the events of the memorable day on which the gallant Willington fell. It is a pleasing spectacle to see the living brave doing honor to the memory of the illustrious dead."

Gen. Wool proceeded to discharge the duty assigned him, and said:

"FELLOW-CITIZENS AND SOLDIERS:—The duty assigned me by the President of the day, in behalf of the citizens of Plattsburgh and the Military Association of the County of Clinton, is no less gratifying to me than it is honorable and magnanimous to its authors, and will furnish an example worthy of imitation for all time to come. It is not less a holy and pious offering to the illustrious dead, than the offspring of noble and generous hearts to a fallen foe, and will furnish themes of praise to the end of time. It will be a healing balm to the wounded hearts of relatives and friends—whilst it will not fail to call forth from every Briton who passes this consecrated spot tears of gratitude as well as tears of sympathy.

"With these brief remarks, I now erect, in behalf of the citizens of Plattsburgh and the Military Association of Clinton County, this monument to the memory of Colonel Willington, who fell the 6th of September, 1814, at Culver's Hill, leading to the charge the advance of the British army marching on Plattsburgh."

The President of the day said:

"FELLOW-CITIZENS:—Our esteemed fellow-citizen, Judge Haile, late a captain in the United States Army, will now proceed to place monuments at the respective graves of Captain Purchase, late of the British Army; Lieut. Runk, late of the 6th Regiment, United States Infantry; and Ensign John Chapman, late of the 3d Buffs."

The President of the day, in designating Judge Haile to perform the duty assigned to him, did so from a full knowledge of the fact that no officer of his rank ever left the army of the United States with a higher and more enviable reputation as a fearless and fighting officer than did Captain Haile.

Judge Haile proceeded to the duty assigned him, with suitable remarks.

The President of the day then said:

" FELLOW-CITIZENS :— The Colonels Miller and Manly and Maj.-Gen. Skinner, all of whom bore a distinguished part in the battles of Beekmantown and Plattsburgh, is assigned the honor of erecting monuments to the memory of Lieutenant Peter Gamble, United States Navy; John Stansbury, United States Navy, and Midshipman James M. Baldwin, United States Navy.

The gentlemen above mentioned proceeded to discharge the duty assigned them, accompanied by appropriate remarks.

The President said—

" To our esteemed fellow-citizen, Platt R. Halsted, Esq., late a Lieutenant in the United States Army, I assign the honor of placing monuments at the graves of Captain Alexander Anderson of the British marines ; Lieutenant William Paul, midshipman ; William Gunn and boatswain Charles Jackson of the British Navy, and Joseph Barron, Pilot on board Commodore Macdonough's ship—all of whom fell in the naval engagement in Cumberland Bay, off Plattsburgh, on the 11th of September, 1814.

" Joseph Barron, Pilot, was personally known to Lieut-Halsted and myself, and was a man held in high estimation for his intelligence and patriotism by all who had the pleasure of his acquaintance."

Lieut. Halsted, in the discharge of the duty assigned him, erected the monuments at the head of the graves of the three Lieutenants of the British Navy, and proceeded to the grave of Joseph Barron, and, as near as we could catch his remarks, spoke as follows :

" I take a melancholy pleasure in erecting this monument at the head of the grave of Joseph Barron, Commodore Macdonough's confidential Pilot. I knew him well—he was about my own age—we were school boys together—a warmer hearted or a braver man never trod the deck of a ship."

Lieut Springer, late of the U. S. Army, was designated by the President of the day, to erect the monument at the head of the grave of Sailing Master Rogers Carter, U. S. Navy, and proceeded to discharge that duty.

A benediction was then pronounced by Rev. Mr. Witherspoon, and the procession returned to Fouquet's Hotel, where the committee of arrangements, the invited guests and the Military Association partook of an excellent dinner, got up in Fouquet's best style.

Among the sentiments offered on this occasion was the following, by General Skinner:

Brig.-general Wool, U. S. Army—The Hero of Beekmantown as well as Queenstown—

" His laurels are green, though his locks are gray."

General Wool, with much feeling, responded to this sentiment as follows :

Mr. PRESIDENT—I rise with a heart overflowing with gratitude to respond to the sentiment just given by my friend at the other end of the table. I find it impossible, however, filled as I am with emotion, to make a speech, or give utterance to my feelings in a manner worthy of the occasion. Were it otherwise, I could say but little that has not already been said. I might speak of the campaigns of 1812 and '13, which closed with the most gloomy forebodings. I might also speak of the campaigns of 1814, when the mantle of darkness was cast off, and a blaze of light shone forth along the frontier from Fort Erie to Plattsburgh, and finally closed, with a brilliancy seldom equalled, on the plains of New Orleans. But these periods have already been noticed and described in the most eloquent and stirring language. Therefore, little remains for me to add, could I give utterance to my feelings, but to express my warmest thanks for the kind partiality with which you have been pleased to allude to my services. I would, however, remark that although at one period of the war darkness and despondency appeared to pervade our beloved country, there was one bright spot exempt from the general gloom. It was here in this place, Plattsburgh, that the patriotic inhabitants never wavered nor quailed before the legions of Great Britain.—They stood by their country in the darkest hour, and never failed to cheer and comfort the war-worn soldier, and to receive him with open arms whether he returned victorious, or was driven back by the force of circumstances. Who that was at Plattsburgh in 1812, '13 and '14, does not remember with delight Mooers, Smith, Sailly, Delord, Bailey, Palmer and Ransom, all patriotic citizens and devoted friends of their country in war as well as in peace, but who now rest in the mansions of eternal bliss. With these few remarks, Mr. President, I would offer this sentiment—

The Citizens of Plattsburgh and the Military Association of Clinton County—This day attests their magnanimity and greatness of soul, by the homage paid to the illustrious dead who fell fighting the battles of their country.

POSITION OF THE GRAVES,

With the Inscriptions on the Monuments erected Sept. 11, 1843.

WEST.

Lieut. G. W. RUNK, 6th Regt. U. S. Army, 8th Sept. 1814.	Colonel WILLINGTON 3d Regt. Buffs, B. Army. 6th Sept. 1814.	Ensign J. CHAPMAN, 3d Buffs, B. Army. 6th Sept. 1814.	Lieut. KINGSBURY, 3d Buffs, B. Army. 6th Sept. 1814.
Lieut. Peter Gamble, U. S. N. 11th Sept. 1814.	Lieut. John Stansbury, U. S. N. 11th Sept. 1814.	Sailing Master Rogers Carter, U. S. N. 11th Sept. 1814.	Midshipman J. M. Baldwin, U. S. N. 11th Sept. 1814.*

SOUTH.

(PINE TREE.)

Pilot
Joseph Barron,
Ship Saratoga.
11th Sept. 1814.

Sacred
to the memory of
GEORGE DOWNIE, Esq.,
A Post Captain in the Royal Brit.
Navy, who gloriously fell on
board His B. M. S. the Confiance, while leading the
vessels under his com-
mand to the
attack of the American Flotilla,
at anchor in Cumberland Bay,
off Plattsburgh,
on the 11th September, 1814.
—
To mark the spot where the remains
of a gallant officer and sincere
friend were honorably interred,
this stone has been erected by his
affectionate Sister-in-Law,
MARY DOWNIE.

(PINE TREE.)

Boatswain
Chas. Jackson,
B. Navy.
11th Sept. 1814.

NORTH.

Capt. Purchase, 76th Regt. B. Army. 11th Sept. 1814.	Alx. Anderson, Capt. Marines, B. Navy, 11th Sept. 1814.	Acting Lieut. William Paul, B. Navy. 11th Sept. 1814.	Midshipman William Gunn, B. Navy. 11th Sept. 1814.

EAST.

* This is an error. Midshipman. Baldwin died in New York City in 1816 from the effects of a wound received on Lake Champlain. (See Plattsburgh *Republican*, Aug. 5, 1816.)

BATTLE OF VALCOUR.

OFFICIAL REPORTS.

GENERAL ARNOLD TO GENERAL GATES.

SCHUYLER'S ISLAND, October 12, 1776.

DEAR GENERAL:—Yesterday morning at eight o'clock,* the enemy's fleet, consisting of one ship mounting sixteen guns, one snow mounting the same number, one schooner of fourteen guns, two of twelve, two sloops, a bomb-ketch and a large vessel (that did not come up) with fifteen or twenty flat-bottomed boats or gondolas, carrying one twelve or eighteen pounder in their bows, appeared off Cumberland Head. We immediately prepared to receive them. The galleys and *Royal Savage* were ordered under way; the rest of our fleet lay at an anchor. At eleven o'clock they ran under the lee of Valcour and began the attack. The schooner, by some bad management, fell to leeward and was first attacked; one of her masts was wounded and her rigging shot away. The captain thought prudent to run her on the point of Valcour, where all the men were saved. They boarded her, and at night set fire to her. At half-past twelve the engagement became gen-

---

*American Archives, Fifth series, vol. ii. 1038. In the same letter, published in the journal of The New York Provincial Congress, vol. ii., p. 344, the time is stated at "10 o'clock."

eral, and very warm. Some of the enemy's ships and
all their gondolas beat and rowed up within musket
shot of us. They continued a very hot fire with round
and grape shot until five o'clock, when they thought
proper to retire to about six or seven hundred yards
distance, and continued the fire till dark.

The *Congress* and *Washington* have suffered greatly,
the latter lost her First Lieutenant killed, Captain and
Master wounded. The *New York* lost all her officers
except the captain. The *Philadelphia* was hulled in,
so many places, that she sunk about one hour after the
engagement was over. The whole killed and wounded
amounted to about sixty. The enemy landed a large
number of Indians on the Island and each shore, who
kept an incessant fire on us but did little damage. The
enemy had, to appearance, upwards of one thousand
men in bateaux prepared for boarding. We suffered
much for want of seamen and gunners. I was obliged,
myself to point most of the guns on board the *Congress*,
which I believe did good execution. The *Congress* received seven shot between wind and water; was hulled
a dozen times; had her main mast wounded in two
places and her yard in one. The *Washington* was
hulled a number of times; her main mast shot through
and must have a new one. Both vessels are very leaky,
and want repairing.

On consulting with General Waterbury and Colonel
Wigglesworth, it was thought prudent to return to
Crown Point, every vessel's ammunition being nearly
three-fourths spent, and the enemy greatly superior to
us in ships and men. At seven o'clock Colonel Wigglesworth, in the *Trumbull*, got under way; the gondolas and small vessels followed, and the *Congress* and
Washington brought up the rear. The enemy did not
molest us. Most of the fleet is this minute come to an
anchor. The wind is small to the southward. The
enemy's fleet is under way to leeward, and beating up.
As soon as our leaks are stopped, the whole fleet will
make the utmost despatch to Crown Point, where I beg
you will send ammunition, and your further orders for

us. On the whole I think we have had a very fortunate escape, and have great reason to return our humble and hearty thanks to Almighty God for preserving
and delivering so many of us from our more than savage enemies.

I am, dear General, your affectionate servant,

B. ARNOLD.

P. S.—I had not moved on board the *Congress* when
the enemy appeared, and lost all my papers and most
of my clothes on board the schooner. I wish a dozen
batteaux, well manned could be sent immediately to
tow up the vessels in case of a southerly wind.

I cannot, in justice to the officers in the fleet, omit
mentioning their spirited conduct during the action.

B. A.

_____

GENERAL ARNOLD TO GENERAL SCHUYLER.

TICONDEROGA, October 15, 1776.

DEAR GENERAL :—I make no doubt before this you
have received a copy of my letter to GeneralGates of the
12th instant, dated at Schuyler's Island, advising of an action between our fleet and the enemy the preceding day,
in which we lost a schooner and a gondola. We remained
no longer at Schuyler's Island than to stop our leaks,
and mend the sails of the *Washington*. At two o'clock
P. M. the 12th, weighed anchor with a fresh breeze to
the southward. The enemy's fleet at the same time got
under way ; our gondola made very little way ahead.
In the evening the wind moderated, and we made such
progress that at six o'clock next morning we were about
off Willsborough, twenty-eight miles from Crown-Point.
The enemy's fleet were very little way above Schuyler's
Island ; the wind breezed up to the southward, so that
we gained very little by beating or rowing, at the same
time the enemy took a fresh breeze from the northeast,
and by the time we had reached Split-Rock, were along-
side of us. The Washington and Congress were in the

rear, the rest of our fleet were ahead except two gondolas sunk at Schuyler's Island. The Washington galley was in such a shattered condition, and had so many men killed and wounded, she struck to the enemy after receiving a few broadsides. We were then attacked in the Congress galley by a ship mounting twelve eighteen-pounders, a schooner of fourteen sixes, and one of twelve sixes, two under our stern, and one on our broadside, within musket-shot. They kept up an incessant fire on us for about five glasses, with round and grape-shot, which we returned as briskly. The sails, rigging, and hull of the Congress were shattered and torn in pieces, the First Lieutenant and three men killed, when, to prevent her falling into the enemy's hands, who had seven sail around me, I ran her ashore in a small creek ten miles from Crown-Point, on the east side when, after saving our small-arms, I set her on fire with four gondolas, with whose crews, I reached Crown-Point through the woods that evening, and very luckily escaped the savages, who waylaid the road in two hours after we passed. At four o'clock yesterday morning I reached this place, exceedingly fatigued and unwell, having been without sleep or refreshment for near three days.

Of our whole fleet we have saved only two galleys, two small schooners, one gondola, and one sloop. General Waterbury, with one hundred and ten prisoners, were returned by Carleton last night. On board of the Congress we had twenty-odd men killed and wounded. Our whole loss amounts to eighty odd.

The enemy's fleet were last night three miles below Crown Point; their army is doubtless at their heels. We are busily employed in completing our lines and redoubts, which I am sorry to say are not so forward as I could wish. We have very few heavy cannon, but are mounting every piece we have. It is the opinion of General Gates and St. Clair that eight or ten thousand Militia should be immediately sent to our assistance, if they can be spared from below. I am of opinion the enemy will attack us with their fleet and army

at the same time. The former is very formidable, a
list of which I am favored with by General Waterbury,
and have enclosed. The season is so far advanced, our
people are daily growing more healthy.

We have about nine thousand effectives, and if properly supported, make no doubt of stopping the career
of the enemy. All your letters to me of late have mis-
carried. I am extremely sorry to hear by General
Gates you are unwell. I have sent you by General
Waterbury a small box containing all my public and
private papers, and accounts, with a considerable sum
of hard and paper money, which beg the favor of your
taking care of.

I am, dear General, your most affectionate, humble
servant, B. ARNOLD.

To Hon. Major General Schuyler.

N. B. Two of the enemy's gondolas sunk by our fleet
the first day, and one blown up with sixty men.

CAPTAIN THOMAS PRINGLE TO MR STEPHENS,
SECRETARY OF THE ADMIRALTY.

On board the Maria, off Crown-Point,
October 15, 1876.

IT is with the greatest pleasure that I embrace this
opportunity of congratulating their Lordships upon
the victory completed the 13th of this month, by his
Majesty's fleet under my command, upon Lake Champlain.

Upon the 11th I came up with the Rebel fleet, commanded by Benedict Arnold; they were at anchor
under the Island Valcour, and formed a strong line,
extending from the island to the west side of the continent. The wind was so unfavorable, that, for a considerable time, nothing could be brought into action
with them but the gun-boats. The Carleton schooner,
commanded by Mr. Dacres, who brings their Lordships
this, by much perseverance, at last got to their assist-

ance ; but as none of the other vessels of the fleet could then get up, I did not think it by any means advisable to continue so partial and unequal a combat; consequently, with the approbation of his Excellency General Carleton, who did me the honor of being on board the Maria, I called off the Carleton and gun-boats, and brought the whole fleet to anchor in a line as near as possible to the Rebels, that their retreat might be cut off; which purpose was however frustrated by the extreme obscurity of the night ; and in the morning the Rebels had got a considerable distance from us up the lake.

Upon the 13th, I again saw eleven sail of their fleet making off to Crown Point, who, after a chase of seven hours, I came up with in the Maria, having the Carleton and Inflexible a small distance astern ; the rest of the fleet almost out of sight. The action began at twelve o'clock, and lasted two hours, at which time Arnold, in the Congress galley, and five gondolas ran on shore, and were directly abandoned and blown up by the enemy, a circumstance they were greatly favored in by the wind being off shore, and the narrowness of the lake. The Washington galley struck during the action, and the rest made their escape to Ticonderoga.

The killed and wounded in His Majesty's fleet, including the artillery in the gun-boats, do not amount to forty ; but from every information I have yet got, the loss of the enemy must indeed be very considerable.

CAPTAIN DOUGLASS, OF THE ISIS, TO MR. STEPHENS.

QUEBEC, October, 21, 1776.

Having for the space of six weeks attended the naval equipments for the important expedition on Lake Champlain, I, on the 4th inst, saw with unspeakable joy the reconstructed ship now called the *Inflexible*, and commanded by Lieutenant Schank, her rebuilder, sail from St. Johns, twenty-eight days after her keel was laid, towards the place of rendezvous, taking in her eighteen twelve-pounders beyond the shoal, which is this side of Isle-aux-Noix, in her way up.

The prodigies of labor which have been effected since the Rebels were driven out of Canada, in creating, re-creating and equipping a fleet of above thirty fighting vessels of different sorts and sizes, and all carrying cannon, since the beginning of July, together with transporting over land, and afterwards dragging up the two rapids of St. Terese and St. Johns, thirty long-boats, the flat-bottomed boats, a gondola weighing about thirty ton and above four hundred-batteaux, almost exceed belief. His Excellency the Commander-in-chief of the army and all the other generals are of the opinion that the sailors of His Majesty's ships and transports, have, far beyond the usual limits of their duty, exerted themselves to the utmost on this great and toilsome occasion; nor has a man of that profession uttered a single word expressive of discontent, amidst all the hardships they have undergone, so truly patriotic are the motives by which they are actuated. To crown the whole, above two hundred prime seaman of the transports, impelled by a due sense of their country's wrongs, did most generously engage themselves to serve in our armed vessels during the expedition, and embarked accordingly. Such having then been our unremittting toils, I am happy beyond expression in hereby acquainting my Lords Commissioners of the Admiralty that the destruction of almost the whole of the Rebel fleet, in two successive battles on the 11th and 13th, instant, is our reward. I have received a letter from Captain PRINGLE, of the *Lord Howe*, armed ship, who commands the officers and seaman on the lake, and who bestows the highest encomiums on their behavior in both engagements. The Rebels did by no means believe it possible for us to get upon Lake Champlain this year; were much surprised at the first sight of the van of our force, but ran into immediate and utter confusion the moment a three-masted ship made her appearance, being a phenomenon they never so much as dreamed of.* Thus have His Majesty's faithful subjects here, contrary to a crude but prevailing idea, by straining every nerve in their country's cause, outdone them in working, as much as in fighting. The ship *Inflexible*, with the *Maria* and *Carleton* schooners, all reconstructions, did the whole of the second day's business, the flat-bottomed rideau, called the *Thunderer*, and the gondola, called the *Royal Convert* with the gun-boats, not having been able to keep up with them. The said gondola was taken from the Rebels the day the seige of Quebec was raised. The loss we have sustained, considering the great superiority of the insurgents, is very small, consisting of between thirty and forty men killed and wounded, seamen, soldiers, artillery-men and all; eight whereof were killed outright and six wounded on board the *Carleton*.

GENERAL WATERBURY TO THE PRESIDENT OF CONGRESS.

STANFORD, October 24, 1776.

HONORED SIR :—I have now returned home on parole. Your Honor has undoubtedly heard of my misfortune of being taken prisoner on the 13th instant, on Lake Champlain. I shall give your Honor a short sketch of our engagement, which is as follows :

On Friday morning, the 11th instant, our alarm guns were fired,that the enemy's fleet were off Cumberland

* Arnold does not seem to have been badly frightened at the appearance of the " three-masted ship," although he had no knowledge that so large a vessel was upon the lake, until she hove in sight off Cumberland Head. WASHINGTON had heard of the vessel from a prisoner, and had transmitted the information to Congress on the 27th of September, but not even a rumor of such a vessel had reached the officers on Lake Champlain. Capt. Douglass was misinformed as to the relative efficiency of the two fleets. The British had a decided superiority both in the experience and discipline of seamen and gunners. and in weight of metal.

Head. I immediately went on board of General Arnold, and told him that I gave it as my opinion that the fleet ought immediately to come to sail, and fight them on the retreat in Main Lake, as they were so much superior to us in number and strength, and we being in such a disadvantageous harbor to fight a number so much superior, and the enemy being able with their small boats to surround us on every side, as I knew they could, we lying between an island and the main : but General Arnold was of the opinion that it was best to draw the fleet in a line where we lay, in the bay of Valcour. The fleet very soon came up with us, and surrounded us, when a very hot engagement ensued, from ten o'clock in the morning till towards sunset, when the enemy withdrew. We immediately held council to secure a retreat through their fleet to get to Crown Point, which was done with so much secrecy that we went through them entirely undiscovered. The enemy finding, next morning, that we had retreated, immediately pursued us,—the wind being against us, and my vessel so torn to pieces that it was almost impossible to keep her above water ; my sails were so short that carrying sail split them from foot to head, and I was obliged to come to anchor at twelve o'clock, to mend my sails. When we had completed that we made sail just at evening. The enemy still pursued all night. I found next morning that they gained upon us very fast, and that they would very soon overtake me. The rest of the fleet all being very much ahead of me, I sent my boat on board of General Arnold to get liberty to put my wounded in the boat and send them forward and run my vessel on shore and blow her up. I received for answer, by no means to run her ashore, but to push forward to Split Rock, where he would draw the fleet in line and engage them again : but when I came to Split Rock, the whole fleet was making their escape as fast as they could, and left me in the rear to fall into the enemy's hands. But before I struck to them, the ship of eighteen twelve pounders and a schooner of fourteen six-pounders had surrounded me which obliged me to strike, and I thought it prudent to surrender myself prisoner of war. As soon as I was taken General Arnold, with four gondolas, ran ashore and blew up the vessels ahead of me. One thing I have omitted in the former part of my letter, that is, the *Royal Savage* ran ashore on the Point of Valcour in the first engagement and was lost.

*　*　*　*　*　*　*　*　*

DAVID WATERBURY, Jr.

FROM HADDEN'S JOURNAL, PUBLISHED BY JOEL MUNSELL'S SONS, ALBANY ; 1884.

[James Murray Hadden was a 2nd lieutenant in the Royal Regiment of Artillery, and had command of a British gun-boat in the naval battle at Valcour Island.]

EXTRACT.—" The 10th Oct'r the fleet proceeded to the southern end of Isle La Motte on the eastern shore of Lake Champlain, which afterwards widens very considerably to about twelve or fifteen miles in many places. The 11th of Oct'r the army arrived at Point Au Fer under General Burgoyne, and early in the morning the fleet under Gen'l Carlton, and Captain Pringle of the navy. A large detachment of savages, under Mayor Carlton, also moved with the fleet in their canoes, which were very regularly ranged. These canoes are made of birch bark, and some of them brought fifteen hundred miles down the country, several of which would contain thirty people. * * About eleven o'clock this morning, one of the enemy's vessels was discovered and immediately pursued into a bay on the eastern [sic.] shore of the lake where the rest of their fleet was found at anchor in the form of a crescent between Valcour Island and the Continent. Their fleet consisted of three row galleys, two schooners, two sloops and eight gondolas, carrying in all ninety guns. That of the

British carried only eighty-seven peices of ordinance including eight howitzers. The pursuit of this vessel was without order or regularity, the wind being fair to go down the lake enabled us to overtake the vessel before she could, by taks, get into the rest of their fleet, but lost to us the opportunity of going in at the upper end of the island and attacking the whole at once. The vessel which proved to be the Royal Savage, taken by them from St. Johns last year, carrying fourteen guns, was run on shore, and most of the men escaped on to Valcour Island, in effecting which they were fired upon by the gun-boats, this firing at one object drew us all in a cluster and four of the enemy's vessels getting under weigh to support the Royal Savage, fired upon the boats with success. An order was therefore given by the commanding officer for the boats to form across the bay : this was soon effected though under the enemy's whole fire, and unsupported, all the King's vessels having dropped too far to leeward. This unequal combat was maintained for two hours, without any aid, when the Carlton schooner of 14 guns, 6 pounders, got into the bay and immediately received the enemy's whole fire, which was continued without intermission for about an hour, when the boats of the fleet towed her off, and left the gun-boats to maintain the conflict. This was done till the boats had expended their ammunition when they were withdrawn, having sunk one of the enemy's gondolas, killed or wounded seventy men, and considerably damaged others, Being small objects the loss in the gun-boats was inconsiderable. Twenty men (a German gun-boat blown up). Each gunboat carried one gun in the bow (or howitzer), 7 Artillery men and 11 seamen, the whole under an Artillery officer. It was found that the boats' advantage was not to come nearer than 700 yards, as whenever they approached nearer, they were greatly annoyed by grape shot, though their case could do little mischief. Each boat had 80 rounds of ammunition, 30 of which were case shot, and could not be used with effect. The boats were now formed between the vessels of the

British fleet, just witnout the enemy's shot, being withdrawn a little before sundown and the Royal Savage blown up. This last was an unnecessary measure, as she might at a more leisure moment have been got off, or, at all events, her stores saved, and in her present position no use could be made of her by the enemy ; night coming on it was determined to make a general attack early next morning. The rebels having no land force the savages took post on the main and Valcour Island. Thus being upon both flanks they were able to annoy them in the working of their guns. This had the effect of now and then obliging the rebels to turn a gun that way, which danger the savages avoided by getting behind trees. The boats having received a small supply of ammunition, were unaccountably ordered to anchor under cover of a small island without the opening of the bay.

" The enemy finding their force diminished and the rest severely handled by little more than one-third the British fleet, determined to withdraw towards Crown Point, and passing through our fleet about ten o'clock at night, effected it undiscovered. This the former position of the gun-boats would probably have prevented. All the enemy's vessels used oars, and on this occasion they were muffled."

---

* In the editions of this compilation, published in 1853 and 1866, it is stated that Arnold, on his retreat, passed around the north end of Valcour. I have made the correction upon the credit of Lieut. Hadden's statement that the gun-boats were withdrawn, thus leaving a passage along the main shore unguarded.

NAVAL BATTLE ON LAKE CHAMPLAIN, 1814.

LETTER, ETC.

NAVY DEPARTMENT,
OCTOBER 3, 1814.

SIR.

IN compliance with your request, I have now the honor to enclose copies of all the documents received from Captain Macdonough, in relation to the brilliant and extraordinary victory achieved by the United States' squadron under his command, over that of the enemy in Plattsburgh Bay, on Lake Champlain.

This action, like that of its prototype on Lake Erie, cannot be portrayed in language corresponding with the universal and just admiration inspired by the exalted prowess, consummate skill, and cool, persevering intrepidity, which will ever distinguish this splendid and memorable event.

This like those brilliant naval victories which preceded it has its peculiar features, which mark it with a distinct character. It was fought at anchor. The firm, compact, and well formed line ; the preparations for all the evolutions of which the situation was susceptible, and the adroitness and decisive effect with which they were performed in the heat of battle, mark no less the judgment which planned, than the valor and skill displayed in the execution.

All these are heightened by the contemplation of a vigorous and greatly superior foe, moving down upon this line, in his own time, selecting his position, and choosing his distance ; animated by the proximity of a powerful army in co-operation, and stimulated by the settled confidence of victory.

To view it in abstract, it is not surpassed by any naval victory on record ; to appreciate its result, it is perhaps one of the most important events in the history of our country.

That it will be justly estimated, and the victors duly honored by the councils of the nation, the justice and liberality hitherto displayed on similar occasions, is a sufficient pledge.

I have the honor to be,
Very respectfully sir,
Your obedient servant,
W. JONES.

The Hon. Charles Tate,
    Chairman of the Naval Committee of the Senate.

(Copy.)   United States' ship Saratoga, off
                            Plattsburgh, Sept. 11, 1814.
SIR,

The Almighty has been pleased to grant us a signal victory on lake Champlain, in the capture of one frigate, one brig, and two sloops of war of the enemy.

I have the honor to be
Very respectfully sir,
Your obedient servant,
T. MACDONOUGH, *com.*

Hon. William Jones, Secretary of the Navy.

(Copy.)   United States' ship Saratoga,
               at anchor off Plattsburgh, Sept. 13, 1814.
SIR,

By lieut. commandant Cassin I have the honor to convey to you the flags of his Brittannic majesty's late squadron, captured on the 11th inst. by the United States' squadron, under my command. Also, my despatches relating to that occurrence, which should have been in your possession at an earlier period, but for the difficulty in arranging the different statements.

The squadron under my command now lies at Plattsburgh—it will bear of considerable diminution, and leave a force sufficient to repel any attempt of the enemy in this quarter. I shall wait your order what to do with the whole or any part thereof, and should it be consistent, I beg you will favor me with permission to leave the lake and place me under command of commodore Decatur, at New York. My health (being some time on the lake,) together with the almost certain inactivity of future naval operations here, are among the causes for this request of my removal.

I have the honor to be,
Sir, with much respect,
Your most ob't servant,
T. MACDONOUGH.

Hon. William Jones, Secretary
    of the Navy, Washington.

(Copy.)   United States' ship Saratoga,
                               Plattsburgh Bay, Sept. 11, 1814

Sir,
    I have the honor to give you the particulars of the action which took place on the 11th inst. on this lake.

For several days the enemy were on their way to Plattsburgh, by land and water; and it being understood that an attack would be made at the same time by their land and naval forces, I determined to await at anchor the approach of the latter.

At 8 A. M. the lookout boat announced the approach

of the enemy. At 9, he anchored in a line ahead at about 300 yards distance from my line ; his ship opposed to the Saratoga, his brig to the Eagle, Captain Robert Henley, his galleys, thirteen in number, to the schooner, sloop, and a division of our galleys ; one of his sloops assisting their ship and brig, the other assisting their galleys. Our remaining galleys with the Saratoga and Eagle. In this situation, the whole force, on both sides, became engaged : the Saratoga suffering much from the heavy fire of the Confiance. I could perceive at the same time, however, that our fire was very destructive to her. The Ticonderoga, lieutenant-commandant Cassin, gallantly sustained her full share of the action. At half-past 10 o'clock, the Eagle, not being able to bring her guns to bear, cut her cable, and anchored in a more eligible position, between my ship and the Ticonderoga, where she very much annoyed the enemy, but unfortunately leaving me exposed to a galling fire from the enemy's brig. Our guns on the starboard side being nearly all dismounted, or not manageable, a stern anchor was let go, the bower cable cut, and the ship winded with a fresh broadside on the enemy's ship, which soon after surrendered. Our broadside was then sprung to bear on the brig, which surrendered in about 15 minutes after.

The sloop that was opposed to the Eagle, had struck some time before, and drifted down the line ; the sloop which was with their galleys having struck also : three of their galleys are said to be sunk, the others pulled off. Our galleys were about obeying, with alacrity, the signal to follow them, when all the vessels were reported to me to be in a sinking state ; it then became necessary to annul the signal to the galleys, and order their men to the pumps.

I could only look at the enemy's galleys going off in a shattered condition, for there was not a mast in either squadron that could stand to make sail on ; the lower rigging, being nearly all shot away, hung down as though it had been just placed over the mast heads.

The Saratoga had fifty-five round shot in her hull ;

the Confiance one hundred and five. The enemy's shot passed principally just over our heads, as there were not twenty whole hammocks in the nettings at the close of the action, which lasted, without intermission, two hours and twenty minutes.

The absence and sickness of Lieut. Raymond Perry, left me without the services of that excellent officer; much ought fairly to be attributed to him for his great care and attention in disciplining the ship's crew, as her first lieutenant. His place was filled by a gallant young officer, Lieutenant Peter Gamble, who, I regret to inform you, was killed early in the action. Acting-Lieutenant Vallette worked the 1st and 2nd divisions of guns with able effect. Sailing master Brum's attention to the springs, and in the execution of the order to wind the ship, and occasionally at the guns, meets with my entire approbation; also Captain Young's commanding the acting marines, who took his men to the guns. Mr. Beale, purser, was of great service at the guns, and in carrying my orders throughout the ship, with Midshipman Montgomery. Master's mate Joshua Justin, had the command of the third division: his conduct during the action was that of a brave and correct officer. Midshipmen Monteith, Graham, Williamson, Platt, Thwing, and Acting Midshipman Baldwin, all behaved well, and gave evidence of their making valuable officers.

The Saratoga was twice set on fire by hot shot from the enemy's ship.

I close, sir, this communication with feelings of gratitude for the able support I received from every officer and man attached to the squadron which I have the honor to command.

I have the honor to be,
With great respect, sir,
Your most obedient servant,
T. MACDONOUGH.

Hon. William Jones, Secretary of the Navy.

P. S. Accompanying this is a list of killed and

wounded, a list of the prisoners, and a precise state,
ment of both forces engaged.   Also letters from Capt.
Henly and Lieut.-Commandant Cassin.   T. M.

(Copy.)   United States' Ship Saratoga.
                                  September 13, 1814.
SIR,
    I have the honor to enclose you a list of the killed
and wounded on board the different vessels of the
squadron under your command in the action of the
11th inst.
    It is impossible to ascertain correctly the loss of the
enemy. From the best information received from the
British officers, from my own observations, and from
various lists found on board the Confiance, I calculate
the number of men on board of that ship at the commencement of the action, at 270, of whom 180, at least,
were killed and wounded; and on board the other captured vessels at least 80 more, making the whole, killed
or wounded, 260. This is doubtless short of the real
number, as many were thrown overboard from the Confiance during the engagement.
    The muster books must have been thrown overboard
or otherwise disposed of, as they are not to be found.
                    I am, sir, respectfully,
                        Your obedient servant,
                            GEORGE BEALE, Jr.,
                                      Purser.

Thomas Macdonough, Esq., Commanding
    United States' Squadron on Lake Champlain.

Return of killed and wounded on board the United States squadron on Lake Champlain in the engagement with the British fleet, on the 11th of September, 1814.

SHIP SARATOGA.

KILLED.—Peter Gamble, lieutenant; Thomas Butler, quarter gunner; James Norberry, boatswain's mate; Abraham Davis, quarter-master; William Wyer, sail-maker; William Brickel, seaman; Peter Johnson, seaman; John Coleman, seaman; Benjamin Burrill, ordinary seaman; Andrew Parmlee, ordinary seaman; Peter Post, seaman; David Bennett, seaman; Ebenezer Johnson, seaman; Joseph Couch, landsman; Thomas Stephens, seaman; Randall McDonald, ordinary seaman; John White, ordinary seaman; Samuel Smith, seaman; Thomas Malony, ordinary seaman; Andrew Nelson, seaman; John Sellack, seaman; Peter Hanson, seaman; Jacob Laraway, seaman; Edward Moore, seaman; Jerome Williams, ordinary seaman; James Carlisle, marine; John Smart, seaman; Earl Hannemon, seaman. Total, 28.

WOUNDED.—James M. Baldwin, acting midshipman; Joseph Barron, pilot; Robert Gary, quarter gunner; George Cassin, quartermaster; John Hollingsworth, seaman; Thomas Robinson, seaman; Purnall Smith, seaman; John Ottiwell, seaman; John Thompson, ordinary seaman; William Tabee, ordinary seaman; William Williams, ordinary seaman; John Roberson, seaman; John Towns, landsman; John Shays, seaman; John S. Hammond, seaman; James Barlow, seaman; James Nagle, ordinary seaman; John Lanman, seaman; Peter Colberg, seaman; William Newton, ordinary seaman; Neil J. Heidmont, seaman; James Steward, seaman; John Adams, landsman; Charles Ratche, seaman; Benjamin Jackson, marine; Jesse Vanhorn, marine; Joseph Ketter, marine; Samuel Pearson, marine. Total, 29.

BRIG EAGLE.

KILLED.—Peter Vandermere, master's mate; John Ribero, seaman; Jacob Lindman, seaman; Perkins Moore, ordinary seaman; James Winship, ordinary seaman; Thomas Anwright, ordinary seaman; Nace Wilson, ordinary seaman; Thomas Lewis, boy; John Wallace, marine; Joseph Heaton, marine; Robert Stratton, marine; James M. Hale, musician; John Wood, musician. Total, 13.

WOUNDED.—Joseph Smith, lieutenant; William A. Spencer, acting lieutenant; Francis Breeze, master's mate; Abraham Walters, pilot; William C. Allen, quartermaster; James Duick, quarter gunner; Andrew McEwen, seaman; Zebediah Concklin, seaman; Joseph Valentine, seaman; John Hartley, seaman; John Micklan, seaman; Robert Buckley, seaman; Aaron Fitzgerald, boy; Purnall Boice, ordinary seaman; John N. Craig, seaman; John McKenny, seaman; Mathew Scriver, marine; George Mainwaring, marine; Henry Jones, marine; John McCarty, marine. Total, 20.

SCHOONER TICONDEROGA.

KILLED.—John Stansbury, lieutenant; John Fisher, boatswain's mate; John Atkinson, boatswain's mate; Henry Johnson, seaman; Deodrick Think, marine; John Sharp, marine. Total, 6.

WOUNDED.—Patrick Cassin, seaman; Ezekiel Goud, seaman; Samuel Sawyer, seaman; William Le Count, seaman; Henry Collin, seaman; John Condon, marine. Total, 6.

SLOOP PREBLE.

KILLED.—Rogers Carter, acting sailing master; Joseph Rowe, boatswain's mate.
WOUNDED.—None.

GUN-BOAT BORER.

KILLED.—Arthur W. Smith, purser s steward; Thomas Gill, boy; James Day, marine.
WOUNDED.—Ebenezer Cobb, corporal of marines.

GUN-BOAT CENTIPEDE.

WOUNDED.—James Taylor, landsman.

GUN-BOAT WILMER.

WOUNDED.—Peter Frank, seaman.

RECAPITULATION.

KILLED.—Saratoga, 28; Eagle, 13; Ticonderoga, 6; Preble, 2; Borer, 3. Total, 52.
WOUNDED.—Saratoga, 29; Eagle, 20; Ticonderoga, 6; Borer, 1; Centipede, 1; Wilmer, 1. Total, 58.

GUN-BOATS.

NONE KILLED OR WOUNDED.—Nettle, Allen, Viper, Burrows, Ludlow, Alwyn, Ballard.

GEORGE BEALE, Jr.,
Purser.

Approved.

T. MACDONOUGH.

LIST OF PRISONERS CAPTURED ON THE 11TH SEPTEMBER, AND SENT TO GREENBUSH.

OFFICERS.—Daniel Pring,* captain; Hicks, Creswick, Robinson, M'Ghie, Drew, Hornsby, lieutenants;

*On parole.

Childs, lieutenant of marines; Fitzpatrick, lieutenant 39th Regt.; Bryden, sailing-master; Clark, Simmonds, master's mates; Todd, surgeon; Giles, purser; Guy, captain's clerk; Dowell, Aire, Bondell, Toorke, Kewstra, midshipmen; Davidson, boatswain; Elvin, Mickel, gunners; Cox, carpenter; Parker, purser; Martin, surgeon M'Cabe, assistant surgeon.

340 seamen.

47 wounded men paroled.

STATEMENT OF THE AMERICAN FORCE ENGAGED ON
THE 11TH SEPTEMBER, 1814.

Saratoga,	8 long 24 pounders,		
	6 42 pound carronades,		
	12 32 do. do. Total, 26 guns.		
Eagle,	12 32 do. do. & 8 long 18 prs. 20		
Ticonderoga,	8 long 12 pounders.		
	4 18 do.		
	5 32 pound carronades. 17		
Preble,	7 long 9 pounders, 7		

Ten Galleys, viz:

Allen,	1 long 24 pr. & 1 18 pr. Columbiad,	2
Burrows,	1	24	do.	do.	2
Borer,	1	24	do.	do.	2
Nettle,	1	24	do.	do.	2
Viper,	1	24	do.	do.	2
Centipede,	1	24	do.	do.	2
Ludlow,	1	12 pounder,	1
Wilmer	1	12 do.	1
Alwyn,	1	12 do.	1
Ballard,	1	12 do.	1

Guns,   86

BECAPITULATION.

14 long 24 pounders,
6 42 pound carronades,
29 32 do. do.
12 long 18 pounders,
12 12 do.
7 9 do.
6 18 pound Columbiads.

Total, 86 guns. Ave. 22 3-4 pounders

T. MACDONOUGH.

STATEMENT OF THE ENEMY'S FORCE ENGAGED ON THE 11TH SEPTEMBER, 1814.

Frigate Confiance, 27 long 24 pounders,
4 32 pound carronades,
6 24 do. do.
2 l. 18 prs. on b. deck. T'l, 39 guns.

Brig Linnet, 16 long 12 pounders, 16
Sloop Chub,* 10 18 pound carronades,
1 long 6 pounder, 11

Finch,* 6 18 pound carronades,
1 18 do. Columbiad,
4 long 6 pounders, 11

Thirteen Galleys, viz :

Sir James Yeo, 1 l. 24 pr. & 1 32 p. carronade, 2
Sir George Prevost, 1 do. do. 2
Sir Sidney Beckwith, 1 do. do. 2
Broke, 1 l. 18 pr. & 1 32 p. do. 2
Murray, 1 do. & 1 18 p. do. 2
Wellington, 1 do. 1

*These sloops were formerly the United States' Growler and Eagle.

Tecumseh,	1	do.		1
Name unknown,	1	do.		1
Drummond,	1	32 pound carronade,		1
Simcoe,	1	do.	do.	1
Unknown,	1	do.	do.	1
Do.	1	do.	do.	1
Do.	1	do.	do.	1

Total, ——
95

RECAPITULATION.

30 long 24 pounders,
  7   18 do.
16   12 do.
  5   6 do.
13 32 pound carronades,
  6 24 pound   do.
17 18 do.   do.
  1 18 do. Columbiad.
——

Total,   95 guns. Ave. about 21 1-5

T. MACDONOUGH.

————

(Copy.)   United States Brig Eagle,
                    Plattsburgh, Sept. 12, 1814.
SIR,

I am happy to inform you that all my officers and men acted bravely, and did their duty in the battle of yesterday, with the enemy.

I shall have the pleasure of making a more particular representation of the respective merits of my gallant officers, to the Honorable the Secretary of the Navy.

I have the honor to be,
Respectfully sir,
Your most obedient servant,
ROBERT HENLEY.

P. S. We had thirty-nine round shot in our hull, (mostly 24 pounders,) four in our lower masts, and we were well peppered with grape. I enclose my boatswain's report.

(Copy.)   Unites States Schooner Ticonderoga,
                                Plattsburgh Bay, Sept. 12, 1814.
SIR,
   It is with pleasure I state that every officer and man under my command, did their duty yesterday.
                        Yours respectfully,
                            STEPHEN CASSIN,
                                Lieutenant-Commandant

Commodore Thomas Macdonough.

                            United States' Ship Saratoga,
                        September 15, 1814, off Plattsburgh.
SIR,
   As Providence has given into my command the squadron on Lake Champlain, of which you were (after the fall of Captain Downie) the commanding officer, I beg you will, after the able conflict you sustained, and evidence of determined valor you evinced on board His Britannic Majesty's brig Linnet, until the necessity of her surrender, accept of your enclosed parole, not to serve against the United States, or their dependencies, until regularly exchanged.
                        I am, &c., &c.,
                            T. MACDONOUGH.

To Captain Pring, Royal Navy.

INDEX.

ABERCROMBIE, MAJ.-GENL.
    Chief Commandant in America...................... 67
    Advances against Ticonderoga..................... 68
    Retreat of....................................... 69

ALGONQUINS.—At war with the Mohawks.................. 19

ALLEN, EBENEZER, CAPT.
    Captures works on Mount Defiance.................. 131

ALLAN, ETHAN, COL.
    Character of...................................... 87
    Expedition against Ticonderoga.................... 88
    Taken prisoner at Montreal....................... 96

AMHERST, MAJ.-GENL.
    Moves against Ticonderoga; builds fort at Crown
        Point; embarks for Canada ; plans expedition
        against Indians; takes Montreal.............. 73–77

ARNOLD, BENEDICT, GENL.—
    Character of...................................... 86
    At Ticonderoga................................... 88
    Expedition against St. Johns...................... 91
    Cruises on Lake................................ 104–5
    Engagement at Valcour and loss of fleet. 108–112

AMERICANS.—Build vessels on lake.................... 104
    Strengthen Ticonderoga..................... 103–118
    Evacuate Ticonderoga............................. 122
    Retake Mt. Defiance.............................. 131
    Invasion of Canada, 1875–6....................... 93
    Retreat from Canada.............................. 100

APPENDIX.
    Graves of officers killed Sept. 1814.............. 218
    Official reports of battle of Valcour.............. 219
    Macdonough's official report..................... 231

BAUM, COL.—Defeated at Bennington.................... 132

BEAUHARNOIS, M. DE.—Erects fort at Crown Point............ 47

BLOOMFIELD, GEN.—Ordered to Champlain frontier............ 161

BOUGAINVILLE, M. DE.—Abandons Isle Aux Noix............ 77

BOURLEMAQUE, M. DE.—Sent to protect Carillon.............. 73
    Destroys fort and retreats to Canada......... 74

BURGOYNE, GENL.
    Assigned to command in Canada..... 116
    Invests Ticonderoga.......................... 117–123
    Surrender of.................................... 132

BIOGRAPHICAL NOTES OF
    Allen, Ebenezer.................................. 138
    Allen, Ira....................................... 139
    Burgoyne, Genl.................................. 133
    Bailey, William.................................. 153
    Macdonough, Com................................ 164
    Macomb, Alex., Genl............................. 187
    Mooers, Benj. Genl.............................. 141
    Izard, Genl..................................... 184
    Pike, Z. M., Genl............................... 162
    Platt, Zephaniah................................ 146
    Platt, Charles.................................. 149
    Sailly, Peter................................... 148
    Smith, Melancton, Judge......................... 144
    Smith, Sidney, Lieut............................ 165
    Smith, Melancton, Col........................... 191
    St. Clair, Genl................................. 118
    Treadwell, Thomas............................... 147
    Woolsey, Melancton L............................ 149

BURLINGTON.—Bell of St. Regis secreted there................ 44
    U. S. troops stationed at in 1812–14............. 168–182
    Fired at by British Gun-boats.................... 170

CANADA.—Condition of in 1689............................. 34
    Ceded to Great Britain........................... 77
    Invasion and retreat of American Army.......... 93–101
    Military Force in 1812........................... 161
    Trade with in 1811.............................. 163

CARIGNAN-SATIERES.—Why so called...................... 25

COURCELLES, M. DE.—Defeated by Mohawks................. 27

CORLEAR.—Intercedes for the French....................... 27
    Drowned in Lake Champlain...................... 32

CARLETON, GUY, GENL.
    Attempt to raise Siege of St. Johns................ 96
    Policy towards prisoners........................ 112
    Menaces Ticonderoga............................ 114
    Returns to Canada.............................. 115

CHAMPLAIN, SAML. DE.
    Sails for America.................................... 17
    Joins expedition against Mohawks through Lake
      Champlain...................................19–21
    Governor of Canada............................... 22
    Character and death............................... 24

CHAMPLAIN, TOWN OF.—Citizens threatened.................. 174
    U. S. Army at..................................... 184
    Sir Geo. Prevost at............................... 189

CHITTENDEN, GOV.
    Dispute with Vermont volunteers.................... 176
    Orders Vermont Militia to Plattsburgh.............. 207

CLARK, ISAAC, COL.—At Missisco Bay........:.............. 173

CUMBERLAND HEAD.—Military Works constructed on........ 184

CROWN POINT.—Occupied by French.......................27–49
    Amherst builds new fort at......................... 74
    Taken possession of by Americans.................. 89
    Condition of Army at, on return from Canada........ 100

DEARBORN MAJ.-GENL.—Command of Northern frontier...... 161

DERBY, VT.—Storehouses and barracks burned................ 174

DEERFIELD.—Destroyed by French and Indians............... 44

DENONVILLE, M. DE.—Makes treaty with Iroquois............ 35

DIESKAU, BARON DE.
    Arrives at Crown Point............................ 59
    Attacks English at Lake George and wounded....... 60

DOWNIE, GEORGE CAPT.
    Commands British fleet in 1814..................... 198
    Killed in action................................... 202
    Buried at Plattsburgh...........................209–218

ENGLISH.—Iroquois' opinion of............................. 57
    Neglect to colonize on Lake Champlain............. 55
    Defeat Arnold at Valcour.......................:... 107
    Capture Ticonderoga............................... 122
    Retreat to Canada................................. 133
    Subsequent appearance on Lake..................... 134
    Henry's mission to New England.................... 157
    Appear off Burlington............................. 170
    Destroy property at Plattsburgh.................... 169
    Appear off Otto Creek............................. 183
    Enter U. S. under Provost......................... 189
    Reach Plattsburgh................................. 194
    Retreat from Plattsburgh.......................... 208

FRONTENAC, COUNT DE.
    Viceroy of Canada................................. 34
    Organizes attack on Schenectady................... 36
    And against Mohawk Village........................ 43

Forsyth, Lt.-Col.—Killed by Indians...................... 185

French.—Repulsed at Ft. Wm. Henry....................... 64
      Abandon Lake Champlain........................ 74
Forts.
      Ann...45, 47
      Carillon built by French.....................62, 64
         Description of................................. 67
         Blown up...................................... 74
      Chambly. 25
         Attacked by Iroquois.......................... 34
         Taken by Americans........................... 95
      Crown Point built by Amherst.................... 74
      Edward......................................58, 64
      George, massacre at............................. 66
      Isle Aux Noix...............94, 102, 167, 184, 186
      Laprairie...................................40, 42
      Nicholson...................................... 45
      Richelieu...................................24, 25
      St. Anne..................................25, 30, 34
      St. Frederic, description of..................... 48
         Seat of French power.......................... 50
         Destroyed..................................... 74
      St. Johns.................................91, 96, 102
      St. Theresa..............................25, 26, 34
      Ticonderoga.........................62, 74, 87, 110
      William Henry...............................62, 64

Hudson, Henry.—Sails up Hudson River................... 23

Hochelaga (Montreal).—Description of.................... 16

Haviland, Col.—Seizes Isle Aux Noix.................... 77

Hubbardton.—Battle of................................. 124

Hale, Col.—Retreat dictated by humanity................. 125

Hampton, Maj.-Genl.
      Abortive invasion of Canada.................... 172
      Dispute with Wilkinson......................... 178
      Removed from command on frontier.............. 179

Indians.—Character of.................................. 18
      At Fort St. Frederic............................ 50
      Number of tribes under Montcalm................ 66
      Burgoyne's war feast to........................ 117
      At Battle of Valcour........................... 228
      With British in war of 1812..................174–185
      Claim of title to land bordering on Lake.......... 154

Johnson, Wm., Sir.
      Marches to Lake George........................ 55
      Defeats Dieskau............................... 60

LAKE CHAMPLAIN.
  General description of............................1-14
  First sail vessel built on........................... 49
  French grants on................................... 51
  French build armed vessels........................ 73
  First settlement on borders of........... 78-84
  Progress of settlement after Revolution.............. 137
  Commerce of....................................... 152
  American and English flotillas on Lake in 1776......106-7
  In 1814...198-9
  Variety of fish in................................. 151
  Sloops on, in 1811......................... 163
  First Steamboat on Lake........................... 163
  French fleet on Lake destroyed..................... 75
  U. S. Gun-boats built in 1812...................... 157
  Loss of Eagle and Growler......................... 165

LACOLLE.—Battle of............................. 180

MOHAWKS.—Description of Villages........................ 31

MONTCALM, M. DE.—Arrives at Ticonderoga; Captures Fort
    George; Defeats Abercrombie.......65-68

MONTGOMERY, MAJ.-GENL.—Invades Canada ; captures St.
    Johns; enters Montreal; killed at Quebec.... 94-98

MACDONOUGH, THOMAS, CAPT.
  Ordered to Lake Champlain....................... 164
  Builds fleet........................... 167-183
  Defeats British.................................... 200

MACOMB, ALEX., GENL.
  In command at Plattsburgh....... 187
  Strength of his Army............................. 188

NICHOLSON, COL.—Plans invasion of Canada.............. 45-47

PARKER, COL.—Captured by French 102

PUTNAM, ISRAEL, CAPT.
  Scout to St. Frederic.............................. 62
  Skirmish with French.............................. 70
  Life saved by Marin............................... 71

PLATTSBURGH.—Murray's raid.............................. 167
  Forts and batteries at 191
  Skirmish on Beekmantown road.................... 193
  Building burned by order of Macomb............... 106
  Loss at Battle of.........................203, 208, 237
  Funeral of officers in Sept., 1814.................... 209
  Sailors buried on Crab Island..................... 210
  Aiken's Volunteers at Battle of.... 195
  Battle of............................... 189-209
  Anniversary of battle.............................. 211
  Official report of Naval engagement................. 231

PLATT, NATHANIEL, CAPT.—Disciplines a Tory Divine....... 85

POINT AU FER.—Fortified by Sullivan....................... 100
    Held by British until after peace................... 136

QUEBEC.—Indian name of.................................. 16

ROGERS, ROBERT, CAPT.—Scout to St. Frederic, on Lake
    Champlain; wounded at Ticonderoga.......... 62–3
    Expedition against St. François Indians............ 78
    Engagement near Rouse's Point.................... 76

ROUSE'S POINT.—Arnold at........................ 104
    Storehouse burned................................ 175
    Battery at, ordered built........................... 184
    Fort Blunder built................................ 11

SCHENECTADY.—Burned.................................. 35
    Families killed near.............................. 39

SCHUYLER, ABRAM, CAPT.—Scout to Chambly.............. 38

SCHUYLER, JOHN, CAPT.—Attacks Laprairie................ 40

SCHUYLER, PHILIP, MAJ.—Surprises Fort Laprairie............ 42

ST. CLAIR, MAJ.-GENL.—In command at Ticonderoga......... 119
    Abandons Ticonderoga............................ 122
    Censured by the people............................ 126
    Ridiculous report against.......................... 138

TRACY, M. DE.—Builds Forts.............................. 225
    Invades Mohawk country........................ 26–30
    Strangles a Mohawk.............................. 29

TRAVASY AND CHASY, CAPTS.—Murdered by Indians......... 29

UNITED STATES.—Difficulty with Great Britain............... 156
    Declaration of war................................ 160

VERMONT.—First settlement of........................ 77
    Admitted into Union............................. 137
    Progress of settlements............................ 138
    Patriotism of inhabitants.......................... 158
    Volunteers dispute with Governor of................ 176
    At Battle of Plattsburgh........................... 207

VALCOUR.—Battle of..................................107–111
    Official reports of battle.......................... 219

WINTHROP, MAJ.-GENL. 39